A

# GRAMMAR

OF THE

# PERSIAN LANGUAGE,

&c. &c. &c.

# A GRAMMAR OF THE PERSIAN LANGUAGE.

TO WHICH ARE SUBJOINED,

SEVERAL DIALOGUES;

WITH AN

ALPHABETICAL LIST

OF THE

ENGLISH AND PERSIAN TERMS OF GRAMMAR;

AND AN

APPENDIX,

ON

THE USE OF ARABIC WORDS.

BY MEERZA MOHAMMAD IBRAHEEM,

PROFESSOR OF ARABIC AND PERSIAN LANGUAGES

AT THE HON. EAST-INDIA COMPANY'S COLLEGE, HAILEYBURY.

LONDON:

W^M. H. ALLEN AND CO.

Booksellers to the Honourable East-India Company,

7, LEADENHALL STREET.

1841.

TO THE HONOURABLE

THE CHAIRMAN, THE DEPUTY CHAIRMAN,

AND THE

COURT OF DIRECTORS

OF THE

HONOURABLE EAST-INDIA COMPANY,

&c. &c. &c.

HONOURABLE SIRS,

THE results of the literary labours undertaken by your own cherished Servants, in their zeal for the well-being of your liberal Institutions, might always with propriety be dedicated to your Honourable Court; but the munificent patronage which you have vouchsafed to the publication of this Volume fully warrants me in inscribing it to you, with the warmest feelings of gratitude.

I have the honour to subscribe myself, with the greatest respect,

HONOURABLE SIRS,

Your most faithful and humble servant,

MOHAMMAD IBRAHEEM.

EAST-INDIA COLLEGE, HAILEYBURY,
*September* 1841.

THE

# PREFACE.

A FOREIGNER, who is under the necessity of addressing the natives of a country in their own language, must throw himself upon their candid and indulgent criticism.

However familiar he may have become with their speech, for the purpose of daily life—whatever pains he may have taken to make himself acquainted with the style of their standard authors—he cannot fail to be aware, that there are peculiarities of expression and construction in all languages, which those who speak them as their native tongues practise unconsciously, but which a stranger can scarcely ever hope to command at will. Impressed, deeply, with a true sense of my own deficiencies, I therefore, with unfeigned humility, solicit the indulgence of my readers to the composition of the following pages; in which, for reasons sufficiently obvious, I, a native of Persia, undertake to communicate the elements of Persian Grammar to English Students, in an English dress. At the same time, I may so far venture to feel confident that my meaning will be found to be intelligibly conveyed, as the kind supervision of a liberal and benevolent friend has removed the likelihood of any material mistakes.

Nor is it only to the outward garb that this beneficial assistance has been directed: the same masterly hand has contributed to improve the substance:—and it is with sentiments of pride and gratitude, that I acknowledge the aid I have received, throughout the whole of my work, from the observations of that unrivalled Persian Scholar, and enlightened

Patron of Persian Literature, NEIL BENJAMIN EDMONSTONE, Esq.;—of whom, I am most grieved to state, the hand of Death has since bereaved me; and to whose honoured memory I now feel it my duty to pay this humble tribute, with extreme reverence and deep sorrow!!

Encouraged by such approbation and aid, I therefore submit this volume to the Students of the Persian Language; trusting they will find it sufficiently accurate and serviceable; and will derive from it facilities for the attainment of the language, which they have hitherto, it is to be apprehended, but imperfectly enjoyed.

No native of any Eastern country has hitherto attempted to exhibit the structure, genius, and idiomatic phraseology of his own language, through the medium of any European dialect. I have, nevertheless, been induced, by the peculiar circumstances of my position in this country, to venture on that arduous undertaking. It happened, that almost immediately after my arrival in England I had the honour of an appointment at the East-India College. At that time I was an entire stranger to the English tongue. I was utterly unable to use it, either for the purposes of reading or of conversation. My first duty therefore, as a Teacher of Persian, was to remedy this defect, by making myself, as speedily as possible, familiar with the native language of my pupils. With this view, I had recourse to the Elementary Works composed by the English Orientalists, for the express purpose of teaching Persian to English Students; in order that, by reversing the process, I might become a learner of English, through their instructions in my own tongue. At the same time, I gladly availed myself of the advantages afforded me by daily intercourse and conversation with the Members of that Learned Body among whom I had the good fortune to be placed :—and, by a persevering use of these resources, I soon had the satisfaction to find myself making rapid progress towards the attainment of my object.

In the course, however, of my studies, and especially of my instructions—now carried on for a period of above fourteen years—I have had frequent reasons to think that the existing system of teaching might be improved, and that a more *idiomatic and living character* might be given to its Rules and Principles.

It must not however be imagined, that this statement is offered with the slightest intention to underrate the labours, or disparage the acquirements, of the Orientalists who have preceded me.

The grammatical works of these distinguished Scholars have undoubtedly been most valuable instruments for the acquisition of an elementary knowledge of the Persian language. They contain, indeed, as much information as can well be derived from the study of literary composition in that language; but still, they are wholly insufficient for the purpose of imparting to the learner any competent knowledge of its *colloquial phraseology* and *idiom*, its *peculiar turns of expression*, and its *various refinements* and *niceties* of diction.

The only extant Persian Grammars are those compiled by European Authors; few of whom have ever even visited the people whose language they undertake to teach; and none of whom have possessed, or could have the means of acquiring, a complete mastery of it, in all its various uses, *literary*, *technical*, and *colloquial*. Without these, however, a writer on Grammar must be necessarily and exclusively dependent upon the resources of prosaic and poetical composition. His work must consequently be, in some respects, erroneous, and in very many points essentially defective. To supply those wants, and to rectify these defects, are the objects which I have principally in view, in the composition of the following work. I seek to teach *the Persian of Persians;*—not the Persian only of *books.* At the same time, I fully acknowledge the value of the efforts made by my learned predecessors: and if I should be found in any degree to have advanced beyond them, it will, in part, be owing to the instruction I have derived both from their merits and their failures; and not merely to the accidental circumstance, that Persian is my native speech.

In the composition of my Grammar, I have not been dependent upon the works of others, but I have endeavoured to draw materials from my own resources. The examples and illustrations which have been cited throughout this work will, therefore, be found to consist of such idiomatic expressions as are used, in their daily intercourse, by those classes of native Persians who speak the language in its greatest purity.

In my efforts, however, I have not sought to supersede, but to assist, the philological labours of others. Their works are not rendered less useful by mine; and while I attempt to correct what appears to me to be erroneous, I endeavour to supply what I consider is deficient in them. I have framed this Grammar chiefly for the use of beginners, to whom the desultory arrangement and the multifarious and complicated rules of the Grammars of the English Authors must present a discouraging obstacle. I do not profess to exhibit a *complete Grammar* of my language, *in all its extended branches and departments:* my purpose is, to give *a compendium of its structure, its idiom and phraseology, by plain rules and simple illustrations.* Although much of what is comprised in European works is, for that reason, omitted in this

Grammar, much also is contained in it that is not to be found in any other; as will appear, especially, on a reference to the various heads of *Pronouns, Prepositions, Conjunctions, Interjections, Adverbs, Diminutive Nouns, and Particles*, the formation of *Compound Epithets*, &c. &c. And I have endeavoured to lay down a more correct and simple system of Verbs and their Conjugations than is adopted in the works of my European predecessors.

The important branch of Syntax—instead of consisting, as in the other Persian Grammars, of a series of elaborate and not always correct rules, exemplified chiefly by quotations from books of Poetry, some of which are almost obsolete—is explained and illustrated in a succession of Dialogues, eight in number, composed for the occasion. The parties chiefly conversing are supposed to be an English Gentleman, who has acquired a competent knowledge of the language of Persia, and is travelling in that country for improvement; and a native Persian friend, who has also resided long enough in England to be able to converse with facility in English. The former occasionally makes mistakes, which the latter corrects;—and an opportunity is thus afforded of exemplifying some of the Rules of Syntax, in a simple, practical, and attractive manner; while, at the same time, the subjects of the several antecedent chapters of the Grammar are illustrated by examples introduced into the Dialogues, and specifically referred to as those examples occur; accompanied also with many explanatory Notes.

My chief object, in the course of these Dialogues, has been to exhibit, to the best of my ability, the genuine idiom and the colloquial and literary phraseology of the language, on a great variety of subjects: and the discussion of those subjects has been conducted with a view to afford as ample and varied a display as possible of national sentiments and manners, and thus to furnish the Student both with instruction and amusement. They are accompanied with an English Translation, as literal as the idiom will admit: and the great difference between the idioms and modes of expression of the two languages are thus advantageously exhibited. The Vowel or Diacritical Points have been used throughout the work, in order to afford the Student the facility of pronouncing the Persian words correctly. A List also has been subjoined, in which the Student will find all the English and Persian Terms of Grammar alphabetically arranged, in parallel columns;—and in an Appendix, the Explanation, the various Forms or Measures, with proper Examples, of all the Arabic words which are of most frequent occurrence in the Persian language.

EAST-INDIA COLLEGE, HAILEYBURY,
*September*, 1841.

# TABLE OF CONTENTS.

TABLE OF CONTENTS.

## APPENDIX.

"The Learner is supposed to be acquainted with the "common terms of Grammar, and to know that the "Persians write their characters from the right-hand to "the left."

Sir William Jones.

# PERSIAN GRAMMAR.

## OF THE ALPHABET.

1. The Persian Alphabet, properly, consists of Twenty-four Letters; of which, Twenty are common to the Persians and the Arabs: but, in consequence of the introduction of so many Arabic words into the Persian Language, Eight more Letters, peculiar to Arabic, have been incorporated with the Persian Alphabet; which at present consists, therefore, of Thirty-two Letters.

2. These Letters, when written singly, appear as follows:—

| Letter | Sound | Name |
|---|---|---|
| ا | A | *alēf* |
| ب | B | *bē* |
| پ | P | *pē* |
| ت | T | *tē* |
| ث | S | *sē* |
| ج | J | *jeem* |
| چ | Ch | *chē* |
| ح | H | *hē* |
| خ | Kh | *khē* (guttural, hard, as the German *Ch*) |
| د | D | *daul* |
| ذ | Z | *zaul* |
| ر ر | R | *rē* |
| ز ز | Z | *zē* |
| ژ ژ | J (*French*) | *jē* |
| س | S | *seen* |
| ش | Sh | *sheen* |
| ص | S | *saud* |
| ض | Z | *zaud* |
| ط | T | *taw* |
| ظ | Z | *zaw* |
| ع | A | *ain* |
| غ | Gh | *ghain* (guttural softly) |
| ف | F | *fē* |
| ق | Ck | *ckauf* (guttural, hard) |
| ک ک | K | *kauf* |
| گ گ | G | *gauf* |
| ل | L | *lawm* |
| م م | M | *meem* |
| ن | N | *noon* |
| و | V | *vawve* |
| ه | H | *hē* |
| ي | Y | *yē* |

3. In composition, some of these letters undergo certain modifications merely in form, and assume somewhat different appearances. But the difference is very trifling; as they never lose their original forms so entirely as not to be recognised by the beginner.

Accordingly, at the beginning of a word they appear thus:

ا بـ پـ تـ ثـ جـ چـ حـ خـ د ذ ر
ز ژ سـ شـ صـ ضـ طـ ظـ عـ غـ فـ قـ
کـ گـ لـ مـ نـ و هـ يـ

In the middle of a word, they appear thus:

ـا ـبـ ـپـ ـتـ ـثـ ـجـ ـچـ ـحـ ـخـ ـد ـذ ـر
ـز ـژ ـسـ ـشـ ـصـ ـضـ ـطـ ـظـ ـعـ ـغـ ـفـ ـقـ
ـکـ ـگـ ـلـ ـمـ ـنـ ـو ـهـ ـيـ

And at the end of a word, they appear thus:

ـا ء ـب ـپ ـت ـث ـج ـچ ـح ـخ ـد ـذ ـر
ـز ـژ ـس ـش ـص ـض ـط ـظ ـع ـغ ـف ـق
ـک ـگ ـل ـم ـن ـو ـه ـي

4. When the letters ل and ا come together, if the former precedes the latter, they are written thus, لا, or لا, or لا. The compound name of *Laum-Alēf*, which of course expresses its own meaning, has been given to this combination; and it is sounded as it is written, "Law."

5. The letter ا, at the end of a word, is sometimes written thus ء, which then goes by the Arabic name *Hamzah*.

It has other uses as well, which shall be duly explained hereafter.

6. Double letters occur in Persian; but to avoid the necessity of writing a letter twice over, the Persians have likewise adopted the Arabic mark ّ *Tashdeed,* "strengthener," which is placed over the letter intended to be double.

7. When two Alēfs come together in the same word, instead of using the mark ّ *Tashdeed,* as in the case of other double letters, this mark ~ is placed over the letter, thus, آ. This is also borrowed from Arabic; and it goes by the name of *Madda,* signifying "to draw out" or "to prolong;" and the ا over which it is placed, is then sounded *aw,* as in the words "paw," "jaw," &c. The *Madda* ~ is, in fact, the second ا horizontally placed over the other. It is sometimes, however, placed parallel to, but somewhat shorter than, the other, thus اٗ: and it answers the same purpose. The Madda is only used when the ا appears at the beginning of a word, as, without this mark, there, it is always short by position; as it is always long in the middle, or at the end of a word, by position likewise.

8. This Arabic mark ْ also is sometimes placed above a consonant, to shew that the syllable ends with it: it is called *Jazm, i.e.* "to conclude," or "to fix."

9. The following eight letters appear only in words purely or originally Arabic; and in many instances will be doubly useful to a beginner, inasmuch as they point out to him the Arabian origin of the words in which they occur. They are—

ث ح ص ض ط ظ ع ق

10. Every letter (of a word) should be connected with that which follows it; except these seven,

ا د ذ ر ز ژ و

### OF THE PRONUNCIATION OF THE ARABIC LETTERS.

11. The beginner cannot fail to observe, that many of the letters, as they are set down in the order of the alphabet, have the same sounds, as

ث س ص   ز ض ظ   ت ط   ع ا   ح ه

which have been marked as S, Z, T, A, and H; and he may naturally wonder at this redundancy. In fact, there is no actual redundancy. Eight of these letters, as already stated (see p. 3), are peculiar to the Arabic, and are sounded in that language very differently from what they are in Persian. They have generally sounds very harsh and rough; some very difficult, and others almost impossible for an English beginner to imitate. Let him be consoled, however, with the assurance, that an exact imitation of these sounds is not only unnecessary, but absolutely useless to a reader of the Persian language; inasmuch as the Persians themselves, in speaking and reading their native tongue, when they come to an Arabic word in which any of those letters occur, never attempt to pronounce them as the Arabs; except, perhaps, the letter ح, which is pronounced with a stronger aspirate than the ہ: they pronounce them merely like as many Persian letters as come the nearest in point of sound to them, exactly as I have set them down in the order of the alphabet. (See the Alphabet, p. 1.)

## OF VOWELS.

12. These thirty-two letters are all consonants; with the exception of ي ا و which serve also as long vowels; but the و is used both as a long and short vowel. When short, it answers to the vowel *u* in English, as in the words "pūt," "pūsh," &c.; and when long, it answers to *oo*, as in the word "boot," or to *u*, as in the word "brute." The ا is long; and it corresponds with "au," as in the word "cause"; or with "aw," as in the word "paw." The ي is also always long; and answers to "*ee*," as in the word "beef"; or to "*ea*," as in the word "beat".*

13. The short vowels are expressed by three small marks; of which, one is placed above the consonant, thus بَ *bă*, and answers to the short *ă* in English, as in the word "bat"; one below the consonant, thus پِ *pĕ*, and answers to the short *ĕ*, as in the word "pĕt"; and the third is somewhat in the front above the consonant, thus شُ *shū*, and answers to the *ū* as pronounced in the word "būll": they are called by the Persians زَبَرْ *zabar*, زِيرْ *zeer*, and پيشْ *peesh* respectively, signifying "above," "below," and "the front"; each of them expressing its own peculiar position with respect to the consonant.

---

* The Indians use the vowel ي sometimes like *ea*, as in the word "bear"; and the vowel و like *oa*, as in the word "boat"; to which و and ي they have given the appellation of مَجْهُولْ *Majhool*, "obscure," in contradistinction to the other instances in which they are used as long vowels, when they are called مَعْرُوفْ *Maaroof*, "distinct." This distinction, however, is not known among the modern Persians.

14. These short vowels are sometimes doubled thus ٌ ٍ they have still the same power; but with this addition, that they are sounded as if the syllable ended with a ن; thus, رً răn, تٍ tĕn, دٌ dūn.

15. Although these double marks are purely and peculiarly Arabic, and the Persians never use them; yet, as they often occur in Arabic passages and quotations, with which a Persian student must frequently meet in the course of his studies, I thought they might as well be explained here. Their collective name (in Arabic of course) is تَنْوِين *Tanween*, signifying "to pronounce or produce the sound of the letter ن"; and, separately, they go by the names نَصْب *Nasb*, جَرّ *Jarr*, and رَفْع *Rafa*, respectively, signifying the same as the short vowels in Persian.

16. Let it be remarked here, that when the letter و in the middle of a word precedes the letter ا, it loses its sound altogether in some instances; as in the words خوابيدَن "to sleep," خواسْتَن "to wish," &c., which are pronounced *khaubeedan*, *khaustan*, &c.: in the same manner, when it precedes the letter ي, as in the word خويش "self," or "relation," which is pronounced *kheesh*. And the ا in the middle of a word is used sometimes as a consonant; in which case the ء *hamzah* is placed over it, to distinguish it from the vowel ا; as, تأمّل *ta-ammūll*, "reflection."

## OF SPELLING AND FORMING WORDS.

17. The beginner can have no difficulty now, in spelling and pronouncing any short Persian words, properly marked with the vowel-points. I advise him, however, to begin by pronouncing single letters; appreciating duly the sound of each consonant, and the power of the vowels, before he attempts the compounds: so let him commence as follows:—

| خَ | حَ | چَ | جَ | ثَ | تَ | پَ | بَ | اَ |
|---|---|---|---|---|---|---|---|---|
| *khă* | *hă* | *chă* | *jă* | *să* | *tă* | *pă* | *bă* | *ă* |

| شِ | سِ | ژِ | زِ | رِ | ذَ | دَ |
|---|---|---|---|---|---|---|
| *shĕ* | *sĕ* | *jĕ* | *zĕ* | *rĕ* | *ză* | *dă* |

| فُ | غِ | عِ | ظِ | طِ | ضِ | صِ |
|---|---|---|---|---|---|---|
| *fŭ* | *ghĕ* | *ĕ* | *zĕ* | *tĕ* | *zĕ* | *sĕ* |

| وُ | نُ | مُ | لُ | گُ | کُ | قُ |
|---|---|---|---|---|---|---|
| *vū* | *nū* | *mū* | *lū* | *gū* | *kū* | *ckū* |

| يُ | هُ |
|---|---|
| *yū* | *hū* |

| حً | چً | جً | ثً | تً | پً | بً | اً |
|---|---|---|---|---|---|---|---|
| *hăn* | *chăn* | *jăn* | *săn* | *tăn* | *păn* | *băn* | *ăn* |

| شٍ | سٍ | ژٍ | زٍ | رٍ | ذٍ | دٍ | خً |
|---|---|---|---|---|---|---|---|
| *shĕn* | *sĕn* | *jĕn* | *zĕn* | *rĕn* | *zĕn* | *dĕn* | *khăn* |

| قٌ | فٌ | غٌ | عٌ | ظٍ | طٍ | ضٍ | صٍ |
|---|---|---|---|---|---|---|---|
| *ckūn* | *fūn* | *ghūn* | *būn* | *zĕn* | *tĕn* | *zĕn* | *sĕn* |

| يٌ | هٌ | وٌ | نٌ | مٌ | لٌ | كٌ |
|---|---|---|---|---|---|---|
| *yūn* | *hūn* | *vūn* | *nūn* | *mūn* | *lūn* | *kūn.* |

## 18. COMPOUNDS OF TWO LETTERS.

| | | | | | |
|---|---|---|---|---|---|
| بِبْ | اِبْ | جَبْ | تَبْ | بَبْ | اَبْ |
| *beb* | *eb* | *jab* | *tab* | *bab* | *ab* |
| حَبَ | كُبْ | نُبْ | دُبْ | حِبْ | ثِبْ |
| *haba* | *kūb* | *nūb* | *dūb* | *heb* | *seb* |
| بَنْ | لِتَ | كِتَ | بَتَ | مَتَ | شَتَ |
| *ban* | *leta* | *keta* | *bata* | *mata* | *shata* |
| هُوَ | فِمَ | زَكْ | رَدْ | جَسَ | بَسْ |
| *hūva* | *fema* | *zak* | *rad* | *jasa* | *bas* |
| جا | با | بَرْ | طِلْ | صَعَ | مُنَ |
| *jaw* | *baw* | *bar* | *tel* | *sa-ă* | *mūna* |
| گَفْ | فَشْ | عَسْ | عَرْ | لا | كا |
| *gaf* | *fash* | *as* | *ar* | *law* | *kaw* |
| خِسْ | بُو | كُو | شِرْ | نَوْ | يا |
| *khes* | *boo* | *koo* | *sher* | *now* | *yaw* |
| نَطْ | بُصْ | اا | آ | ما | يَرْ |
| *nat* | *būs* | *aw* | *aw* | *maw* | *yar* |
| يَجْ | بِخْ | ژَنْ | دِهْ | عِضْ | سُبَ |
| *yaj* | *bekh* | *jan* | *deh* | *ez* | *sūba* |
| كِرْ | طَشَ | صَسْ | نِي | قِمْ | نَچْ |
| *ker* | *tasha* | *sas* | *nee* | *ckem* | *nach* |

| لَنْ | لِبْ | ها | پَژْ | يُتَ | فِي |
|---|---|---|---|---|---|
| *lan* | *leb* | *haw* | *paj* | *yūta* | *fee* |
| هِمْ | هَجْ | مَيْ | رِكَ | غِشْ | لُو |
| *hem* | *haj* | *may* | *reka* | *ghesh* | *loo* |
| مُغْ | شِدَ | لَذْ | بَكْ | بَدْ | هُنْ |
| *mūgh* | *sheda* | *laz* | *bak* | *bad* | *hūn* |
| فُدَ | ضُكَ | صُبَ | صُلْ | جَيْ | سُغْ |
| *fūda* | *zūka* | *sūba* | *sūl* | *jay* | *sūgh* |
| ثِمَ | كُشْ | تُرْ | لُرْ | عُذْ | قِدْ |
| *sema* | *kūsh* | *tūr* | *lūr* | *oz* | *cked* |
| گُوْ | يُوْ | پِسَ | هُلِ | بِفُ | نَدُ |
| *goo* | *yoo* | *pesa* | *hūlē* | *befū* | *nadū* |
| ظَيْ | طُرْ | غِمَ | شا | شُوَ | كِيَ |
| *zay* | *tūr* | *ghema* | *shaw* | *shūva* | *keya* |

19. The sounds of the consonants, and the power of the vowels, (according to the examples already given), being perfectly regular and uniform in Persian, the beginner is now enabled, by the perusal of the preceding pages, to combine as many letters as he pleases together, and, by supplying them with the vowels as they are marked, form them into words of as many syllables as he likes. He will do well now to store his memory with as many Persian words as he can, out of those which I shall set down for him, before he begins to learn the parts of speech and the rules for the formation of sentences. Let him first learn the Persian numerals.

## OF THE NUMERALS.

20. Twenty-eight of the thirty-two letters of the Alphabet are expressed in eight words; thus:

| سَعفَص | كَلَمَن | حُطي | هَوَز | اَبجَد |
|---|---|---|---|---|
| *să-afăs* | *kalaman* | *Hŭt-tee* | *Hav-vaz* | *Abjad* |

| ضَظَغ | ثَخَذ | قَرَشَت |
|---|---|---|
| *zazegh* | *sakh-khez* | *Ckarashat* |

21. These letters have their numerical values; and, taking the order in which they are now arranged, the first nine, that is, from ا to ط, are the units; the second nine, that is, from ي to ص, are the tens; the third nine, that is, from ق to ظ, are the hundreds; and the remaining letter غ is one thousand. By the combination of these letters, according to their values of course, any number may be expressed.

22. The Persians also use figures, which is a much simpler way of calculating, having only nine units (as the English); with which, of course, combinations may be found indefinitely. These figures are arranged, and calculated, from left to right; thus:

| ١ | ٢ | ٣ | ۴ | ۵ | ٦ | ٧ | ٨ | ٩ | ١٠ |
|---|---|---|---|---|---|---|---|---|---|
| 1 | 2 | 3 | 4 | 5 | 6 | 7 | 8 | 9 | 10 |

and they are expressed as follows:

يَك دُو سِه چهار پَنج شِش هَفت هَشت نُه دَه

23. The following lines will shew how the numbers are formed, both with letters and with figures, as well as how they are pronounced in Persian.

| پَنْج | چَهارْ | سِهْ | دُو | يَكْ |
|---|---|---|---|---|
| ه | د | ج | ب | ا |
| ٥ | ٤ | ٣ | ٢ | ١ |
| 5 | 4 | 3 | 2 | 1 |
| دَهْ | نُهْ | هَشْتْ | هَفْتْ | شِشْ |
| ي | ط | ح | ز | و |
| ١٠ | ٩ | ٨ | ٧ | ٦ |
| 10 | 9 | 8 | 7 | 6 |
| پانْزْدَهْ | چَهارْدَهْ | سيزْدَهْ | دَوازْدَهْ | يازْدَهْ |
| يه | دي | جب | يب | يا |
| ١٥ | ١٤ | ١٣ | ١٢ | ١١ |
| 15 | 14 | 13 | 12 | 11 |
| بيسْتْ | نُوزْدَهْ | هَجْدَهْ | هَفْدَهْ | شانْزْدَهْ |
| ك | يط | يح | يز | يو |
| ٢٠ | ١٩ | ١٨ | ١٧ | ١٦ |
| 20 | 19 | 18 | 17 | 16 |
| بيسْتُ وچَهارْ | بيسْتُ وسِهْ | بيسْتُ ودُو | بيسْتُ ويَكْ | |
| كد | كج | كب | كا | |
| ٢٤ | ٢٣ | ٢٢ | ٢١ | |
| 24 | 23 | 22 | 21 | |
| بيسْتُ وهَشْتْ | بيسْتُ وهَفْتْ | بيسْتُ وشَشْ | بيسْتُ وپَنْج | |
| كح | كز | كو | كه | |
| ٢٨ | ٢٧ | ٢٦ | ٢٥ | |
| 28 | 27 | 26 | 25 | |
| سي ودُو | سي ويَكْ | سيْ | بيسْتُ ونُه | |
| لب | لا | ل | كط | |
| ٣٢ | ٣١ | ٣٠ | ٢٩ | |
| 32 | 31 | 30 | 29 | |

| سي وُشِشْ | سي وُپَنْج | سي وُچَهارْ | سي وُسِهْ |
|---|---|---|---|
| لو | له | لد | لج |
| ۳۶ | ۳۵ | ۳۴ | ۳۳ |
| 36 | 35 | 34 | 33 |

| چِهِلْ | سي وُنُهْ | سي وُهَشْتْ | سي وُهَفْتْ |
|---|---|---|---|
| م | لط | لح | لز |
| ۴۰ | ۳۹ | ۳۸ | ۳۷ |
| 40 | 39 | 38 | 37 |

| چِهِلُ وُچَهارْ | چِهِلُ وسِهْ | چِهِلُ ودُوْ | چِهِلُ ويَكْ |
|---|---|---|---|
| مد | مج | مب | ما |
| ۴۴ | ۴۳ | ۴۲ | ۴۱ |
| 44 | 43 | 42 | 41 |

| چِهِلُ وهَشْتْ | چِهِلُ وهَفْتْ | چِهِلُ وشِشْ | چِهِلُ وَپنْج |
|---|---|---|---|
| مح | مز | مو | مه |
| ۴۸ | ۴۷ | ۴۶ | ۴۵ |
| 48 | 47 | 46 | 45 |

| نَوَدْ | هَشْتادْ | هَفْتادْ | شَسْتْ | پَنْجاهْ | چِهِلُ ونُهْ |
|---|---|---|---|---|---|
| ص | ف | ع | س | ن | مط |
| ۹۰ | ۸۰ | ۷۰ | ۶۰ | ۵۰ | ۴۹ |
| 90 | 80 | 70 | 60 | 50 | 49 |

| پانْصَدْ | چَهارْصَدْ | سيصَدْ | دُوصَدْ or دَوِيسْتْ | صَدْ |
|---|---|---|---|---|
| ث | ت | ش | ر | ق |
| ۵۰۰ | ۴۰۰ | ۳۰۰ | ۲۰۰ | ۱۰۰ |
| 500 | 400 | 300 | 200 | 100 |

| هَزارْ | نُهْصَدْ | هَشْصَدْ | هَفْصَدْ | شَشْصَدْ |
|---|---|---|---|---|
| غ | ظ | ض | ذ | خ |
| ۱۰۰۰ | ۹۰۰ | ۸۰۰ | ۷۰۰ | ۶۰۰ |
| 1000 | 900 | 800 | 700 | 600 |

24. The Persian Ordinals are expressed thus:

| پَنجُم | چَهارُم | سِیُوم | دُوُم | اَوَّل |
|---|---|---|---|---|
| 5th | 4th | 3d | 2d | 1st |
| دَهُم | نُهُم | هَشتُم | هَفتُم | شَشُم |
| 10th | 9th | 8th | 7th | 6th |
| پانزدَهُم | چَهاردَهُم | سیزدَهُم | دَوازدَهُم | یازدَهُم |
| 15th | 14th | 13th | 12th | 11th |
| بیستُم | نوزدَهُم | هَجدَهُم | هَفدَهُم | شانزدَهُم |
| 20th | 19th | 18th | 17th | 16th |
| شَصتُم | پَنجاهُم | چِهِلُم | سی اُم | بیستُ ویَکُم |
| 60th | 50th | 40th | 30th | 21st |

| صَدُم | نَوَدُم | هشتادُم | هَفتادُم |
|---|---|---|---|
| 100th | 90th | 80th | 70th |

25. The days of the week are thus named in Persian:

| چهار شَنبه | سه‌شنبه | دوشَنبه | یَکشَنبه | شَنبه |
|---|---|---|---|---|
| Wednesday. | Tuesday. | Monday. | Sunday. | Saturday |

| جُمعَه or آدینَه | پَنج شَنبه |
|---|---|
| Friday. | Thursday. |

They are collectively called اَیّامِ هَفتَه *i.e.* "the seven days of the week."

### OF SINGLE SIGNIFICANT WORDS.

26. I now proceed to put down a number of words, which, as I shall mark them with Vowel-points, as well as place under each word its exact meaning in English, will serve the

double purpose of storing the memory of a beginner with a good many useful and common words in the Persian language, and of teaching him, at the same time, how to pronounce them: and, in order to point out the words that are of Arabic origin, they shall be distinguished by the letter (A). The student is recommended, therefore, to learn and remember as many of these words as he can, before he goes any further. They will be found very useful hereafter, in the course of his study.

| | | | |
|---|---|---|---|
| A. مَلَك<br>Angel. | A. اِمام<br>a Leader in Religion. | پَیغَمبَر<br>Prophet. | خُدا<br>God. |
| آسمان<br>sky. | A. مَذهَب<br>creed. | A. دِین<br>Religion, Faith. | فِرِشتَه<br>Angel. |
| مَرد<br>man. | دُوزَخ<br>Hell. | بِهِشت<br>Paradise. | زَمِین<br>Earth. |
| بِرادَر<br>brother. | مادَر<br>mother. | پِدَر<br>father. | زَن<br>woman. |
| دُختَر<br>girl, daughter. | پِسَر<br>boy, son. | فَرزَند<br>offspring, child. | خواهَر<br>sister. |
| A. عَمّه<br>paternal aunt. | A. عَم<br>paternal uncle. | A. جَدّه<br>grandmother. | A. جَد<br>grandfather. |
| نان<br>bread. | خویش<br>relation, kindred. | A. خالَه<br>maternal aunt. | A. خال<br>maternal uncle. |
| مَي<br>wine. | رَوغَن<br>butter. | گُوشت<br>meat, flesh. | آب<br>water. |

| | | | |
|---|---|---|---|
| اَنگُور<br>grapes. | مِیوَه<br>fruit. | A. شَرْبَت<br>drink. | A. شَراب<br>wine. |
| سَبْزِي<br>vegetables. | شِیر<br>milk. | گُلابِي<br>pear. | سِیب<br>apple. |
| باغْبان<br>gardener. | باغ<br>fruit-garden. | دِرَخْت<br>tree. | گُل<br>flowers, rose. |
| A. کُرْسِي<br>chair. | A. حُجْرَه<br>room. | خانَه<br>house. | باغْچَه<br>flower-garden. |
| A. قَلَم<br>pen. | کاغَذ<br>paper. | A. کِتاب<br>book. | A. مَدْرَسَه<br>college. |
| A. شَمْع<br>candle. | لاك<br>sealing-wax. | دَوات<br>inkstand. | A. مُرَکَّب<br>ink. |
| سُوزَن<br>needle. | مِقْراض<br>scissors. | چاقُو<br>penknife. | مُهْر<br>seal, signet. |
| اوسْتادْ<br>master. | آبْرِیشَم<br>silk. | رِیسْمان<br>thread. | سُنْجاق<br>pin. |
| A. طَلَبَه<br>student. | شاگِرْد<br>pupil. | A. مُدَرِّس<br>lecturer. | A. مُعَلِّم<br>teacher, schoolmaster. |
| نَماز<br>prayer. | A. مَسْجِد<br>church, chapel, mosque. | A. دَرْس<br>lecture. | A. سَبَق<br>lesson. |
| A. نَصِیحَت<br>advice. | A. وَعْظ<br>preaching. | A. مَوْعِظَه<br>exhortation. | A. دُعا<br>supplication. |

| | | | |
|---|---|---|---|
| دِه<br>village. | شَهر<br>city. | تَوبیخ<br>reproof. | A. مَشوَرَت<br>council. |
| شاه or پادِشاه<br>king. | A. وَلایَت<br>dominion. | A. مَملَکَت<br>kingdom. | A. قَریَه<br>hamlet. |
| A. کاتِب<br>scribe. | A. دَبیر<br>counsellor. | A. وَزیر<br>minister. | A. مَلِکَه<br>queen. |
| سِپَهسالار<br>commander-in-chief. | A. اَمیر<br>commander, a prince. | سِپاهی<br>soldier. | سِپاه<br>army. |
| A. عَقل<br>wisdom. | دانِش<br>learning. | A. حِکمَت<br>science, philosophy. | A. عِلم<br>knowledge. |
| خاک<br>dust, earth. | باد<br>wind. | آتَش<br>fire. | خِرَد<br>understanding. |
| A. جَنوب<br>south. | A. مَغرِب<br>west. | A. مَشرِق<br>east. | A. هَوا<br>air. |
| زیر<br>under. | راست<br>right. | چَپ<br>left. | A. شَمال<br>north. |
| میز<br>table. | پائین<br>below. | زَبَر<br>upon. | بالا<br>above. |
| نَمَک<br>salt. | میزبان<br>host. | مِهمان<br>guest. | سُفرَه<br>table-cloth. |
| A. کاسَه<br>basin. | A. ظَرف<br>vessel. | خورِش<br>eatable. | A. طَعام<br>food. |

| | | | |
|---|---|---|---|
| گُوسالَه<br>calf. | گاو<br>ox. | بَرَه<br>lamb. | گُوسفَند<br>sheep. |
| قاطِر<br>mule. | مادِیان<br>mare. | اَسب<br>horse. | شُتُر<br>camel. |
| خَرگوش<br>hare. | آهو<br>antelope. | گامیش<br>buffalo. | خَر<br>ass. |
| رُوباه<br>fox. | گُرگ<br>wolf. | پَلَنگ<br>leopard. | شیر<br>lion. |
| بِیابان<br>desert. | باز<br>hawk. | تَذَرو<br>pheasant. | کَبک<br>partridge. |
| بیشَه<br>forest. | چَمَن<br>lawn. | مَرغزار<br>meadow. | صَحرا A.<br>field. |
| جاشو<br>sailor. | کَشتي<br>ship. | دَریا<br>sea. | کُوه<br>mountain. |
| سَیل , سَیلاب<br>torrent. | رُود , رُودخانَه<br>river. | ناخُدا<br>captain, pilot. | مُعَلِّم A.<br>mate. |
| بَرف<br>snow. | باران<br>rain. | جُوي<br>brook. | نَهر A.<br>stream. |
| طُوفان A.<br>flood, deluge. | بَرق A.<br>lightning. | رَعد A.<br>thunder. | تَگَرگ , ژالَه<br>hail. |
| چَشم<br>eye. | سَر<br>head. | پاي or پا<br>foot. | دَست<br>hand. |
| زَبان<br>tongue. | دَندان<br>tooth. | دَهَن<br>mouth. | گُوش<br>ear. |

| | | | |
|---|---|---|---|
| مُوْيْ<br>hair. | رُوْيْ<br>face. | اَنْگُشْتْ<br>finger. | دِلْ<br>heart. |
| رانْ<br>thigh. | بازُوْ<br>arm. | A. كَفْ<br>the palm (of the hand). | ساعِدْ<br>wrist. |
| سِينَهْ<br>breast. | شانَهْ<br>shoulder. | گَرْدَنْ<br>neck. | زانُوْ<br>knee. |
| پِيشانِي<br>forehead. | دِماغْ<br>brain. | بِينِي<br>nose. | رِيشْ<br>beard. |
| لَبْ<br>the lip. | زَنَخْ<br>chin. | اَبْرُوْ<br>eyebrow. | مِژْگان<br>eyelid, eyelash. |
| زَهْرَهْ<br>gall-bladder. | جِگَرْ<br>liver. | شُشْ<br>the lungs. | گُلُو<br>the throat. |
| A. كَوْكَبْ *or* سِتارَهْ<br>a star. | ناخُنْ<br>nail of the hand or foot. | پَنْجَهْ<br>the fist, the five fingers. | رُودَهْ<br>bowels. |

| | | |
|---|---|---|
| A. عُطارِدْ *or* تِيرْ<br>Mercury. | A. قَمَرْ *or* ماهْ<br>the Moon. | A. شَمْسْ *or* آفْتابْ<br>the Sun. |
| A. مُشْتَرِي *or* بِرْجِيسْ<br>Jupiter. | A. مِرِّيخْ *or* بَهْرامْ<br>Mars. | A. زُهْرَهْ *or* ناهِيدْ<br>Venus. |

| | | | |
|---|---|---|---|
| گَرْمْ<br>warm. | A. سَيّاراتْ<br>the planets. | A. ثَوابِتْ<br>the fixed stars. | A. زُحَلْ *or* كِيوانْ<br>Saturn. |
| تُرُشْ<br>sour | شِيرِينْ<br>sweet. | تَلْخْ<br>bitter. | سَرْدْ<br>cold. |

| | | | |
|---|---|---|---|
| باریك<br>slender. | دُرُشت<br>coarse, thick, severe. | نازُك<br>fine, nice, delicate. | چَرب<br>oily, rich. |
| A. قَوي<br>strong. | لاغَر<br>thin, lean. | فَربِه<br>fat. | كُلُفت<br>stout, thick. |
| سُرخ<br>red. | سیاه<br>black. | سَفید<br>white. | A. ضَعیف<br>weak. |
| بِنَفش<br>violet colour. | كَبُود<br>blue. | سَبز<br>green. | زَرد<br>yellow. |
| آهَن<br>iron. | مِس<br>copper. | A. نُقرَه *or* سیم<br>silver. | A. طلا *or* زَر<br>gold. |
| جیوَه *or* A. زَیبَق<br>quicksilver. | A. قَلع *or* اَرزیز<br>tin. | رُوي<br>zinc. | سُرب<br>lead. |
| چَنگال<br>a fork. | كارد<br>a knife. | فُولاد<br>steel. | بِرِنج<br>brass. |
| پیشگیر<br>napkin. | نَلبَكي<br>a saucer. | فِنجان<br>a cup. | بُشقاب<br>a plate. |
| كَباب<br>roasted. | بِریان<br>fried. | A. حَلوا<br>sweetmeat *or* sweet cake. | A. خَلال<br>toothpick. |
| بیمَزَه<br>tasteless, insipid. | خام<br>raw. | پُختَه<br>cooked *or* baked. | جُوشیدَه<br>boiled. |
| شَكَر<br>sugar. | چاي<br>tea. | A. قَهوَه<br>coffee. | A. لَذیذ<br>delicious. |
| تُند<br>(too) fast. | كَلید<br>key. | زَنجیر<br>chain. | A. ساعَت<br>a watch. |

| | | | |
|---|---|---|---|
| میانه<br>middling. | بد<br>bad. | خوب<br>good. | کند<br>(too) slow. |
| شام<br>evening. | صبح .A<br>morning. | روز<br>day. | شب<br>night. |
| غروب .A<br>sunset. | عصر .A<br>afternoon. | ظهر .A<br>noontide. | چاشت<br>mid-day. |
| در<br>door. | دیر<br>late. | زود<br>quick. | وقت .A<br>time. |
| فرش .A<br>carpet. | درگاه<br>gateway. | آستانه<br>threshold. | دیوار<br>wall. |
| بازار<br>market. | بالش<br>pillow. | خوابگاه<br>bedstead. | بستر<br>bed *or* pillow. |
| جوراب<br>stocking. | کفش .A<br>shoe. | متاع .A<br>goods. | دوکان<br>shop. |
| پیراهن<br>shirt. | قبا .A<br>coat. | دستار<br>turban. | کلاه<br>hat *or* cap. |
| کمربند<br>sash, belt. | شال .A<br>shawl. | جامه<br>close. | شلوار<br>trowsers. |
| هیزم<br>fire-wood. | گلگیر<br>snuffers. | شمعدان<br>candlestick. | کیسه .A<br>purse. |
| بارگاه<br>court. | تاج<br>crown. | تخت .A<br>throne. | چوب<br>stick. |
| غله .A<br>corn. | گدا<br>beggar. | دشمن<br>enemy. | دوست<br>friend. |
| سگ<br>dog. | مواشی .A<br>cattle. | چارپا<br>quadruped. | انبار<br>barn. |

| | | | |
|---|---|---|---|
| رَوشَن<br>light. | خُوك or گُراز<br>hog (wild *or* tame). | مُوش<br>mouse. | گُربَه<br>cat. |
| حَوض A.<br>pond. | شيشَه<br>glass *or* bottle. | آيِنَه<br>looking-glass. | تاريك<br>dark. |
| دَوا<br>medicine. | ماهي<br>fish. | غاز<br>goose. | بَط A.<br>duck. |
| دَلّاك A.<br>barber. | عَطّار A.<br>druggist. | جَرّاح A.<br>surgeon. | طَبيب A.<br>physician. |
| خَيّاط A.<br>tailor. | بَزّاز A.<br>draper. | بَقّال A.<br>grocer. | حَمّام A.<br>bath. |
| عَصّار A.<br>oilman. | طَبّاخ A.<br>cook. | خَبّاز A.<br>baker. | سَرّاج A.<br>saddler. |
| نَسّاج A.<br>weaver. | خَرّاط A.<br>turner. | نَجّار A.<br>carpenter. | خَرّاز A.<br>pedlar. |
| حَدّاد A.<br>blacksmith. | كَفّاش A.<br>shoemaker. | صَبّاغ A.<br>dyer. | قَصّاب A.<br>butcher. |
| حَكّاك A.<br>engraver. | قَنّاد A.<br>confectioner. | طَبّاع A.<br>printer. | صَحّاف A.<br>bookbinder. |
| صَيّاد A.<br>hunter. | شَمّاع A.<br>chandler. | نَقّاش A.<br>painter. | صَرّاف A.<br>banker *or* money-changer. |
| دَلّال A.<br>horse &c. *or* cattle dealer. | عَلّاف A.<br>corn-chandler. | خَمّار A.<br>wine-merchant. | فَلّاح A.<br>husbandman. |
| رَقّاص A.<br>a dancer. | حَمّال A.<br>a porter. | رَزّاز A.<br>rice-merchant. | هَلّاج A.<br>cotton-carder. |

غَوّاص A.
a diver.

## OF NOUNS.

27. The form and construction of the Persian Nouns are extremely simple and regular: there are no varieties of "Declension," or of "Articles"; nor is there any difference of termination, to mark the Gender, either in Substantives or Adjectives. All inanimate things are neuter: rational beings have different names to distinguish the sexes; as, مَرْدْ "man," زَنْ "woman," پِسَرْ "boy," دُخْتَرْ "girl," &c.; and animals have either the Adjectives, نَرْ "male," and مادَهْ "female," affixed or prefixed to them, to mark their genders; as, شيرِنَرْ "a lion," شيرِمادَهْ "a lioness"; مادَهْ گاو "a cow," گاوِنَرْ "a bull"; or, in some cases, they have also their proper names; as, ميشْ "an ewe," غُوچْ "a ram," نَرِيانْ "a horse," مادِيانْ "a mare," خُرُوسْ "a cock," ماكِيانْ "a hen," &c.

### OF THE CASES.

28. The Cases are decided by certain Particles, prefixed or affixed to the Noun: the Nominative never, and the Genitive but seldom, stands in need of such addition: the Dative is obtained by prefixing the syllable بِ to the Noun; and the Accusative, by affixing the particle را; though sometimes it is affixed to the Dative as well; in which case, of course, no prefix is used. The Ablative Case is formed by placing the Particle اَزْ, and the Vocative by placing the Particle اَيْ, before the Noun.

*EXAMPLES.*

### پِدَر "A Father."

| | | |
|---|---|---|
| N. & G. | پِدَر | the father. |
| D. | بِپِدَر | to the father. |
| Ac. | پِدَررا | the father. |
| Ab. | اَزپِدَر | from the father. |
| V. | اَيْ پِدَر | O father ! |

### بِرَادَر "A Brother."

| | | |
|---|---|---|
| N. & G. | بِرَادَر | the brother. |
| D. | بِبِرَادَر | to the brother. |
| Ac. | بِرَادَررا | the brother. |
| Ab. | اَزبِرَادَر | from the brother. |
| V. | اَيْ بِرَادَر | O brother ! |

### پِسَر "A Boy."

| | | |
|---|---|---|
| N. & G. | پِسَر | the boy. |
| D. | بِپِسَر | to the boy. |
| Ac. | پِسَررا | the boy. |
| Ab. | اَزپِسَر | from the boy. |
| V. | اَيْ پِسَر | O boy ! |

### دُخْتَر "A Girl."

| | | |
|---|---|---|
| N. & G. | دُخْتَر | the girl. |
| D. | بِدُخْتَر | to the girl. |
| Ac. | دُخْتَررا | the girl. |
| Ab. | اَزدُخْتَر | from the girl. |
| V. | اَيْ دُخْتَر | O girl ! |

### REMARKS ON A FEW EXCEPTIONS.

29. The above rules are quite regular ; and general enough for a beginner to be always on the safe side, if he observes them in the formation of the different Cases of any Persian Substantive or Adjective, Noun or Pronoun : but, at the same time, he will do well to peruse the following remarks, and to commit as many of them as he can to memory : they will be of great use to him in the course of his studies.

30. A Noun may be put in the Dative Case by affixing the Particle را, *instead* of placing the بِ before it ; as, for

instance, پسرْرا دِيدَمْ "I saw the boy," or پِسَرْرا گُفْتَمْ "I spoke *to* the boy"; the Noun پِسَرْ having the affix را in both the Accusative and Dative Cases: but when the Particle بِ is prefixed, the Noun is always in the Dative Case, and never in the Accusative.

31. When the Accusative is used indefinitely, the Particle را is altogether omitted; as, مي نُوشيدَمْ "I drank wine," instead of مَيْ را نُوشيدَمْ "I drank *the* wine."

32. A Noun may also be put in the Vocative Case by affixing the long آ, instead of prefixing the Particle اَيْ; but this form generally implies supplication, entreaty, or some such emphatic address; as, پَرْوَرْدِگار "the Lord," پَرْوَرْدِگارا "O Lord!" پادِشاهْ "the king," پادِشاها "O king!" دُوسْتْ "a friend," دُوسْتا "O friend!"

33. When two Nouns come together in Persian, in some instances, the short vowel (ِ) زِيرْ is placed under the last letter of the preceding Noun: this takes place when one Noun governs another, as in the Genitive Case; as, پَدَرِ دُخْتَرْ "the girl's father," or "the father of the girl." Here we see the vowel (ِ) placed under (ر), the last letter of the Noun پَدَرْ, which precedes and governs the other Noun دُخْتَرْ in the Genitive: but if this letter happen to be a quiescent ه, or a ي, instead of placing the (ِ) under it, the short Alēf (ٔ) or the Hamzah is placed over it, and the ۀ and ئ, so accented, are, in both instances, pronounced "*yē*"; as, بَنْدَۀ خُدا "the servant of God"; خانۀ پَدَرْ "the father's house"; ماهِئ دَرْيا "the fish of the sea"; &c.

34. Should the last letter be an ا, as جا "place," or و, as بُو "fragrance," the letter ي — either with the (ِ) under it, or with the (ٔ) over it—is added to the end of the word; as, جايِ پَدَر or جائِ پَدَر "the place of the father," بوِيِ گُل or بوئِ گُل "the fragrance of the rose." The latter form, however, is the most common of the two.

35. If the preceding Noun, however, be a part of the following one, as شَمْشيرِ فُولاد "a sword of steel," the Genitive may be obtained by placing the Particle اَز before the second Noun; but in such instances, the preceding Noun should be made definite, either by adding the ي of unity to the end of it, or placing a Numeral before it; as, شمشيري اَزفُولاد "*a* sword of steel," or دُوشَمْشِير اَزفُولاد "*two* swords of steel," *i.e.* swords made *out of* the steel.

## OF THE PLURALS.

36. In Persian, Rational beings, whether masculine or feminine, form their Plurals by adding آن (*awn*) to the Singular; as, مَرد "a man," مَردان "men"; زَن "a woman," زَنان "women": Inanimate things, by adding ها (*haw*); as, گُل "a flower," گُلها "flowers": and Animals, either by adding آن, as in the case of rational beings, or ها, as in that of inanimate things; as, اَسْب "a horse," اَسْبان or اَسْبها "horses." It depends upon the taste and the choice of the judicious writer which to prefer, as being more suitable to the occasion; though I may safely recommend the learner always to prefer the ها in all prose writings, as is generally done by the Persian writers themselves; but in poetry, the Muses are the best instructors. The celebrated bard سَعْدي (*Sādy*) himself has yielded to their authority, and sacrificed at their

altar: in one instance (but I believe the only one in all his writings) he has indeed been compelled, as it were, to form the Plural even of an inanimate thing, by adding آن to the Singular; — a transgression, of which none but himself (though only for once) could venture to be guilty; and for which, nothing but the splendid composition in which it occurs could have secured him against the censure of the Learned. It occurs in a beautiful couplet, in one of the author's most famous poems on the Praises of the Divinity. The couplet runs thus:

برگِ درختانِ سبز در نظرِ هوشیار
هر ورقي دفتريست معرفتِ کردگار

I translate it word for word, thus:

"The foliage of the verdant *trees*, in the sight of an intelligent being;"
"Every leaf is a volume on the knowledge of the Divinity."

The reader will observe the second word درختان "*trees*," in the couplet just cited, is the Plural of درخت "a tree," to which, in this instance, آن, instead of ها, has been added by the poet.

37. When a Noun, the Plural of which may be formed in آن, ends in the Singular Number, in ا or و, the letter ي is, for the most part, interposed between such final letter and the Particle آن, in forming the Plural Number; as, گدا "a beggar," گدایان "beggars"; بدگو "an evil-speaker," بدگویان "evil-speakers": and those Nouns that end in quiescent ه form their Plurals in گان when the ه is omitted, except they be written separately, which, however, is seldom or never the case; as, فرشته "an angel," فرشتگان "angels"; بچه "an infant," بچگان "infants," which are hardly ever written فرشته گان or بچه گان.

38. In imitation of the Feminine Plural of Arabic words, which is invariably formed by the affix آتْ, some modern writers, of no great authority however, have formed the Plurals of a few Persian Nouns of the Neuter Gender in آتْ also; or, if the Singular ends with the quiescent ه, in جاتْ; as, نَوازِش "a favour," نَوازِشاتْ "favours"; نِوِشْتَهْ "a letter," نِوِشْتَجاتْ "writings." The instances are, luckily, very few; and it is too vulgar to encourage imitation.

39. The Cases of a Noun in the Plural Number are formed in the same manner, and by the same Particles, as in the Singular.

EXAMPLES OF RATIONAL BEINGS.

SINGULAR.

| مَرْدْ | زَنْ | بَچَهْ | گَدا | بَدْگو |
|---|---|---|---|---|
| "A Man." | "A Woman." | "An Infant." | "A Beggar." | "Evil-speaker." |

PLURAL.

| | "Men" | "Women" | "Infants" | "Beggars" | "Evil-speakers" |
|---|---|---|---|---|---|
| N. & G. | مَرْدانْ | زَنانْ | بَچَگانْ | گَدایانْ | بَدْگویانْ |
| D. | بِمَرْدانْ | بِزَنانْ | بِبَچَگانْ | بِگَدایانْ | بِبَدْ گویانْ |
| Ac. | مَرْدانْ را | زَنانْ را | بَچَگانْ را | گَدایانْ را | بَدْ گویانْ را |
| Ab. | أَزْمَرْدانْ | أَزْزَنانْ | أَزْبَچَگانْ | أَزْگَدایانْ | أَزْبَدْ گویانْ |
| V. | اَيْ مَرْدانْ | اَيْ زَنانْ | اَيْ بَچَگانْ | اَيْ گَدایانْ | اَيْ بَدْ گویانْ |

## 40. OF IRRATIONAL BEINGS.

SINGULAR.

| | شيرِ نَر | شيرِ مادَه | بَرَه | آهُو |
|---|---|---|---|---|
| | "A Lion." | "A Lioness." | "A Lamb." | "An Antelope." |

PLURAL.

| | | | | |
|---|---|---|---|---|
| N. & G. | شيرهايِ نَر or شيرانِ نَر | شيرهايِ مادَه or شيرانِ مادَه | بَرَها or بَرَگان | آهُوها or آهُويان or آهُوان |
| D. | بِشيرهايِ نَر or بِشيرانِ نَر | بِشيرهايِ مادَه or .... &c. | بِبَرَها or ... &c. | .... or بِآهُوها or .... &c. |
| Ac. | شيرهايِ نَررا or شيرانِ نَررا | شيرهايِ مادَه‌را or .... &c. | بَرَهارا or ... &c. | .... or آهُوهارا or .... &c. |
| Ab. | اَزشيرهايِ نَر or اَزشيرانِ نَر | اَزشيرهايِ مادَه or .... &c. | اَزبَرَها or ... &c. | .... or اَزآهُوها or .... &c. |
| V. | اَيْ شيرهايِ نَر or اَيْ شيرانِ نَر | اَيْ شيرهايِ مادَه or .... &c. | اَيْ بَرَها or ... &c. | .... or اَيْ آهُوها or .... &c. |

## 41. OF INANIMATE THINGS.

SINGULAR.

| | نان | آفتاب | خانَه | گُو | مَي |
|---|---|---|---|---|---|
| | "Bread." | "The Sun." | "A House." | "A Ball." | "Wine." |

PLURAL.

| | | | | | |
|---|---|---|---|---|---|
| N. & G. | نانها | آفتابها | خانَها | گُويها | مَيها |
| D. | بِنانها | بِآفتابها | بِخانَها | بِگُويها | بِمَيها |
| Ac. | نانهارا | آفتابهارا | خانَهارا | گُويهارا | مَيهارا |
| Ab. | اَزنانها | اَزآفتابها | اَزخانَها | اَزگُويها | اَزمَيها |
| V. | اَيْ نانَها | اَيْ آفتابها | اَيْ خانَها | اَيْ گُويها | اَيْ مَيها |

42. In conclusion, let the reader remember, that what has been stated with regard to Rational Beings forming their Plurals in آن, یان, or گان, refers more strictly to poetry, and the higher classes of prose compositions. In the ordinary writings of the day, or even in refined conversation, it is by no means forbidden (or it is even better) to form all the Persian Plurals, of whatever kind, uniformly in ها. Nothing is more common in conversation, in Persia, than to say مَردها "men," زَنها "women," بچها "children," گدَاها "beggars," and numerous similar instances of ها implying the Plurals of both Rational and Irrational Beings. I shall only add, that if a foreigner, speaking good Persian, adheres uniformly to the use of the ها, in forming the Plural, he will be much nearer the mark than one who attempts to put the rigid rules of grammar into practice with regard to the Plurals of the three different classes of Nouns; as I am quite sure that the latter will many times oftener appear pedantic, than the former will fall into a slight error of idiom.

## OF ADJECTIVES.

43. The Persian Adjectives, whether of Number or otherwise, admit of no variation, but in the degrees of comparison: in other respects, they uniformly follow the Substantive, without partaking of the changes which the latter may undergo in Number or Case; excepting in the Accusative Case, when the Particle را is affixed to the Adjective, instead of being affixed to the Substantive; as will be seen in the following examples:—

جَوان "young." پیر "old." بیمار "sick."
خوب "good." بَد "bad."

| SINGULAR. | PLURAL. |
|---|---|
| مَردِ خُوبْ "a good man." | مَردانِ خُوبْ "good men." |
| بِمَردِ خُوبْ "to a good man." | بِمَردانِ خُوبْ "to good men." |
| مَردِ خُوبْ را "the good man." | مَردانِ خُوبْ را "the good men." |
| اَز مَردِ خُوبْ "from a good man." | اَز مَردانِ خُوبْ "from the good men." |
| اَي مَردِ خُوبْ "O good man!" | اَي مَردانِ خُوبْ "O good men!" |

In like manner, اَسْبْ "a horse," اَسْبِ بَدْ, اَسْبهايِ بَدْ, اَسْبِ بَدْرا; &c.

44. Simple Adjectives are frequently used *in the Plural*, to express *qualified* Substantives; as, خوبانْ "good *men*," بَدانْ "bad *men*"; جَوانانْ "youths," پيرانْ "old men"; بيمارانْ "sick persons; but these Plurals (which, be it remembered, must always be formed in آنْ) invariably signify Rational Beings, and, chiefly, those of the Masculine Gender. But when Compound Adjectives are thus used as Qualified Substantives (though forming their Plurals in آنْ), they are not confined to any particular Gender: they may be either Masculine or Feminine, as the expression itself may indicate; as, دِلْبَران "the ravishers of hearts"; which is evidently intended to be Feminine; دِلْ آوَرانْ "the bold-hearted," "heroes," which is obviously Masculine; and دِلْ خَسْتَگانْ "the afflicted in heart," which may belong to either Gender.

OF COMPARISON.

45. There are two Particles of Comparison in Persian, تَرْ and تَرِينْ. The Positive is made Comparative by affixing تَرْ, and Superlative by adding تَرِينْ; as, بِهْ "well," بِهْتَرْ "better";

بِهْتَرِينْ "best"; بَدْ "bad," بَدْتَرْ "worse," بَدْتَرِينْ "worst"; جَوانْ "young," جَوانْتَرْ "younger," جَوانْتَرِينْ "youngest"; &c. The Particle اَزْ, in Persian, is an equivalent to "*than*" expressed in English after a Comparative; with this difference only, that in Persian it may be expressed either after or before the Comparative; as, پِدَرْ جَوانْتَرْ اَزْ مادَرْ "the father (is) younger than the mother"; which may also be expressed, پِدَرْ اَزْ مادَرْ جَوانْتَرْ, &c.

The following are a few more Examples:

[N. B. The reader will observe, that, in all the following sentences, *no Verbs* have been employed: the reason of the omission is, that the reader being supposed to be as yet unacquainted with the Persian Verbs, I did not like to introduce any, before he had received instructions on the subject. He can place any verb he pleases (as soon as he has learned the Verbs) at the end of each of these sentences, to make them complete.]

COMPARATIVE.

| | |
|---|---|
| كِتابْ اَزْ بازِي بِهْتَرْ | Book (*i.e.* reading) (is) better than play. |
| هِنْدْ اَزْ اِنْگِلِسْتانْ گَرْمْ تَرْ | India (is) warmer than England. |
| پِدَرْ اَزْ پِسَرْ جاهِلْ تَرْ | The father (was) more ignorant than the son. |
| اِنْگِلِسْتانْ آبادْ تَرْ اَزْ رُوسْ | England (became) more populous than Russia. |
| زَنانْ نازُكْ تَرْ اَزْ مَرْدانْ | Women (are) more delicate than men. |
| فارْسِي آسانْ تَرْ اَزْ عَرَبِي | Persian (is not) easier than Arabic. |
| دُوسْتانْ مِهْرَبانْ تَرْ اَزْ خْوِيشانْ | Friends (are not) kinder than relations. |

SUPERLATIVE.

| | |
|---|---|
| خُدا بِهْتَرِينِ ياوَرانْ | God (is) the best of helpers. |
| وَفا خُوبتَرِينِ صِفَتْها | Fidelity (is) the best of qualities. |
| دانِشْ بِهْتَرِينِ گَنْجْها | Knowledge (is) the best of treasures. |
| سَگْ مِهْرَبان تَرِينِ جانْوَرانْ | The dog (is) the most affectionate of animals. |
| طَمَعْ بَدْتَرِينِ عَيْبْها | Avarice (is) the worst of vices. |
| شيرِينْ تَرِينِ مِيوَها اَنْگُور | The sweetest of fruits (is) the grape. |
| بَدْتَرِينِ گُناهانْ دُرُوغْ | The worst of crimes (is) falsehood. |

## 46. OF DEFINITE AND INDEFINITE NOUNS.

The Persian Nouns are for the most part generic, and Definite in their significations. For instance, مَرْدْ, زَنْ, اَسْبْ, كِتابْ, "man," "woman," "horse," "book": each of these Nouns, as it now stands by itself, signifies its own kind in general; and in composition, when used in this form, each would signify a particular one, or, if used in the plural, a particular collection of its kind; as in English would be expressed, "the man," "the woman," &c.

47. These Nouns may be made Indefinite, or, to express unity by adding the letter ي; termed يايِ تَنْكير, the indefinite ي; or يايِ وَحْدَتْ, that of unity; as, مَرْدي, زَني, اَسْبي, كِتابي, "a certain man," "a certain woman," &c. If the Noun, however, ends in the quiescent ه, as بَچَه "an infant," instead of adding the ي, the Hamzah (ٔ) is placed over the ه; as, بَچَهٔ and pronounced "*bacha-ee*," "a certain infant."

48. Abstract Nouns are formed in the same manner; as, دُوسْت "a friend," دُوسْتي "friendship," مَردي "manliness," &c. An Abstract Noun is easily distinguished from an Indefinite Noun, when properly pronounced. In an Indefinite Noun, the accent is placed on the last syllable but one; that is, upon مَر, and upon دُو, in the words مَردي and دُوستي: and in the other instance, it is placed on the last syllable; that is, upon دي and تي in the same words; or upon شا and هي in the word پادِشاهي "a certain king *or* sovereignty": and, to distinguish them in writing, it is better always to place the Hamzah (ء) over the final ي in the Abstract Nouns; thus, بيكارئ "idleness," مِهمانئ "entertainment," &c. The quiescent ه is changed for the letter گ in Abstract Nouns, instead of placing the ء over it, as in Indefinite Nouns; thus, بَچَگي "infancy," هَرزگي "foolery," &c.

49. Another use of this ي at the end of a Noun, is to denote connection or relation; as, حافِظِ شيرازي "Haufez (the Poet) of Shiraz"; زَنانِ بَغدادي "the women of Bagdad." In this case, the accent is placed on the last syllable, that is, upon زي and دي in شيرازي and بَغدادي, without the Hamzah (ء) when they are used as Adjectives, as in the above instance: but when such Nouns are used as Substantives, the ء (Hamzah) is interposed between the last letter of the Noun (which must have the (ِ) زير under it) and the final ي: and the accent is then placed upon the (ء) Hamzah, in pronouncing the word; thus, شيرازِئي "a certain person of Shiraz," &c.

50. Although this ي, termed ياي نَسبَت, that is, of con-

nection or patronymic, is purely Arabic, yet it is so extensively used in Persian as to render it quite necessary for a beginner to understand the nature of it.

51. يايِ لَياقَتْ the ي is sometimes added to a Verbal Noun, to express fitness, suitableness, &c.; as, كَرْدَنِي "fit to be done," خوردَني "fit to eat," &c.: and sometimes to intimate an event or circumstance; as, روزيِ كِه "the day *that* or *which*," &c., وَقْتيِ كِه "the time *when*"; meaning, *in both places*, to describe some event or circumstance. It is, in this sense, called the يايِ اِشارَتْ, that is, of Intimation.

52. This ي has also several other little uses in Persian; but they being either very rare, or purely poetical, I have not thought it necessary to detain the reader in order to explain them.

## OF PRONOUNS.

53. The Persian Pronouns have also two Numbers, Singular and Plural; and there is no difference of Gender, except in the Third Persons of irrational and inanimate things. The Pronouns belonging to these two are the same, and may also be used for rational beings; but such as are peculiar to the latter should not be used for any other.

The following are the separate Personal Pronouns:

| SINGULAR. | PLURAL. |
|---|---|
| مَن "I." | ما "We." |
| تُو "Thou." | شُما "You." |
| اُو "He" *or* "She." | ايشان "They." |
| وَي "He" *or* "She." | — |
| آن "It." | آنها "They." |

54. These are declined as any other Nouns; except that the letter ن in the First Person, and the letter و in the Second Person Singular, are left out when the Particle را is added to the Pronoun: and in the Third Person of both numbers, in the Dative Case, the letter د may also be interposed between the Particle ب and the first ا, which in some instances is altogether omitted; as will be seen in the following examples:

SINGULAR.

| | | | | |
|---|---|---|---|---|
| N. & G. | مَن | تُو | وَي or اُو | آن |
| D. | بِمَن | بِتُو | بِوَي , بِدُو or بِاُو | بِآن or بِدان |
| Ac. | مَرا | تُرا | وَيرا or اُورا | آنرا |
| Ab. | اَزمَن | اَزتُو | اَزوَي  اَزاُو | اَزآن |
| V. | اَي مَن | اَي تُو | اَي اُو  اَي اُو | اَي آن |

PLURAL.

| | | | | |
|---|---|---|---|---|
| N. & G. | ما | شُما | اِيشان | آنها or آنان |
| D. | بِما | بِشُما | بِايشان or بِديشان | بِآنها or بِدانها or بِآنان |
| Ac. | مارا | شُمارا | ايشانرا | آنهارا or آنانرا |
| Ab. | اَزما | اَزشُما | اَزايشان | اَزآنها  اَزآنان |
| V. | اَي ما | اَي شُما | اَي ايشان | اَي آنها  اَي آنان |

55. The RECIPROCAL PRONOUN خُود "self" or "own," applicable to *persons* of both sexes, as well as to *things*, may be declined in the same manner: it may also be added to the Personal Pronouns, in all the Cases, for the sake of emphasis; as,

| SINGULAR. | PLURAL. |
|---|---|
| مَن خُود | ما خُود |
| تُو خُود | شُما خُود |
| اُو *or* وَي خُود | ايشان خُود |
| آن خُود | آنها *or* آنان خُود |

56. The POSSESSIVE PRONOUNS may be rendered in two ways in Persian;—by declining a Noun before the Nominative Cases of all the Personal Pronouns, excepting the Accusative, where the affix را is added to the Pronoun; or by declining a Noun with the Personal Pronouns constructed as it were thus, اَمْ "My," اَتْ "Thy," اَشْ "His," مان "Our," تان "Your," شاْن "Their." The ا in the three former is omitted, and the Nouns joined only to م, ت, ش, excepting when the Noun ends in quiescent ه; as will be seen in the following examples: خانهٔ اَمْ "My house," خانهٔ اَتْ "Thy house," &c.

| SINGULAR. | PLURAL. |
|---|---|
| پِدَرِمَن or پِدَرَمْ "My father." | پِدَرِمانْ or پِدَرِما "Our father." |
| پِدَرِتُو or پِدَرَتْ "Thy father." | پِدَرِشُما or پِدَرِتانْ "Your father." |
| پِدَرِوي or پِدَرِاُوْ or پِدَرَشْ "His father." | پِدَرِشانْ or پِدَرِاِيْشانْ "Their father." |

To which, also, the Reciprocal Pronoun may be added; thus:

| | |
|---|---|
| كِتابِ خُودَمْ "My own book." | كتابِ خُودَشْ "His own book." |
| كِتابِ خُودَتْ "Thine own book." | كتابِ خُودِمانْ &c. &c. |
| كِتابْهايِ خُودَمْ "My own books." | كِتابْهايِ خُودِمانْ "Our own books." |
| دُوستَمْ or دُوستِ مَن "My friend." | دُوستِ خُودَمْ "My own friend." |
| بِرادَرَتْ or بِرادَرِتُو "Thy brother." | بِرادَرِ خُودَتْ "Thine own brother." |
| اَسْبَشْ or اَسْبِ اُوْ "His horse." | اَسبِ خُودَشْ "His own horse." |
| باغْهايَمْ or باغهايِ مَن "My gardens." | باغهايِ خُودَمْ "My own gardens." |
| شُتُرهاتانْ or شُتُرهايِ شُما "Your camels." | شُتُرهايِ خُودِتانْ "Your own camels," |

&c. &c. &c.

57. The three Pronouns may also be used together; thus:

| SINGULAR. | | PLURAL. | |
|---|---|---|---|
| مَن خُودَمْ | "I, myself." | ماخُودِمانْ | "We, ourselves." |
| تُوخُودَتْ | "Thou, thyself." | شُماخُودِتانْ | "You, yourselves." |
| أُوخُودَشْ | "He, himself." | ايشانْ خُودِشانْ | "They, themselves." |

## 58. OF DEMONSTRATIVE PRONOUNS.

The following are the Demonstrative Pronouns.

| | | | |
|---|---|---|---|
| اينْ | "This" (rational, or otherwise). | آنْ | "That" (rational, or otherwise). |
| اينْها | "These" (rational, or otherwise). | آنْها | "Those" (rational, or otherwise). |
| اينانْ | "These" (rational beings only). | آنانْ | "These" (rational beings only). |

59. These Pronouns may also be declined like any other of the preceding kinds, and with or without the Reciprocal or Possessive Pronouns, or with the Reciprocals alone; as,

*EXAMPLES.*

| SINGULAR. | | PLURAL. | |
|---|---|---|---|
| اينْ خُودْ | This, him, her, *or* it—self. | اينانْ خُودْ *or* اينها &c. | These, themselves, &c. |
| بِدينْ خُودْ | To this, him, her, *or* it—self. | بِاينانْ خُودْ *or* بِدينها &c. | To these, themselves, &c. |
| أَزينْ خُودْ | From this, him, her, *or* it—self. | أَزينانْ خُودْ *or* أَزاينْها &c. | From these, themselves, &c. |
| اينْ خُودَشْ | This, him, her, *or* it—self. | اينانْ خُودِشانْ *or* اينها &c. | These, themselves, &c. |

| SINGULAR. | | PLURAL. | |
|---|---|---|---|
| اینْ خُودَشْ را | This, him, her, *or* it—self. | اینانْ خُودِشانْرا *or* اینها &c. | These, themselves. |
| اَزینْ خُودَشْ | From this, him, her, *or* it—self. | اَزاینانْ خُودِشانْ *or* اَزاینها &c. | From these, themselves. |
| آنْ خُودْ | That, him, her, *or* it—self. | آنانْ خُودْ *or* آنها &c. | Those, themselves. |
| بِدانْ خُودْ *or* بِانْ خُودْ | To that, him, her, *or* it—self. | بِآنانْ خُودْ *or* بِدانها &c. | To those, themselves. |
| اَزآنْ خُودْ | From that, him, her, *or* it—self. | اَزآنانْ خُودْ. *or* اَزآنها &c. | From those, themselves. |
| آنْ خُودَشْ | That, him, her, *or* it—self. | آنانْ خُودِشانْ *or* آنها &c. | Those, themselves. |
| آنْ خُودَشْ را | That, him, her, *or* it—self. | آنانْ خُودِشانْرا *or* آنها &c. | Those, themselves. |
| اَزآنْ خُودَشْ | From that, him, her, *or* it—self. | اَزآنانْ خُودِشانْ *or* اَزآنها &c. | From those, themselves. |

60. When اینْ "This" is prefixed to a Noun, so as to form one word altogether, it is sometimes changed into اِمْ; as, اِمْروزْ "This day," اِمْشَبْ "This night," اِمْسالْ "This year," &c. I do not, however, recollect any other instance in which اینْ is so changed; and I rather believe that these are the only instances that could be cited.

## 61. OF RELATIVE PRONOUNS.

The Relative Pronouns are two, in Persian: كِه "Who," relating to Persons more particularly, but sometimes to Animals, and to Things also; and چِه "Which," relates exclusively to Things. They may be declined with any one, or all, of the Personal, Possessive, Demonstrative, and Reciprocal Pronouns; thus:

[N. B. It is superfluous to observe, that, to make sense of these Examples, *a Verb* must be added.]

| SINGULAR. | | PLURAL. | |
|---|---|---|---|
| مَن كِه خُودَم | I, who, myself. | ما كِه خُودمان | We, who, ourselves. |
| تُو كِه خُودَت | Thou, who, thyself. | شُما كِه خُودتان | You, who, yourselves. |
| اُو كِه خُودَش | He (*or* she) who, himself (*or* herself). | ايشان كِه خُودِشان | They, who, themselves. |

| | |
|---|---|
| پِدَرِ مَن كِه | My father, who &c. |
| پِدَرَم كِه خُودَش | My father, who, himself &c. |
| پِدَرِ تُو كِه خُودرا | Thy father, who —— himself &c. |
| پِدَرِ اُو كِه خُودَش را | His (*or* her) father, who —— himself &c. |
| بِرادَرِ مَن كِه بِخُود | My brother, who —— to himself &c. |
| خواهَرَت كِه بِخُودَش | Thy sister, who —— to herself &c. |
| مادَرَش كِه بِمَن | His mother, who —— to me &c. |
| دُوسْتِ تُورا كِه اَزْمَن | Thy friend, whom —— from me &c. |
| كِتابِ مَن كِه بِاُو خُود | My book, which —— to he himself &c. |

| | |
|---|---|
| خانۂ کِه اَزْ پِدَرِ خُودَمْ | The house, which, —— from my own father &c. |
| آنْ اَسْبْ کِه اَزْ بِرادَرَمْ خُودَشْ | That horse, which, from my brother himself &c. |
| اَسْبْها کِه بِخُودِتانْ | The horses, which, —— to yourselves &c. |
| کِتابْها کِه اَزْ خُودِمانْ | The books, which, —— from ourselves &c. |

&c. &c.

INANIMATE THINGS.

| | |
|---|---|
| آنْچِه بِدُو خُودْ | *That,* which, —— to himself &c. |
| آنْچِه بِایْشانْ خُودِشانْ | *That,* which, —— to themselves &c. |
| آنْچِه ما خُودِمانْ اَزْتُو | *That,* which, we ourselves —— from thee &c. |
| آنْچِه شُما خُودْ اَزْاُو | *That,* which, you yourselves —— from him &c. |
| آنْچِه اِیْشانْ خُودِشانْ بِمَنْ | *That,* which, they themselves —— to me &c. |
| آنْچِه پِدَرَمْ خُودَشْ بِوَیْ | *That,* which, my father himself —— to him &c. |
| آنْچِه بِرادَرانِتْ خُودْ اَزْ اِیْشانْ | *That,* which, thy brothers themselves —— from them &c. |
| آنْچِه خُودْ اَزْ خانَۂ پِدَرِ خُودِشْ | *That,* which he, —— from the house of his own father &c. |

62. When the Relative Pronoun کِه comes after an Indefinite Noun, the Noun, although it may have the Indefinite Particle ي, still will become Definite; as, پادِشاهي "A certain king," پادِشاهي کِه "That king, who," مَرْدي "A certain man," مَرْديکِه "The man, who," چيزي "Any thing," چيزيکِه "The thing, which": and the same in the Plural, &c.

## 63. OF INTERROGATIVE PRONOUNS.

The Pronouns کِه and چِه may also be used Interrogatively; as, "Who?" and "What?" In the Oblique Cases of these Pronouns, however, the final ه is absorbed before the syllable را; as, کِرا "Whom?" "To whom?" or "Who for?" and چِرا "Why?" or "What for?" And in the former of these, the ه may be changed into ي also; as, كِي "Who," for persons only: and when reference is made to more than one object, the Pronouns کُدام or کُدامین must be used; as, کُدام مَرد "Which man?" کُدامین زَن "Which woman?" کُدام راه "Which road?" کُدامین خانَه "Which house?" In all these instances, the meaning is "which" particular *one*, out of *many* things of the same kind.

64. The Interrogative Pronouns may be used along with the others; as follows:

[N.B. An Interrogative sentence can hardly be rendered perfect without a Verb; but as the beginner is supposed to be, as yet, unacquainted with the Persian Verbs, a vacant place is left, thus ——, where the Verb ought to come, in all the following sentences: the corresponding places in the English, however, are supplied with Verbs, printed in *Italics*.]

| | |
|---|---|
| كي —— آن مَردِکه خُودَش | Who *was* that man who himself &c.? |
| تُو اَز کِه اِین اَسب را —— | Of whom didst thou *purchase* this horse? |
| شُما چِرا اِمرُوز بِخانَهٔ من —— | Why did you to-day *come* to my house? |

| | |
|---|---|
| تُو خُودْ اَزْ كِي بِهْتَرْ —— | Thou thyself, than whom better *art* thou? |
| اَيْشَانْ اَزْ مَا چِهْ —— | What do they *wish* from us? |
| كُدَامْ اَزْ بِرَادَرَانَتْ رَا —— | Which of thy brothers *did he beat*? |
| كِرَا خُودْ بِخَانَهٔ مَنْ —— | Whom didst thyself *bring* to my house? |
| تُو اَزْ بِرَادَرَشْ چِهْ —— | What *didst* thou *ask* of her brother? |
| اِيْنهَا رَا تُو خُودْ اَزْ كِهْ —— | Of whom didst thou *learn* these things? |
| كِهْ — آن مَرْدِ كِه اِيْن رَا —— | Who *was* the man who *did* this? |
| بِهْتَرْ اَزْ اِيْنهَا كُدَامْ —— | Which *is* better than these? |
| اِيْن گُلْ رَا دَرْ زَبَانِ فَارْسِي چِهْ — | What *do they call* this flower in the Persian tongue? |
| آنْ زَنْ چِرَا خُودَشْ بِتُو —— | Why *did not* that woman herself *say* to thee? |
| پِدَرَتْ اَزْ كِي بِهْتَرْ | Than whom *is* thy father better? |
| اَزْ شَهْرهَايِ فَرَنْگْ كُدَامْ بُزُرْگْتَرْ —— | Of the cities of Europe, which *is* the larger? |
| مَنْ خُودْ اَزْ كِي كَمْتَرْ —— | Less than whom *am* I myself? |
| چِهْ — آنكِهْ تُو خُودْ اَزْ اُو —— | What *was* that which thou thyself *didst take* from him? |
| كُدَامْ رَاهْ بِلَنْدَنْ نَزْدِيكْتَرْ —— | Which road *is* nearer to London? |
| مَرْدِي كِهْ شُمَا رَا —— كِي —— | The man who *saw* you, who *was* he? |
| اَسْبهَايِ مَا رَا كِهْ بِيرُونْ —— | Who *took* out our horses? |
| دَرْ خَانَهٔ خُودَتْ چِهْ —— | In thine own house what *wast thou doing*? |
| كُدَامْ يَكْ اَزْ اِيْن كِتَابْهَا كِتَابِ تُو | Which of these books *is* thy book? |

65. The English Pronouns "Whosoever," "Whatsoever," &c., are thus expressed in Persian:

| | | | |
|---|---|---|---|
| هَرکِه | "Whosoever." | هَرچیز | "Every thing," *or* "Whatsoever thing." |
| هَرچِه | "Whatsoever." | هَرکَس | "Every body." |
| هَرکُدام | "Whichsoever." | هرجا | "Every place." |
| هَروَقت | "Whensoever." | هرروز | "Every day." |
| هَرکُجا *or* هَرجا | "Wheresoever." | هَرشَب | "Every night." |
| بِهَرحال | "However," *or* "In whatever manner." | هردو | "Both." |
| | | هَریَك | "Each." |
| | | هَمَه | "All." |

## OF THE PERSIAN VERBS.

66. Before discussing the subject of the Persian Verbs fully, the student will do well to learn by heart the Personal Terminations. No Persian Verb or Participle, of any kind, whether Active or Passive, can be formed without them; inasmuch as by them alone the Numbers and the Persons of all the Verbs and Participles are decided. These Personal Terminations (as the name itself denotes) uniformly appear at the end of the word, and are six in number; three for the Singular, and three for the Plural; thus:

| SINGULAR. | | PLURAL. | |
|---|---|---|---|
| اَم | "Am." | ایم | "Are." |
| یْ | "Art." | اید | "Are." |
| اَست | "Is." | اَند | "Are." |

67. In composition, however, the first letter in every one of these is omitted (except when the words ends in quiescent ه), and the word prefixed to the remaining portion; viz. to م , ي , ست , يم , يد , ند.

68. The Termination, Third Person Singular, ست is omitted in the Imperfect, the Pluperfect, and the Simple-Preterite Tenses; and it is changed into د in the Future, the Aorist, and the Present Tense, as well as in the Imperative Mood; as will be presently seen, in conjugating the Verbs.

69. Let us first join these Terminations to the Personal Pronouns; thus:

| SINGULAR. | PLURAL. |
|---|---|
| مَنَم "I am." | مايَمْ "We are." |
| تُوئِي "Thou art." | شُمائِيد "You are." |
| اُوسْتْ "He (*or* she) is." | ايْشانَنْد "They are." |

70. They may also be joined to any Abstract Noun; such, for instance, as هَسْتِي "existence," شادي "gladness," دِليري "boldness," &c. In such cases, the final ي is always dropped; and the remaining part, which then becomes an Adjective, only, as هَسْت* "existent," شادْ "glad," دِلير "bold," is prefixed to the Personal Terminations; thus:

---

* It is a mistake to suppose this to be the Present Tense of the Auxiliary Verb "*To be*," which in Persian is بُودَن i.e. "*To be*" in a certain *condition, manner, mood, place,* &c.; and not هَسْتَن, erroneously supposed to be the Infinitive, a word which does not exist in the Persian language.

| SINGULAR. | | PLURAL. | |
|---|---|---|---|
| هَستَم | I exist. | هَستيم | We exist. |
| هَستي | Thou existest. | هَستيد | You exist. |
| هَست | He (*or* she) exists. | هَستَند | They exist. |
| شادَم | I am glad. | شاديم | We are glad. |
| شادي | Thou art glad. | شاديد | You are glad. |
| شاداَست | * He (*or* she) is glad. | شادَند | They are glad. |
| دِليرَم | I am bold. | دِليريم | We are bold. |
| دِليري | Thou art bold. | دِليريد | You are bold. |
| دِليراَست | He (*or* she) is bold. | دِليراَند | They are bold. |

71. All the Persian Verbs are to be considered, in their origin, as so many abstract terms, denoting certain acts or states of things; but the manner in which the act is performed, the time of performance, the agent or person who performed it, and the object of it, are all determined by certain Auxiliaries added to these abstract terms; or by certain modifications which they must undergo, before they can express their own meanings exactly and definitively. It is necessary, therefore, for a beginner to understand the

---

* What has been stated with regard to the Third Person Singular of the Personal Termination اَست, viz. to be left out altogether in some Tenses, does not apply to these kinds of Adjectives. And the ا in the Pronouns اَست and اَند, in many instances of composition, may be omitted.

nature of these Auxiliaries well, before he attempts to go any further in learning the Verbs.

72. Some of these Auxiliaries are in themselves a species of Verbs, and are called "Auxiliary Verbs"; of some of which the following are the Infinitives, or Verbal Nouns: بُودَن "To be," شُدَن "To become," داشْتَن "To have," كَرْدَن "To do," خواسْتَن "To will," &c.; and these are the Auxiliary Verbs chiefly employed in conjugating other Persian Verbs, Active or Passive.

73. The Persian Verbs have but one conjugation; and the Infinitives always end in ن. The antecedent letter of them, invariably, is either a دَ *dă*, or a تَ *tă*, enunciated with a (َ) زَبَر; as shewn in the Infinitives of the Auxiliary Verbs already cited.

73. With regard to the formation of the different Tenses of Persian Verbs, attempts have been made by some ingenious writers to lay down certain rules by which to deduce all the Tenses of a Verb from the Infinitive.

Recourse has been had, therefore, to various complicated systems of classification; which, in their turns, have given birth to so many exceptions, as to make the *Irregulars* almost as numerous as the Regular Verbs; to the great discouragement of the beginners of a new language, who, in consequence, may, at the very outset, despair of ever acquiring a competent knowledge of one of the most essential parts of his task; namely, the conjugation of a Verb.

This unnecessary obstruction seems to have been caused by a desire to imitate the Arabian Grammarians; who, according to the genius of the Arabic language, which admits of such an arrangement, denominate the Infinitive مَصْدَر, or source whence all Tenses and Moods flow.

The great beauty of the Persian language is its extreme simplicity, and the admirable facility with which the different Parts of Speech can be combined and understood.

74. The reader is therefore requested to observe, that in the Persian language there are *two sources*, from which the different Moods and Tenses of a Verb are derived; viz. the Infinitive, and the Imperative or Aorist. From the former, the Preterites, the Past Participle, and the Future Tense of a Verb are deduced; and from the latter, the Present Tense, the Aorist, the Participle Active, and the Participle Present.

75. It is always easy to recognise the Infinitives, by the final نْ, in the manner already described: and, as an additional aid, I subjoin a Table, where almost all the Imperatives will be found alphabetically arranged.* The reader will have only to look for any Infinitive that he wishes, and he will find the Imperative directly opposite to the same.

AUXILIARY VERBS.

76. Now, we begin by conjugating the AUXILIARY VERBS.

First: بُودْ "*Being.*"

| INFINITIVE. | IMPERATIVE. |
|---|---|
| بُودَن "To be." | بَاشْ "Be thou." |

By rejecting the last syllable of the Infinitive, the Third Person Singular of the Simple Preterite is obtained, and the remaining Persons of the same Tense are formed by adding the Personal Terminations to the word so obtained†; thus:

---

* See the Index. † See the Personal Terminations, p. 43.

## INDICATIVE MOOD.

### SIMPLE PRETERITE.

| SINGULAR. | | PLURAL. | |
|---|---|---|---|
| بُودَم | I was. | بُودِيم | We were. |
| بُودِي | Thou wast. | بُودِيد | You (*or* ye) were. |
| بُود | He (*or* she) was. | بُودَند | They were. |

77. The COMPOUND PRETERITE is formed by adding the quiescent ه to the Simple Preterite; as, from بُود , بُودَه.

| | | | |
|---|---|---|---|
| بُودَه اَم | I have been. | بُودَه ايم | We have been. |
| بُودَهٔ | Thou hast been. | بُودَه ايد | You have been. |
| بُودَه اَست | He (*or* she) has been. | بُودَه اَند | They have been. |

78. The PRETERITE IMPERFECT is formed by prefixing مي or هَمي to the Simple Preterite; as, from بود , مي بُود.

| | | | |
|---|---|---|---|
| ميبودَم | I used to be. | ميبوديم | We used to be. |
| ميبودي | Thou usedst to be. | ميبوديد | You used to be. |
| ميبُود | He (*or* she) used to be. | ميبودَند | They used to be. |

79. This Verb has no Pluperfect Tense. In other Verbs, this Tense is formed by prefixing the Compound Preterite to the different Persons of the Auxiliary بُودَن; and if this Verb had a Pluperfect Tense, it would likewise be formed by prefixing بُودَه, which is the Compound Preterite of the Verb we are now conjugating, to the Persons of the Simple

Preterite of the Auxiliary; and the Tense would then be as follows:—

| SINGULAR. | | PLURAL. | |
|---|---|---|---|
| بُودَه بُودَم | I had been. | بُودَه بُودِيم | We had been. |
| بُودَه بُودِي | Thou hadst been. | بُودَه بُودِيد | You had been. |
| بُودَه بُود | He (*or* she) had been. | بُودَه بُودَند | They had been. |

80. The Past Participle is always the same in form as the Compound Preterite; which, in this Verb, is بُودَه.

81. The Future Tense is formed by prefixing the different Persons of the Aorist of the Auxiliary Verb خواستَن to the Simple Preterite of the Verb; thus:

| | | | |
|---|---|---|---|
| خواهَم بُود | I will *or* shall be. | خواهِيم بُود | We will *or* shall be. |
| خواهِي بُود | Thou wilt *or* shalt be. | خواهِيد بُود | You will *or* shall be. |
| خواهَد بُود | He (*or* she) shall be. | خواهَند بُود | They will *or* shall be. |

82. Excepting in Poetical writings, when a syllable often will be found in the way, no Persian Imperative is ever used without prefixing the Particle بِ: in which case there will be no difference of form between the Imperative Mood and the Aorist, excepting in the Second Person Singular, when the former has not the Personal Termination; as, باش or بِباش "Be thou": and the latter has it as usual; as, باشِي or بِباشِي "You be," or "You may be."

## 83. IMPERATIVE MOOD.

| SINGULAR. | PLURAL. |
|---|---|
| باشْ or بِباشْ "Be thou. | باشِيْدْ or بِباشِيْدْ "Be ye." |

84. The Aorist is formed from the Contracted Imperative by prefixing the Particle ب; as from باشْ, بِباشْ, adding the Terminations.

| | | | |
|---|---|---|---|
| بِباشَمْ | I be. | بِباشِيْم | We be. |
| بِباشِيْ | Thou beest. | بِباشِيْدْ | You be. |
| بِباشَدْ | He (*or* she) be. | بِباشَنْدْ | They be. |

85. When the Aorist is used as the Subjunctive, the Particle is omitted; thus:

| | | | |
|---|---|---|---|
| باشَمْ | I may be. | باشِيْم | We may be. |
| باشِيْ | Thou mayst be. | باشِيْدْ | You may be. |
| باشَدْ | He (*or* she) may be. | باشَنْدْ | They may be. |

86. The Present Tense is formed by prefixing to the Contracted Imperative the Particle مِيْ; as, from باش, we have مي باش or مِيْباشْ.

| | | | |
|---|---|---|---|
| مِيْباشَمْ | I am. | مِيْباشِيْم | We are. |
| مِيْباشِيْ | Thou art. | مِيْباشِيْدْ | You are. |
| مِيْباشَدْ | He (*or* she) is. | مِيْباشَنْدْ | They are. |

87. There are two PARTICIPLES in Persian, in the Active Voice—the PRESENT, and the ACTIVE OR SUBSTANTIVE PARTICIPLE. By the Present Participle is meant, all those Participles which in English end in *-ing;* as, "writ*ing*," "walk*ing*," "speak*ing*," &c., when the agent, to whom the act is attributed, is, at the moment, performing the action: and by the Active Participle, all those which end in *-er;* as, "writ*er*," "walk*er*," "speak*er*," &c., when the agent may or may not be at the moment performing the action.

88. The PRESENT PARTICIPLE is formed by adding آن to the Contracted Imperative; as from باش, باشان, adding the Personal Terminations.

| SINGULAR. | | PLURAL. | |
|---|---|---|---|
| باشانم | I am being &c. | باشانیم | We are being &c. |
| باشانی | Thou art being &c. | باشانید | You are being &c. |
| باشانست | He (*or* she) is being &c. | باشانند | They are being &c. |

89. The ACTIVE OR SUBSTANTIVE PARTICIPLE is formed by adding انده to the Contracted Imperative; thus:

| | | | |
|---|---|---|---|
| باشنده ام | I am &c. | باشنده ایم | We are &c. |
| باشنده | Thou art &c. | باشنده اید | You are &c. |
| باشنده است | He (*or* she) is &c. | باشنده اند | They are &c. |

90. The reader will observe, that this Verb بودن "To be" is not quite perfect. Many of the Tenses and Moods which I have here laid down, for example's sake, are forced, and are not to be met with in the language; such as, the Pluperfect Tense بوده بودم, and the Active and Present Parti-

ciples, باشَنْدَه and باشانْ: but, as my object was to lay down for the beginner a model for the conjugation of the Persian Verbs in general, and had begun with one of the most useful of the Auxiliary Verbs, I did not like to break off by pointing out defects in a Verb which, in its nature, cannot possibly be perfect in all the Tenses and Moods; and as it might lead a beginner to suppose that the rules I was laying down for him were imperfect, since exceptions were stated at the very outset. The reader will find, however, the model here laid down for him perfectly applicable to all the Persian Verbs susceptible of the Tenses and Moods of the Active Voice, Indicative Mood.

91. The Verb شُدَنْ "*To become.*"

| INFINITIVE. | IMPERATIVE. |
|---|---|
| شُدَنْ | شَوْ "Be thou." شَوِيدْ "Be ye." |

INDICATIVE MOOD.

SIMPLE PRETERITE.

Reject the ن of the Infinitive, and add the Personal Terminations; thus:

| SINGULAR. | PLURAL. |
|---|---|
| شُدَمْ I became. | شُدِيمْ We became. |
| شُدِي Thou becamest. | شُدِيدْ You became. |
| شُدْ He (*or* she) became. | شُدَنْدْ They became. |

92. COMPOUND PRETERITE.

Add the quiescent ه to the Simple Preterite with the Personal Terminations; thus:

| | |
|---|---|
| شُدَه اَمْ I have become. | شُدَه ايمْ We have become. |
| شُدَه Thou hast become. | شُدَه ايدْ You have become. |
| شُدَه اَسْتْ He (*or* she) has become. | شُدَه اَنْدْ They have become. |

### 93. IMPERFECT TENSE.

Prefix the Simple Preterite with مي, and add the Personal Terminations; thus:

| SINGULAR. | | PLURAL. | |
|---|---|---|---|
| میشدم | I was becoming. | میشدیم | We were becoming. |
| میشدي | Thou wast becoming. | میشدید | You were becoming. |
| میشد | He (*or* she) was becoming. | میشدند | They were becoming. |

### 94. PLUPERFECT TENSE.

Put the Compound Preterite before all the Persons of the Simple Preterite of the Verb بودن; *i.e.* before بود.

| | | | |
|---|---|---|---|
| شده بودم | I had become. | شده بودیم | We had become. |
| شده بودي | Thou hadst become. | شده بودید | You had become. |
| شده بود | He (*or* she) had become. | شده بودند | They had become. |

### 95. FUTURE TENSE.

Put the different Persons of the Aorist of the Auxiliary Verb خواستن before the Third Person Singular of the Simple Preterite of the Verb*; thus:

| | | | |
|---|---|---|---|
| خواهم شد | I will *or* shall become. | خواهیم شد | We will *or* shall become. |
| خواهي شد | Thou wilt *or* shalt become. | خواهید شد | You will *or* shall become. |
| خواهد شد | He (*or* she) will *or* shall become. | خواهند شد | They will *or* shall become. |

---

* See the following Verb, خواستن "To will," or "To wish."

### 96. THE AORIST.

Put بِ before the Imperative; and add the Personal Terminations; thus:

| SINGULAR. | | PLURAL. | |
|---|---|---|---|
| بِشَوَم | I may become. | بِشَوِيم | We may become. |
| بِشَوِي | Thou mayst become. | بِشَوِيد | You may become. |
| بِشَوَد | He (*or* she) may become. | بِشَوَند | They may become. |

### 97. PRESENT TENSE.

Put مي before the Imperative, and add the Personal Terminations; thus:

| | | | |
|---|---|---|---|
| ميشَوَم | I become. | ميشَوِيم | We become. |
| ميشَوِي | Thou becomest. | ميشَوِيد | You become. |
| ميشَوَد | He (*or* she) becomes. | ميشَوَند | They become. |

98. The PRESENT PARTICIPLE, corresponding in English with "I am becoming," is in Persian wanting in this Verb.

### 99. THE ACTIVE OR SUBSTANTIVE PARTICIPLE.

Add اَنْدَه to the Imperative, with the Personal Terminations; thus:

| | | | |
|---|---|---|---|
| شَوَنْدَه اَم | I am becom*er* &c.* | شَوَنْدَه ايم | We are becom*ers* &c. |
| شَوَنْدَه | Thou art becom*er* &c. | شَوَنْدَه ايد | You are becom*ers* &c. |
| شَوَنْدَه اَسْت | He (*or* he) is becom*er*. | شَوَنْدَه اَند | They are becom*ers* &c. |

* This termination is intended to give the Persian model, in which language this form is considered a Participle; though in English it bears the character of a Substantive.

## 100. The Verb خواستن "*To Will*," or "*To Wish*."

### IMPERATIVE MOOD.

| SINGULAR. | | PLURAL. | |
|---|---|---|---|
| خواه | Wish thou. | خواهید | Wish ye. |

### INDICATIVE MOOD.

#### SIMPLE PRETERITE TENSE.*

| | | | |
|---|---|---|---|
| خواستم | I wished. | خواستیم | We wished. |
| خواستي | Thou wishedst. | خواستید | You wished. |
| خواست | He (*or* she) wished. | خواستند | They wished. |

#### COMPOUND PRETERITE.

| | | | |
|---|---|---|---|
| خواسته ام | I have wished. | خواسته ایم | We have wished. |
| خواستهٔ | Thou hast wished. | خواسته اید | You have wished. |
| خواسته است | He (*or* she) has wished. | خواسته اند | They have wished. |

#### IMPERFECT TENSE.

| | | | |
|---|---|---|---|
| میخواستم | I was wishing. | میخواستیم | We were wishing. |
| میخواستي | Thou wast wishing. | میخواستید | You were wishing. |
| میخواست | He (*or* she) was wishing. | میخواستند | They were wishing. |

#### PLUPERFECT TENSE.

| | | | |
|---|---|---|---|
| خواسته بودم | I had wished. | خواسته بودیم | We had wished. |
| خواسته بودي | Thou hadst wished. | خواسته بودید | You had wished. |
| خواسته بود | He (*or* she) had wished. | خواسته بودند | They had wished. |

* See the Rules in Verb بودن p. 49.

### PAST PARTICIPLE.

خواسْتَهْ Wished.

### FUTURE TENSE.

| SINGULAR. | | PLURAL. | |
|---|---|---|---|
| خواهَمْ خواسْتْ | I will *or* shall wish. | خواهيم خواسْتْ | We will *or* shall wish. |
| خواهيْ خواسْتْ | Thou wilt *or* shalt wish. | خواهيد خواسْتْ | You will *or* shall wish. |
| خواهَدْ خواسْتْ | He (*or* she) will *or* shall wish. | خواهَنْد خواسْتْ | They will *or* shall wish. |

### THE AORIST.

| | | | |
|---|---|---|---|
| بِخواهَمْ | I may wish. | بِخواهيم | We may wish. |
| بِخواهيْ | Thou mayst wish. | بِخواهيدْ | You may wish. |
| بِخواهَدْ | He (*or* she) may wish. | بِخواهَنْدْ | They may wish. |

### PRESENT TENSE.

| | | | |
|---|---|---|---|
| مَيخواهَمْ | I wish. | ميخواهيم | We wish. |
| ميخواهيْ | Thou wishest. | ميخواهيدْ | You wish. |
| ميخواهَدْ | He (*or* she) wishes. | ميخواهَنْدْ | They wish. |

### PRESENT PARTICIPLE.

| | | | |
|---|---|---|---|
| خواهانَمْ | I am wishing. | خواهانيْمْ | We are wishing. |
| خواهاني | Thou art wishing. | خواهانيْدْ | You are wishing. |
| خواهانَسْت | He (*or* she) is wishing. | خواهانَنْد | They are wishing. |

### ACTIVE OR SUBSTANTIVE PARTICIPLE.

| | | | |
|---|---|---|---|
| خواهَنْدهاَمْ | I am wisher &c. | خواهَنْدَهايم | We are wishers &c. |
| خواهَنْدَهٔ | Thou art wisher &c. | خواهَنْدَهايْد | You are wishers &c. |
| خواهَنْدهاسْت | He (*or* she) is wisher &c. | خواهَنْدَهاَنْد | They are wishers &c. |

## 101. The Verb داشتن "*To Have.*"

### IMPERATIVE MOOD.

| SINGULAR. | PLURAL. |
|---|---|
| دار Have thou. | دارید Have you. |

### INDICATIVE MOOD.

#### SIMPLE PRETERITE.*

| | |
|---|---|
| داشتم I had. | داشتیم We had. |
| داشتی Thou hadst. | داشتید You had. |
| داشت He (*or* she) had. | داشتند They had. |

#### COMPOUND PRETERITE.

| | |
|---|---|
| داشته ام I have had. | داشته ایم We have had. |
| داشتهٔ Thou hadst had. | داشته اید You have had. |
| داشته است He (*or* she) has had. | داشته اند They have had. |

#### PRETERITE IMPERFECT.

| | |
|---|---|
| میداشتم I was having. | میداشتیم We were having. |
| میداشتی Thou wast having. | میداشتید You were having. |
| میداشت He (*or* she) was having. | میداشتند They were having. |

#### PRETERITE PLUPERFECT.

| | |
|---|---|
| داشته بودم I had had. | داشته بودیم We had had. |
| داشته بودی Thou hadst had. | داشته بودید You had had. |
| داشته بود He (*or* she) had had. | داشته بودند They had had. |

---

* See the Auxiliary Verb بودن p. 47.

### FUTURE TENSE.

| SINGULAR. | | PLURAL. | |
|---|---|---|---|
| خواهم داشت | I will *or* shall have. | خواهيم داشت | We will *or* shall have. |
| خواهي داشت | Thou wilt *or* shalt have. | خواهيد داشت | You will *or* shall have. |
| خواهد داشت | He (*or* she) will *or* shall have. | خواهند داشت | They will *or* shall have. |

### PAST PARTICIPLE.

داشته Having had.

### PRESENT TENSE.

| | | | |
|---|---|---|---|
| ميدارم | I have. | ميداريم | We have. |
| ميداري | Thou hast. | ميداريد | You have. |
| ميدارد | He (*or* she) has. | ميدارند | They have. |

### AORIST.

| | | | |
|---|---|---|---|
| بدارم | I may have. | بداريم | We may have. |
| بداري | Thou mayst have. | بداريد | You may have. |
| بدارد | He (*or* she) may have. | بدارند | They may have. |

### PRESENT PARTICIPLE.

| | | | |
|---|---|---|---|
| دارانم | I am having. | دارانيم | We are having. |
| داراني | Thou art having. | دارانيد | You are having. |
| دارانست | He (*or* she) is having. | دارانند | They are having. |

### ACTIVE OR SUBSTANTIVE PARTICIPLE.

| | | | |
|---|---|---|---|
| دارنده ام | I am haver, | دارنده ايم | We are havers, |
| دارنده | Thou art haver, | دارنده ايد | You are havers, |
| دارنده است | He (*or* she) is haver, | دارنده اند | They are havers, |

*i.e.* possessors.

## 102. كَرْدَنْ "*To Do.*"

### IMPERATIVE MOOD.

| SINGULAR. | PLURAL. |
|---|---|
| كُنْ Do Thou. | كُنِيدْ Do ye. |

### INDICATIVE MOOD.

#### SIMPLE PRETERITE.*

| | |
|---|---|
| كَرْدَمْ I did. | كَرْدِيمْ We did. |
| كَرْدِي Thou didst. | كَرْدِيدْ You did. |
| كَرْدْ He (*or* she) did. | كَرْدَنْدْ They did. |

#### COMPOUND PRETERITE.

| | |
|---|---|
| كَرْدَهْ اَمْ I have done. | كَرْدَهْ ايمْ We have done. |
| كَرْدَهٔ Thou hast done. | كَرْدَهْ ايدْ You have done. |
| كَرْدَهْ اَسْتْ He (*or* she) has done. | كَرْدَهْ اَنْدْ They have done. |

#### IMPERFECT TENSE.

| | |
|---|---|
| ميكَرْدَمْ I was doing. | ميكَرْدِيمْ We were doing. |
| ميكَرْدِي Thou wast doing. | ميكَرْدِيدْ You were doing. |
| ميكَرْدْ He (*or*) she was doing. | ميكَرْدَنْدْ They were doing. |

#### PRETERITE PLUPERFECT.

| | |
|---|---|
| كَرْدَهْ بُودَمْ I had done. | كَرْدَهْ بُودِيمْ We had done. |
| كَرْدَهْ بُودِي Thou hadst done. | كَرْدَهْ بُودِيدْ You had done. |
| كَرْدَهْ بُودْ He (*or* she) had done. | كَرْدَهْ بُودَنْدْ They had done. |

---

* See the Auxiliary Verb بُودَنْ p. 47.

### FUTURE TENSE.

| SINGULAR. | | PLURAL. | |
|---|---|---|---|
| خواهَمْ كَرْدْ | I will *or* shall do. | خواهيم كَرْدْ | We will *or* shall do. |
| خواهي كَرْدْ | Thou wilt *or* shalt do. | خواهيدْ كَرْدْ | You will *or* shall do. |
| خواهَدْ كَرْدْ | He (*or* she) will *or* shall do. | خواهَنْدْ كَرْدْ | They will *or* shall do. |

### PAST PARTICIPLE.

كَرْدَهْ Having done.

### PRESENT TENSE.

| | | | |
|---|---|---|---|
| ميكُنَمْ | I do. | ميكُنيمْ | We do. |
| ميكُني | Thou doest. | ميكُنيدْ | You do. |
| ميكُنَدْ | He (*or* she) do. | ميكُنَنْدْ | They do. |

### AORIST.

| | | | |
|---|---|---|---|
| بِكُنَمْ | I may do. | بِكُنيمْ | We may do. |
| بِكُني | Thou mayst do. | بِكُنيدْ | You may do. |
| بِكُنَدْ | He (*or* she) may do. | بِكُنَنْدْ | They may do. |

### PRESENT PARTICIPLE.

| | | | |
|---|---|---|---|
| كُنانَمْ | I am doing. | كُنانيمْ | We are doing. |
| كُنانيْ | Thou art doing. | كُنانيدْ | You are doing. |
| كُنانَسْتْ | He (*or* she) is doing. | كُنانَنْدْ | They are doing. |

### ACTIVE OR SUBSTANTIVE PARTICIPLE.

| | | | |
|---|---|---|---|
| كُنَنْدَه اَمْ | I am do*er*. | كُنَنْدَه ايمْ | We are do*ers*. |
| كُنَنْدَهْ | Thou art do*er*. | كُنَنْدَه ايدْ | You are do*ers*. |
| كُنَنْدَه اَسْتْ | He (*or* she) is do*er*. | كُنَنْدَه اَنْدْ | They are do*ers*. |

## OF THE SUBJUNCTIVE AND POTENTIAL MOODS.

103. As neither of these Moods could properly be expressed in Persian without certain particular Auxiliaries or peculiar modes of phraseology, I have reserved the examination of them until I had explained some of the Ordinary and Auxiliary Verbs, and laid down the rules for conjugating them.

104. By SUBJUNCTIVE MOOD is meant a thing represented under a condition, motive, wish, supposition &c.; and it is preceded usually by a Conjunction; as, اَگَر "if": by an Interjection; as, كاش "Would that!" or "May it be granted!" &c.: or by an Adverb; as, اَگَرچِه "although;" شايَد "perhaps," &c.: and it is generally accompanied with another Verb; as, اَگَر بِخواهي اُو خواهَد كَرد "If thou shouldst ask, he (or she) will do it": مَن اين را نَميكُنَم اَگَرچِه اُو مَرا بِكُشَد "I shall not do this, although he should kill me," &c.

105. It is not always necessary that the Subjunctive should have the Particle بِ placed before it. This is only the case in the Aorist of the Subjunctive, as in the two preceding examples.

106. The following will be a model for conjugating any Verb in the Subjunctive Mood, in Persian. There will be only one Tense of each of the Verbs given as a specimen; but the reader can easily supply the rest, or change the forms according to his own fancy.

## SUBJUNCTIVE MOOD.

### FOR TIME PAST.

| SINGULAR. | | PLURAL. | |
|---|---|---|---|
| اگر بودم *or* بودمي | Had I been, *or* If I had been. | اگر بوديم | Had we been, *or* If we had been. |
| اگر بودي | Hadst thou been, *or* If thou hadst been. | اگر بوديد | Had you been, *or* If you had been. |
| اگر بود *or* بودي | Had he, she, *or* it, been. | اگر بودند *or* بودندي | Had they been, *or* If they had been. |

---

| | | | |
|---|---|---|---|
| كاش بودم *or* بودمي | Would that I had! *or* I wish I had been! | كاش بوديم | Would that we had been! *or* I wish we had been! |
| كاش بودي | Would that thou hadst been! | كاش بوديد | Would that you had been! |
| كاش بود *or* بودي | Would that he, she, *or* it, had been! | كاش بودند *or* بودندي | Would that they had been! |

---

| | | | |
|---|---|---|---|
| اگرچه بودم *or* بودمي | Although I was *or* had been. | اگرچه بوديم | Although we were *or* had been. |
| اگرچه بودي | Although thou wast *or* had been. | اگرچه بوديد | Altho' you were &c. |
| اگرچه بود *or* بودي | Although he, she, *or* it, had been. | اگرچه بودند *or* بودندي | Altho' they were &c. |

---

| | | | |
|---|---|---|---|
| شايد بودم *or* بودمي | Perhaps I was *or* may have been. | شايد بوديم | Perhaps we were *or* may have been. |
| شايد بودي | Perhaps thou wast *or* mayst have been. | شايد بوديد | Perhaps you were &c. |
| شايد بود *or* بودي | Perhaps he, she, *or* it, was *or* may &c. | شايد بودند *or* بودندي | Perhaps they were &c. |

107. The Particle مي may be placed before all these Verbs; or the quiescent ه added to the end of all of them, as in the Compound Preterite and Imperfect Tenses; or to render the Pluperfect Tense in the Subjunctive Mood; as,

| | |
|---|---|
| اگر خواسته ام | If I have wished *or* desired. |
| کاش کرده بودي | Would that, *or* I wish thou hadst done it! |
| اگرچه میکرد | Altho' he was doing. |
| شاید کرده بودم | Perhaps I had done. |
| اگر شده ایم | If we are *or* have become. |
| کاش میداشتید | Would that, *or* I wish you were having! |
| اگرچه کرده بودند | Altho' they had done. |
| شاید خواسته بودیم | We may have wished. |

### 108. FOR TIME TO COME.

**SINGULAR.**

| | |
|---|---|
| اگر خواهم کرد | If I should *or* would wish to do. |
| شاید خواهي بود | Thou mayst wish to be. |
| اگرچه خواهد شد | Although he, she, *or* it, would become. |

**PLURAL.**

| | |
|---|---|
| شاید خواهیم کرد | Perhaps we would do. |
| اگرچه خواهید بود | Altho' you would be. |
| اگر خواهند داشت | If they would have. |

### 109. AORIST.

| | |
|---|---|
| اگر کنم<br>اگر بکنم | If I should do. |
| شاید باشي | Thou mayst be. |
| اگرچه دارم<br>اگرچه بدارم | Although I may *or* should have been. |
| اگر باشیم | If we should be. |
| شاید بخواهیم | Perhaps we may wish. |
| کاش بشوند | Would that, *or* I wish they may become! |

### 110. PRESENT TENSE.

| | |
|---|---|
| اگرچه میکنم | Although I do. |
| اگر میخواهي | If thou doest wish. |
| شاید میدارم | I may perhaps have. |
| اگر میباشند | If they are *or* should be. |
| شاید میخواهند | Perhaps they may *or* do wish. |
| اگرچه میشویم | Although we do become. |

### 111. PARTICIPLE PRESENT AND ACTIVE.

| | |
|---|---|
| اگرچه خواهانم | Although I am desiring. |
| اگر دارنده است | If he is a possessor. |
| شاید خواهنده | Perhaps thou art a wisher. |
| شاید دارانند | Perhaps they are having. |
| اگر خواهنده اند | If they are wishers. |
| اگرچه کنانند | Although they are doers. |

112. The power and the uses of these Subjunctives, especially of the Participles, will be better understood in Compounds, when these Verbs &c. perform their proper offices of Auxiliaries: thus, for instance:—

شايَدْ اَيشانْ دادْ خواهانَنْدْ Perhaps they are *seeking* justice.

اَگَر اُوْدارَنْدَهٔ مالَسْتْ If he is, or should be, the *possessor* of wealth.

اَگَرچِهْ كُشْتَهْ بِشَوَمْ Although I may *or* should be killed.

113. The Potential Mood implies "possibility," "liberty," "power," "will," or "obligation," which are expressed in Persian by certain words generally placed before the Verb; as, تَوانْ "possible," "can," or "may"; تَوانِسْتْ "might," or "could"; بايَدْ "necessary," "must," or "shall"; بايِسْتْ "ought," or "should."

114. A Verb may be rendered Potential in various ways: the Past Tenses may be expressed by adding the Personal Terminations to تَوانِسْتْ or بايِسْتْ, and placing them before the Contracted Infinitive of any Verb, with or without prefixing مي to either; as:

مِيتَوانِسْتَمْ *or* تَوانِسْتَمْ كَرْدْ I might *or* could do, *or* have done.

مِيتَوانِسْتِي *or* تَوانِسْتِي خواسْتْ Thou mightest *or* couldst wish, *or* have wished.

مِيتَوانِسْتْ *or* تَوانِسْتْ دِيدْ He, she, *or* it, might, *or* could see, *or* have seen.

The same with بايِسْتْ.

115. The Separate Pronouns, in the Nominative Form,

may at the same time be placed before تَوانِسْت and ميتَوانِسْت: and, in the Accusative Form, before بايِسْت and ميبايِسْت; as,

IN THE NOMINATIVE FORM.

مَنْ توانِسْتَمْ ,مَنْ ميتَوانِسْتَمْ *or* مَنْ تَوانِسْتَمِي

تَو تَوانِسْتِي ,تُومِيتَوانِسْتِي *or* تُوتَوانِسْتِي

اُو تَوانِسْت ,اُومِيتَوانِسْت *or* اُوتَوانِسْتِي

ما تَوانِسْتِيم ,مامِيتَوانِسْتِيم *or* ما تَوانِسْتِيمِي

شُما تَوانِسْتِيد ,شُماميتَوانِسْتِيد *or* شُما تَوانِسْتِيدِي

ايْشان تَوانِسْتَنْد ,ايْشان ميتَوانِسْتَنْد *or* ايْشان تَوانِسْتَنْدِي

IN THE ACCUSATIVE FORM.

مَرابايِسْت ,مَرامِيبايِسْت *or* مَرابايِسْتِي

تُرابايِسْت ,تُرامِيبايِسْت *or* تُرابايِسْتِي

اُورابايِسْت ,اُورامِيبايِسْت *or* اُورابايِسْتِي

مارابايِسْت ,مارامِيبايِسْت *or* مارابايِسْتِي

شُمارابايِسْت ,شُمارامِيبايِسْت *or* شُمارابايِسْتِي

ايْشانْرابايِسْت ,ايْشانْرامِيبايِسْت *or* ايْشانْرابايِسْتِي

116. The Possessive Pronouns may be added to بايِسْت *only*; as,

| | |
|---|---|
| بايِسْتَمْ *or* ميبايِسْتَمْ | بايِسْتِمان *or* ميبايِسْتِمان |
| بايِسْتَت *or* ميبايِسْتَت | بايِسْتِتان *or* ميبايِسْتِتان |
| بايِسْتَش *or* ميبايِسْتَش | بايِسْتِشان *or* ميبايِسْتِشان |

If we substitute تَوانْ for تَوانِسْتْ in all the places, when the latter appears in the preceding examples, and also بايَدْ for بايِسْتْ in the same manner, we shall have all the Aorists and Future Potentials: in these instances, however, we may also substitute sometimes the Aorist Tense of the Verb (which is intended to be made Potential) for the Contracted Infinitive; as,

| | |
|---|---|
| مْيتَوانَمْ *or* تَوانَمْ گُفْتْ<br>مْيتَوانَمْ *or* تَوانَمْ بِگُوْيَمْ | I can, am able, *or* may speak. |
| شُما تَوانِيدْ *or* مْيتَوانيدْ داشْتْ<br>شُما تَوانِيدْ *or* مْيتَوانيدْ بِدارِيدْ | You can, are able, *or* may have. |

When no Personal Terminations, or Pronouns of any kind, are added, the Verbs are termed Impersonal, لا يُسَمَّ الفاعِلْ; as,

| | |
|---|---|
| تَوانْ دِيدْ | One could, *or*, it is possible to, see. |
| مْيتَوانْ خواسْتْ | It is possible to, *or* one may, wish. |
| بايَدْ *or* مْيبايَدْ كَرْدْ | One must, *or* ought to, do. |

117. A Verb may be Potential and Subjunctive at the same time; as,

| | |
|---|---|
| اَگَرْ تَوانَمْ بِتُوخواهَمْ دادْ | If I should be able, *or* if I can, I will give you. |
| اَگَرْچِه مْيتَوانِسْتيمْ كَرْدْ | Although we might have done. |
| شايَدْ اينْ را اَزْ ماتَوانَنْدْ گِرِفْتْ | Perhaps they can take this from us. |
| كاشْ تَوانِسْتَمي پِدَرَتْ را دِيدْ | I wish I had been able to see thy father! |
| اِمْرُوزْ اَگَرْ مْيتَوانِي سَوارْ شَوْ | To-day, if thou art able, take a ride. |

| | |
|---|---|
| اگرچه بیمار بودم اما دو سه قدم میتوانستم رفت | Although I was sick, yet I could have gone two or three steps. |
| کاشکی هرگز ما را ندیده بودند تا چنین نمیتوانستند کرد | Would that they had never seen us, so that they might not be able to do thus! |
| از من نشنیدی اگرچه هزار بار بتو گفتم که هرگز آنرا نمیتوانی دید | Thou wouldst not hear it from me, although I told thee a thousand times that thou couldst never see that. |

### OPTATIVE MOOD.

118. In Persian, when a person wishes another either good or bad luck, or when he blesses or curses, he interposes the letter Alĕf (ا) between the penultimate and final letter of the Third Person Singular of the Aorist, chiefly of one of the following Verbs; viz. کردن "To do"; شدن "To become"; گردانیدن "To cause to become"; دادن "To give"; and بودن "To be": thus, کند, شود, گرداند, دهد, and بود become کناد, شواد, گرداناد, دهاد, and بواد, or باد; and they are then thus joined to a sentence, or a phrase.

*EXAMPLES:*

| | |
|---|---|
| عمرت دراز باد | May your life be long! |
| خدا ترا روزی دهاد | My God give thee fortune! |
| رحمت حق براو باد | May the mercy of God be upon him *or* her! |
| خدا دلش را شاد گرداناد | May God make his, *or* her, heart rejoice! |
| طالع ویرا مدد کناد | May good luck assist him, *or* her! |
| بختش برگشته شواد | May his, *or* her, fortune be reversed! |

| | |
|---|---|
| دلِ دُوستانِتان خُوش بادْ | May the hearts of your friends be delighted! |
| خانهٔ دُشمَنانِمان خَراب شَوادْ | May the abodes of our enemies be desolate! |
| خُدا ایشان را خَیر دِهادْ | May Heaven grant them blessings! |
| اَزْ گَردِشِ روزِگارِتان آسیب مَبادْ | May you never receive harm from the revolutions of fate! |
| خُدا شُمارا عافیَت دِهادْ | May God give you good health! |
| بَخْت مارا مَدَدْ کُنادْ | May good fortune help us! |

119. It is by no means necessary, however, that these forms of the Verbs should always be employed in expressions of this kind: the Aorist alone, without any alteration or addition, may be, and is much more frequently, used optatively: indeed, except in Poetry, and on occasions of particular formality, it is rather pedantic to say بادْ, دِهادْ, شَوادْ &c.; and the Persians generally employ باشَدْ, دِهَدْ, کُنَدْ, گَرْدانَدْ, &c.; the context being of itself quite sufficient to shew that it is used in an optative sense.

## OF NEGATIVE VERBS.

120. The formation of these Verbs is very simple. The letter نَ, put before any Tense, Mood, or Person of a Verb, makes the same Negative; excepting the Imperative, to which the letter مَ must be prefixed; as,

نَگُفْتَنْ "*Not to Speak.*"

### IMPERATIVE MOOD.

| | |
|---|---|
| مَگُوی Speak not thou. | مَگُوئِیدْ Speak not ye. |

نَگُفتَم I spoke not.
نَگُفتَهٔ Thou hast not spoken.
نَمیگُفت He, *or* she, was not speaking.
نَگُفتَهٔ بُودیم We had not spoken.
نَخواهید گُفت You will not speak.
نَمیگُویَند They do not speak.
&c. &c. &c.

## OF THE PASSIVE VOICE.

121. In the whole range of Persian Grammar (easy and simple as it is), there is no part perhaps so easy and simple as the formation of the Passive Verbs. The student has only to place the Past Participle of any Active Verb (which Past Participle is to be formed, as already stated, by changing the ن of the Infinitive into ه) before the different Tenses and Moods throughout the Auxiliary Verb شُدَن "To become."* For instance: let us take پُرسیدَه, the Past Participle of the Verb پُرسیدَن "To ask," and place it, first of all, before the Infinitive of the Auxiliary, and we shall obtain the Compound Infinitive پُرسیدَه شُدَن "To be, *or* to become, asked";— next, before the Imperative, and we shall have پُرسیدَه شَو "Be thou asked," پُرسیدَه شَوید "Be ye asked."

### INDICATIVE MOOD.

SIMPLE PRETERITE.

| SINGULAR. | | PLURAL. | |
|---|---|---|---|
| پُرسیدَه شُدَم | I was asked. | پُرسیدَه شُدیم | We were asked. |
| پُرسیدَه شُدي | Thou wast asked. | پُرسیدَه شُدید | You were asked. |
| پُرسیدَه شُد | He (*or* she) was asked. | پُرسیدَه شُدَند | They were asked. |

* See the Auxiliary Verb شُدَن, p. 52.

### COMPOUND PRETERITE.

| SINGULAR. | | PLURAL. | |
|---|---|---|---|
| پُرسیده شُده‌اَم | I have been asked. | پُرسیده شُده‌ایم | We have been asked. |
| پُرسیده شُده | Thou hast been asked. | پُرسیده شُده‌اید | You have been asked. |
| پُرسیده شُده اَست | He (*or* she) has been asked. | پُرسیده شُده‌اَند | They have been asked. |

### PRETERITE IMPERFECT.

| | | | |
|---|---|---|---|
| پُرسیده میشُدم | I was being asked. | پُرسیده میشُدیم | We were being asked. |
| پُرسیده میشُدي | Thou was being asked. | پُرسیده میشُدید | You were being asked. |
| پُرسیده میشُد | He (*or* she) was being asked. | پُرسیده میشُدند | They were being asked. |

### PRETERITE PLUPERFECT.

| | | | |
|---|---|---|---|
| پُرسیده شُده بُودم | I had been asked. | پُرسیده شُده بُودیم | We had been asked. |
| پُرسیده شُده بُودي | Thou hadst been asked | پُرسیده شُده بُودید | You had been asked. |
| پُرسیده شُده بُود | He (*or* she) had been asked. | پُرسیده شُده بُودند | They had been asked. |

### FUTURE TENSE.

| | | | |
|---|---|---|---|
| پُرسیده خواهم شُد | I will *or* shall be asked. | پُرسیده خواهیم شُد | We will *or* shall be asked. |
| پُرسیده خواهي شُد | Thou wilt *or* shalt be asked. | پُرسیده خواهید شُد | You will *or* shall be asked. |
| پُرسیده خواهد شُد | He *or* she will *or* shall be asked. | پُرسیده خواهند شُد | They will *or* shall be asked. |

### PRESENT TENSE.

| | | | |
|---|---|---|---|
| پُرسیده میشوم | I am being asked. | پُرسیده میشویم | We are being asked. |
| پُرسیده میشوي | Thou art being asked. | پُرسیده میشوید | You are being asked. |
| پُرسیده میشود | He (*or* she) is being asked. | پُرسیده میشوند | They are being asked. |

### AORIST.

| SINGULAR. | | PLURAL. | |
|---|---|---|---|
| پرسیدہ بِشَوم | I may be asked. | پرسیدہ بِشَویم | We may be asked. |
| پرسیدہ بِشَوي | Thou mayst be asked. | پرسیدہ بِشَوید | You may be asked. |
| پرسیدہ بِشَود | He (*or* she) may be asked. | پرسیدہ بِشَوَند | They may be asked. |

### SUBJUNCTIVE MOOD.

With اَگَر , اَگَرچِہ , شایَد , *or* کاش and کاشکي ; and also with or without مي .

| | | | |
|---|---|---|---|
| پرسیدہ شُدہ باشَم | I may have been asked. | پرسیدہ شُدہ باشیم | We may have been asked. |
| پرسیدہ شُدہ باشي | Thou mayst have been asked. | پرسیدہ شُدہ باشید | You may have been asked. |
| پرسیدہ شُدہ باشد | He (*or* she) may have been asked. | پرسیدہ شُدہ باشَند | They may have been asked. |

### POTENTIAL MOOD.

With تَوان , بایَد , تَوانِست , or بایِست ; and also with or without مي .

| | | | |
|---|---|---|---|
| پرسیدہ تَوانَم شُد | I can *or* could be asked. | پرسیدہ تَوانیم شُد | We can *or* could be asked. |
| پرسیدہ تَواني شُد | Thou canst *or* couldst be asked. | پرسیدہ تَوانید شُد | You can *or* could be asked. |
| پرسیدہ تَوانَد شُد | He (*or* she) can *or* could be asked. | پرسیدہ تَوانَند شُد | They can *or* could be asked. |

All other forms of Subjunctives and Potentials can now easily be imagined by the student himself.

## OF CAUSAL VERBS.

122. Besides the Transitive (فِعلِ مُتَعَدّی) and Intransitive (فِعلِ لازِم) Verbs, there is also in Persian a species of Derivative Verbs (فِعلِ مُشتَق), which may be termed "Causal," as the agent is forced (as it were) or caused by others to perform the action. In English, such meanings are expressed by two Verbs; as, "I *made* him *bring* it"; "He *caused* me to *give* it up," &c. In Persian, generally, though not always, they are expressed by a single Verb; which is derived from the Present Participle of the Primitive Verb denoting the action.

The Second Person Plural of the Present Participle of the Primitive Verb is, then, the root from which all the Past Tenses, the Past Participle, and the Future Tense of the Causal Verb are derived; and the Present Participle itself of the Primitive Verb (without a Person) is the other root from which the Participle Active, the Present Tense, and the Aorist, are formed:—the first, with the final ن attached to it, is the Infinitive; and the second, the Imperative: and from these two, in the same manner as has already been stated with reference to other Verbs,* the reader will proceed to form the rest; thus:

---

تَرسیدَن "*To fear.*"

---

IMPERATIVE MOOD.

تَرس Fear thou.

The Present Participle, as we have said, is formed from the Imperative, by adding آن; thus: تَرسان "Fearing";

---

* See the Rules for Conjugating a Verb, p. 47.

تَرْسانَم "I am fearing"; تَرْسانِي "Thou art fearing"; تَرْسانَست "He, *or* she, is fearing"; تَرْسانِيم "We are fearing"; تَرْسانِيد "You are fearing." This last word, by adding the final ن, becomes the Infinitive of the Causal Verb تَرْسانِيدَن "To cause another to fear" *or* "to frighten," &c.; تَرْسان "Frighten thou," is the Imperative.

---

## INFINITIVE.

تَرْسانِيدَن "*To frighten.*"

---

### IMPERATIVE MOOD.

| SINGULAR. | PLURAL. |
|---|---|
| تَرْسان Frighten thou. | تَرْسانِيد Frighten ye. |

### INDICATIVE MOOD.

#### SIMPLE PRETERITE.

| | |
|---|---|
| تَرْسانِيدَم I frightened. | تَرْسانِيدِيم We frightened. |
| تَرْسانِيدِي Thou frightenedst. | تَرْسانِيدِيد You frightened. |
| تَرْسانِيد He (*or* she) frightened. | تَرْسانِيدَند They frightened. |

#### COMPOUND PRETERITE.

| | |
|---|---|
| تَرْسانِيدَه اَم I have frightened. | تَرْسانِيدَه ايم We have frightened. |
| تَرْسانِيدَه Thou hast frightened. | تَرْسانِيدَه ايد You have frightened. |
| تَرْسانِيدَه اَسْت He (*or* she) has frightened. | تَرْسانِيدَه اَنْد They have frightened. |

#### PRETERITE IMPERFECT.

| | |
|---|---|
| ميتَرْسانِيدَم I was frightening. | ميتَرْسانِيدِيم We were frightening. |
| ميتَرْسانِيدِي Thou wast frightening. | ميتَرْسانِيدِيد You were frightening. |
| ميتَرْسانِيد He (*or* she) was frightening. | ميتَرْسانِيدَند They were frightening. |

### PRETERITE PLUPERFECT.

| SINGULAR. | | PLURAL. | |
|---|---|---|---|
| ترسانیده بودم | I had frightened. | ترسانیده بودیم | We had frightened. |
| ترسانیده بودي | Thou hadst frightened. | ترسانیده بودید | You had frightened. |
| ترسانیده بود | He (*or* she) had frightened. | ترسانیده بودند | They had frightened. |

### PAST PARTICIPLE.

ترسانیده Being, or having been, frightened.

### PRESENT TENSE.

| | | | |
|---|---|---|---|
| میترسانم | I am frightening. | میترسانیم | We are frightening. |
| میترساني | Thou art frightening. | میترسانید | You are frightening. |
| میترساند | He (*or* she) is frightening. | میترسانند | They are frightening. |

### AORIST.

| | | | |
|---|---|---|---|
| بترسانم | I may frighten. | بترسانیم | We may frighten. |
| بترساني | Thou mayst frighten. | بترسانید | You may frighten. |
| بترساند | He (*or* she) may frighten. | بترسانند | They may frighten. |

### PARTICIPLE ACTIVE.

| | | | |
|---|---|---|---|
| ترساننده ام | I am frighten*er*. | ترساننده ایم | We are frighten*ers*. |
| ترساننده | Thou art frighten*er*. | ترساننده اید | You are frighten*ers*. |
| ترساننده است | He (*or* she) is frighten*er*. | ترساننده اند | They are frighten*ers*. |

Causal Verbs have no Present or Substantive Participles.

## The Causal Verb, from دَوِيدَن "*To run.*"

### INFINITIVE.

دَوانِيدَن To urge, *or* To cause to run.

### IMPERATIVE MOOD.

| SINGULAR. | | PLURAL. | |
|---|---|---|---|
| دَوان | Cause thou to run. | دَوانِيد | Cause ye to run. |

### SUBJUNCTIVE MOOD.

#### SIMPLE PRETERITE.

SINGULAR.

| | |
|---|---|
| اَگَر اُو مَرا دَوانِيد | If he, *or* she, made me run. |
| اَگَر اُو تُرا دَوانِيد | If he, *or* she, made thee run. |
| اَگَر اُو اُورا دَوانِيد | If he, *or* she, made him, *or* her, run. |

PLURAL.

| | |
|---|---|
| اَگَر اِيشان مارا دَوانِيدَند | If they made us run. |
| اَگَر اِيشان شُمارا دَوانِيدَند | If they made you run. |
| اَگَر اِيشان اِيشانرا دَوانِيدَند | If they made them run. |

#### COMPOUND PRETERITE.

SINGULAR.

| | |
|---|---|
| شايَد مَن اُورا دَوانِيدَه اَم | Perhaps I have made him, *or* her, run. |
| شايَد تُو اُورا دَوانِيدَه | Perhaps thou hast made him, *or* her, run. |
| شايَد وَي اُورا دَوانِيدَه اَست | Perhaps he, *or* she, has made him, *or* her, run. |

PLURAL.

| | |
|---|---|
| شايَد اِيشان مَرا دَوانِيدَه اَند | Perhaps they have made me run. |
| شايَد اِيشان تُورا دَوانِيدَه اَند | Perhaps they have made thee run. |
| شايَد اِيشان اُورا دَوانِيدَه اَند | Perhaps they have made him, *or* her, run. |

### PRETERITE IMPERFECT.

SINGULAR.

| | |
|---|---|
| اَگَرْچِه مَرا مْیدَوانْیدْ | Although he, *or* she, was urging me to run. |
| اَگَرْچِه تُرا مْیدَوانْیدْ | Although he, *or* she, was urging thee to run. |
| اَگَرْچِه اُورا مْیدَوانْیدْ | Although he, *or* she, was urging him, *or* her, to run. |

PLURAL.

| | |
|---|---|
| اَگَرْچِه مارا مْیدَوانْیدَنْدْ | Although they were urging us to run. |
| اَگَرْچِه شُمارا مْیدَوانْیدَنْدْ | Although they were urging you to run. |
| اَگَرْچِه اِیْشانْرا مْیدَوانْیدَنْدْ | Although they were urging them to run. |

### PRETERITE PLUPERFECT.

SINGULAR.

| | |
|---|---|
| کاشْ تُرادَوانْیدَهْ بُودَمْ | I wish I had made thee run. |
| کاشْ شُمارادَوانْیدَهْ بُودَمْ | I wish I had made you run. |
| کاشْ اِیشانْرادَوانیدَهْ بُودَمْ | I wish I had made them run. |

PLURAL.

| | |
|---|---|
| کاشْ تُرادَوانْیدَهْ بُودَنْدْ | I wish they had made thee run. |
| کاشْ شُمارادَوانْیدَهْ بُودَنْدْ | I wish they had made you run. |
| کاشْ اِیْشانْرادَوانْیدَهْ بُودَنْدْ | I wish they had made them run. |

### FUTURE TENSE.

SINGULAR.

| | |
|---|---|
| شایَدْ خواهَمْ تُرادَوانْیدْ | Perhaps I will, *or* may, make thee run. |
| شایَدْ خواهَمْ اُورادَوانْیدْ | Perhaps I will, *or* may, make him, *or* her, run. |
| شایَدْ خواهَمْ وَیْرادَوانْیدْ | Perhaps I will, *or* may, make him, *or* her, run. |

PLURAL.

شايَدْ خواهَنْد مارادَوانْيدْ Perhaps they will, *or* would, make us run.

شايَدْ خواهَنْد شُمارادَوانْيدْ Perhaps they will, *or* would, make you run.

شايَدْ خواهَنْد ايْشانْرادَوانْيدْ Perhaps they will, *or* would, make them run.

PRESENT TENSE.

SINGULAR.

اَگَرْ تُرا مْيدَ وانَمْ If I do urge thee to run.

اَگَرْ اُورا مْيدَ وانَمْ If I do urge him, *or* her, to run.

اَگَرْ وَيْرا مْيدَ واني If thou urgest him, *or* her, to run.

PLURAL.

اَگَرْ اُورا مْيدَ وانْيمْ If we do urge him, *or* her, to run.

اَگَرْ تُرا مْيدَ وانْيمْ If we do urge thee to run.

اَگَرْ ايْشانْرا مْيدَ وانْيمْ If we do urge them to run.

AORIST.

SINGULAR.

كاشْ مَرابِدَواني I wish thou wouldst make me run.

كاشْ اُورابِدَواني I wish thou wouldst make him *or* her run.

كاشْ وَيْرابِدَواني I wish thou wouldst make them run.

PLURAL.

كاشْ مارابِدَوانَنْدْ I wish they would make us run.

كاشْ شُمارابِدَوانَنْدْ I wish they would make you run.

كاشْ ايْشانْرابِدَوانَنْدْ I wish they would make them run.

The reader cannot fail to observe, by the foregoing examples, what an infinite variety of Subjunctive Verbs could be formed in Persian, by the aid of the Particles, the Pronouns, and the changing of their positions.

### The Causal Verb, from گُذَشْتَنْ "*To pass.*"

#### INFINITIVE.

گُذَرانِیدَنْ To cause to pass.

#### IMPERATIVE MOOD.

گُذَرانْ Cause thou to pass. | گُذَرانِیدْ Cause ye to pass.

#### POTENTIAL MOOD.

##### SIMPLE PRETERITE.

SINGULAR.

| | |
|---|---|
| تَوانِسْتَمْ اُورا گُذَرانِیدْ | I could, *or* might, cause him, *or* her, to pass. |
| تَوانِسْتِي اُوْرا گُذَرانِیدْ | Thou couldst, *or* mightst, cause him, *or* her, to pass. |
| تَوانِسْتْ اُوْرا گُذَرانِیدْ | He, *or* she, could, *or* might, cause him, *or* her, to pass. |

PLURAL.

| | |
|---|---|
| تَوانِسْتِیم اِیْشانْ را گُذَرانِید | We could, *or* might, cause them to pass. |
| تَوانِسْتِیدْ اِیشانْ را گُذَرانِیدْ | You could, *or* might, cause them to pass. |
| تَوانِسْتَنْدْ اِیْشانْ را گُذَرانِیدْ | They could, *or* might, cause them to pass. |

##### IMPERFECT TENSE.

SINGULAR.

| | |
|---|---|
| اُوْرا مْیتَوانِسْتَمْ گُذَرانِیدْ | I could, *or* might, have caused him, *or* her, to pass. |
| اُوْرا مْیتَوانِسْتِي گُذَرانِیدْ | Thou couldst, *or* mightst, have caused him, *or* her, to pass. |
| اُوْرا مْیتَوانِسْتْ گُذَرانِیدْ | He, *or* she, could, *or* might, have caused him, *or* her, to pass. |

PLURAL.

| | |
|---|---|
| آنْهارا مْیتَوانْسِتیم گُذَرانیدْ | We could, *or* might, have caused them to pass. |
| آنْهارا مْیتَوانْسِتید گُذَرانیدْ | You could, *or* might, have caused them to pass. |
| آنْهارا مْیتَوانْسِتَنْد گُذَرانیدْ | They could, *or* might, have caused them to pass. |

PRETERITE IMPERFECT.

SINGULAR.

| | |
|---|---|
| اینْرا بایْسِتَم گُذَرانیدْ | I ought to have caused this (thing) to pass. |
| اینْرا بایْسِتَت گُذَرانیدْ | Thou oughtst to have caused this (thing) to pass. |
| اینْرا بایْسِتَش گُذَرانیدْ | He, *or* she, ought to have caused this (thing) to pass. |

PLURAL.

| | |
|---|---|
| اینهارا بایْسِتِمان گُذَرانیدْ | We ought to have caused these (things) to pass. |
| اینهارا بایْسِتِتان گُذَرانیدْ | You ought to have caused these (things) to pass. |
| اینهارا بایْسِتِشان گُذَرانیدْ | They ought to have caused these (things) to pass. |

PRESENT TENSE.

SINGULAR.

| | |
|---|---|
| مَنْ تُرا مْیتَوانَم گُذَرانیدْ | I can cause thee to pass. |
| تُو مَرا مْیتَوانی گُذَرانیدْ | Thou canst cause me to pass. |
| اُو مارا مْیتَوانَدْ گُذَرانیدْ | He, *or* she, can cause us to pass. |

PLURAL.

| | |
|---|---|
| ماشُمارا مْیتَوانیم گُذَرانیدْ | We can cause you to pass. |
| شُماmارا مْیتَوانید گُذَرانیدْ | You can cause us to pass. |
| ایشانْ ماوَشُمارا مْیتَوانَنْد گُذَرانیدْ | They can cause us and you to pass. |

### AORIST POTENTIAL.

#### SINGULAR.

برادَرَتْ تَوانَدْ مَرا بِگُذَرانَدْ Thy brother can, *or* may, cause me to pass.

برادَرَمْ تَوانَدْ تُرا بِگُذَرانَدْ My brother can, *or* may, cause thee to pass.

بِرادَرَش تَوانَدْ شُمارا بِگُذَرانَدْ His, *or* her, brother can, *or* may, cause you to pass.

#### PLURAL.

ایْشانْ تَوانَنْدْ پِدَرَمْرا بِگُذَرانَنْدْ They can cause my father to pass.

ایْشانْ تَوانَنْدْ پِدَرَتْرا بِگُذَرانَنْدْ They can cause thy father to pass.

ایْشانْ تَوانَنْدْ پِدَرَشْرا بِگُذَرانَنْدْ They can cause his, *or* her, father to pass.

### FUTURE, SUBJUNCTIVE, AND POTENTIAL.

اَگَرْ بِتَوانَمْ تُرا خواهَمْ گُذَرانِیدْ If I can, I will cause thee to pass.

اَگَرْ بِتَوانِي مَرا خواهِي گُذَرانِیدْ If thou couldst, thou wouldst cause me to pass.

اَگَرْ بِتَوانَدْ مَرا خواهَدْ گُذَرانِیدْ If he *or* she could, he *or* she would cause me to pass.

### PRESENT, SUBJUNCTIVE, AND POTENTIAL.

اَگَرْچِهْ مِیتَوانَمْ تُرا بِگُذَرانَمْ Although I can cause thee to pass.

اَگَرْچِهْ مِیتَوانِي مَرا بِگُذَرانِي Although thou canst cause me to pass.

اَگَرْچِهْ مِیتَوانَدْ اُورا بِگُذَرانَدْ Although he, *or* she, can cause him, *or* her, to pass.

### AORIST, SUBJUNCTIVE, AND POTENTIAL.

شایَدْ مارا تَوانَنْدْ گُذَرانِیدْ They may perhaps be able to cause us to pass.

شایَدْ شُمارا تَوانَنْدْ گُذَرانِیدْ They may perhaps be able to cause you to pass.

شایَدْ ایْشانْرا تَوانَنْدْ گُذَرانِیدْ They may perhaps be able to cause them to pass.

PRETERITE PLUPERFECT.

کاش تَوانِسته بودم بِگُذَرانَمت I wish I had been able to have caused thee to pass!

کاش تَوانِسته بودي بِگُذَرانيم I wish thou hadst been able to have caused me to pass!

کاش تَوانِسته بود بِگُذَرانَدش I wish he, *or* she, had been able to have caused him, *or* her, to pass!

PRESENT TENSE.

تُرا گُذَرانيدَن تَوانَم To cause thee to pass, I can.

اُورا گُذَرانيدَن تَواني To cause him, *or* her, to pass, thou canst.

مارا گُذَرانيدَن تَوانَند To cause us to pass they can.

## OF INTERROGATIVE VERBS.

123. There is no particular form employed for the purpose of putting a Verb *interrogatively* in Persian. In the English language, in which the general rule for the Affirmative, in ordinary Verbs, is, that they should come after the Nominative, as, "*I* did," "*You* will," "*He* shall," &c., by transposing this order, and putting the Verb before the Nominative, the Verb becomes Interrogative; as, "Did I?" "Will you?" "Shall he?" But in Persian there are no such forms; and Interrogatives are differently expressed. A Simple or a Compound Adverb of Interrogation (such as, چرا "Why?" چون "How?" مَگَر "Perhaps?" كَي "When?" كُو "Where?" كُجا "What place?" &c.*) is very often employed to express the query.

124. The context very often shews the Verb to have been

* See the Index, for Persian Adverbs.

interrogatively put: for instance, if I say to a person in Persian, شُما اِنگلیسی مِیدانید "You know English?" if he is a Persian himself, or knows the Persian language, he perceives at once that I am asking him whether he knows the English language or not.

125. The third mode, and by far the most general, of asking a question in Persian, is, that the speaker softens his voice and expresses the Verb in an accent quite peculiar to the occasion, which leaves no doubt on the minds of those who hear him that he is asking a question: this, I believe, may be done, and is perhaps done in all languages, whether there be at the same time any particular form for expressing a Verb *interrogatively* or not. But in Persian, the Interrogation may at the same time be rendered quite complete and decided, by adding یانَه "or not" (a Disjunctive added to a Negative Particle) to the end of the sentence; thus: پِدَرِشُما آنجارَفت یانَه "Did your father go there, *or not?*" شُمافارسی مِیدانید یانَه "Do you know [or speak] Persian, *or not?*" &c. &c.

126. We now proceed to conjugate a Verb Interrogatively with the Adverb چِرا "Why?"

INFINITIVE MOOD.

گُفتَن "*To Say,*" or "*To Speak.*"

IMPERATIVE MOOD.

| SINGULAR. | PLURAL. |
|---|---|
| گوی "Say thou." | گوئید "Say ye." |

## INDICATIVE MOOD.

### SIMPLE PRETERITE.

| SINGULAR. | | PLURAL. | |
|---|---|---|---|
| چِرا گُفتم | Why said I? | چِرا گُفتيم | Why said we? |
| چِرا گُفتي | Why saidst thou? | چِرا گُفتيد | Why said you? |
| چِرا گُفت | Why said he, *or* she? | چِرا گُفتند | Why said they? |

### COMPOUND PRETERITE.

| | | | |
|---|---|---|---|
| چِرا گُفته ام | Why have I said? | چِرا گُفته ايم | Why have we said? |
| چِرا گُفته | Why hast thou said? | چِرا گُفته ايد | Why have you said? |
| چِرا گُفته است | Why has he, *or* she, said? | چِرا گُفته اند | Why have they said? |

### PRETERITE IMPERFECT.

| | | | |
|---|---|---|---|
| چِرا ميْگُفتم | Why was I saying? | چِرا ميْگُفتيم | Why were we saying? |
| چِرا ميْگُفتي | Why wast thou saying? | چِرا ميْگُفتيد | Why were you saying? |
| چِرا ميْگُفت | Why was he, *or* she, saying? | چِرا ميْگُفتند | Why were they saying? |

### PRETERITE PLUPERFECT.

| | | | |
|---|---|---|---|
| چِرا گُفته بودم | Why had I said? | چِرا گُفته بوديم | Why had we said? |
| چِرا گُفته بودي | Why hadst thou said? | چِرا گُفته بوديد | Why had you said? |
| چِرا گُفته بود | Why had he, *or* she, said? | چِرا گُفته بودند | Why had they said? |

### FUTURE TENSE.

| | | | |
|---|---|---|---|
| چِرا خواهم گُفت | Why will, or shall, I say? | چِرا خواهيم گُفت | Why will, *or* shall, we say? |
| چِرا خواهي گُفت | Why wilt, *or* shalt, thou say? | چِرا خواهيد گُفت | Why will, *or* shall, you say? |
| چِرا خواهد گُفت | Why will, *or* shall, he, *or* she, say? | چِرا خواهند گُفت | Why will, *or* shall, they say? |

### PRESENT TENSE.

| SINGULAR. | | PLURAL. | |
|---|---|---|---|
| چرا میگویم | Why say I? | چرا میگوئیم | Why say we? |
| چرا میگوئی | Why sayest thou? | چرا میگوئید | Why say you? |
| چرا میگوید | Why says he, *or* she? | چرا میگویند | Why say they? |

### AORIST.

| | | | |
|---|---|---|---|
| چرا بگویم | Why may *or* should I say? | چرا بگوئیم | Why may *or* should we say? |
| چرا بگوئی | Why mayst *or* shouldst thou say? | چرا بگوئید | Why may *or* should you say? |
| چرا بگوید | Why may *or* should he, *or* she, say? | چرا بگویند | Why may *or* should they say? |

### PRESENT PARTICIPLE.

| | | | |
|---|---|---|---|
| چرا گویانم | Why am I saying? | چرا گویانیم | Why are we saying? |
| چرا گویانی | Why art thou saying? | چرا گویانید | Why are you saying? |
| چرا گویانست | Why is he, *or* she, saying? | چرا گویانند | Why are they saying? |

### ACTIVE OR SUBSTANTIVE PARTICIPLE.

| | | | |
|---|---|---|---|
| چرا گوینده ام | Why am I say*er*? | چرا گوینده ایم | Why are we say*ers*? |
| چرا گوینده | Why art thou say*er*? | چرا گوینده اید | Why are you say*ers*? |
| چرا گوینده است | Why is he, *or* she, say*er*? | چرا گوینده اند | Why are they say*ers*? |

[N. B. When the Interrogative Particle چرا is placed before a Verb (as in the above instance), the Disjunctive Negative یانه cannot be added to the end of the sentence.]

## OF COMPOUND VERBS.

127. The Persian Verbs are very often compounded with Nouns, either Substantive or Adjective; with Participles; with Prepositions; or with other Particles; as, سُخَن گُفتَن "To speak" or "to utter words;" دادْخواستَن "To seek justice"; نیك ورزیدن "To do good," or, "To exercise virtue"; بیمارشدن "To become sick"; خرّم ساختن "To make happy"; رَنگ آمیختن "To mix colours," or "To be deceptive"; جوینده گردیدن "To be," or "become, a searcher"; پویان بودن "To be walking" or "travelling, in quest of"; خَندان نِشَستَن "To sit smiling"; بالارفتن "To go up"; پائین آمدن "To come down"; برخاستن "To rise"; &c. &c.

128. The Persian Verbs of Arabic extraction are always Compounds of an Arabic Verbal Noun, Participle, or Adjective, and a Persian Verb, which, in all its inflexions, is joined to the other;—the former expressing the meaning in abstract; and the latter deciding the Mood, the Tense, and the Person of the Verb. The Arabic words so compounded undergo, of course, no inflexions.

129. The Verbs chiefly used in these combinations, especially when Arabic words are adopted, are,

| | | | |
|---|---|---|---|
| کردن | To do, *or* To make. | آوردن | To bring. |
| خوردن | To devour, *or* To suffer. | کشیدن | To draw, *or* To undergo. |
| داشتن | To have. | ساختن | To make. |
| زدن | To strike. | فرمودن | To order. |
| آمدن | To come, *or* To become. | شدن, گشتن, گردیدن | To be changed into, *or* become. |

| | | | |
|---|---|---|---|
| بُرْدَن | To bear. | گِرِفْتَن | To take. |
| نِمُودَن | To shew. | يافْتَن | To find. |
| خواسْتَن | To wish, *or* To ask. | جُسْتَن | To search, *or* To find. |
| بُودَن | To be. | نِشَسْتَن | To sit. |

*EXAMPLES.*

| | | | |
|---|---|---|---|
| تَمام كَرْدَن | To complete. | اِنْتِظار كَشيدَن | To expect. |
| رُجُوع نِمُودَن | To return. | حَسَد بُرْدَن | To envy. |
| غُصّه خُورْدَن | To be grieved. | اِعْتِقاد داشْتَن | To believe. |
| عُذْر خواسْتَن | To apologize. | هُجُوم آوَرْدَن | To assault. |
| مُتَعَجِّب گَرديدَن | To be astonished. | ضَرْبَت زَدَن | To strike. |
| اِحْسان فَرمُودَن | To be beneficent. | طالِع آمَدَن | To appear. |
| هِجْران ديدَن | To be bereaved. | نَفْع گِرِفْتَن | To take profit. |
| عَيْب جُسْتَن | To find fault. | مَريض شُدَن | To be sick. |
| مَغْمُوم بُودَن | To be sorrowful. | مَحْرُوم يافْتَن | To find (others) disappointed. |

130. The student will observe, that, in forming these Compounds, he need not always be restricted to special Persian Verbs in combination with any particular Arabic word; for تَمام فَرمُودَن ,تَمام ساخْتَن ,تَمام نِمُودَن all mean "To complete," as well as تَمام كَرْدَن; and in the same manner, as مُنْتَظِر نِشَسْتَن ,مُنْتَظِر بُودَن ,مُنْتَظِر گَرديدَن ,اِنْتِظار داشْتَن ,اِنْتِظار بُرْدَن, as well as اِنْتِظار كَشيدَن would signify "To expect"; as would اِعْتِقاد داشْتَن ,اِعْتِقاد نِمُودَن ,اِعْتِقاد آوَرْدَن ,اِعْتِقاد كَرْدَن all alike signify "To believe"; just as تَعَجُّب كَرْدَن ,تَعَجُّب نِمُودَن ,مُتَعَجِّب شُدَن, تَعَجُّب داشْتَن ,عَجَب آوَرْدَن ,مُتَعَجِّب گَرديدَن and, all may mean "To wonder," or "To be astonished": and so with the

rest, &c. In fact, these Persian Verbs, when united with any Arabic word so as to form a Compound Verb, in many instances completely lose their own primitive meanings, and serve merely as Auxiliaries, to shew, as already observed, the Arabic Verbs to be in the same inflexions as themselves.

131. The following exhibit a few examples of the Compound Verbs of both kinds,—Persian and Persian, and Persian and Arabic united.

## COMPOUND VERB—BOTH PARTS PERSIAN.

### INFINITIVE MOOD.

پاسْ داشْتَنْ "*To Watch*," or "*To keep Watch.*"

### IMPERATIVE MOOD.

| SINGULAR. | PLURAL. |
|---|---|
| پاسْ دارْ Watch thou. | پاسْ دارِيدْ Watch ye. |

### INDICATIVE MOOD.—ACTIVE VOICE.

#### SIMPLE PRETERITE.

| | |
|---|---|
| پاسْ داشْتَمْ I watched. | پاسْ داشْتِيمْ We watched. |
| پاسْ داشْتِي Thou watchedst. | پاسْ داشْتِيدْ You watched. |
| پاسْ داشْت He, *or* she, watched. | پاسْ داشْتَنْدْ They watched. |

#### COMPOUND PRETERITE.

| | |
|---|---|
| پاسْ داشْتَه اَمْ I have watched. | پاسْ داشْتَه ايمْ We have watched. |
| پاسْ داشْتَه Thou hast watched. | پاسْ داشْتَه ايدْ You have watched. |
| پاسْ داشْتَه اَسْتْ He, *or* she, has watched. | پاسْ داشْتَه اَنْدْ They have watched. |

### IMPERFECT TENSE.

| SINGULAR. | | PLURAL. | |
|---|---|---|---|
| پاسْ مِيداشْتَمْ | I was watching. | پاسْ مِيداشْتِيمْ | We were watching. |
| پاسْ مِيداشْتِي | Thou wast watching. | پاسْ مِيداشْتِيدْ | You were watching. |
| پاسْ مِيداشْتْ | He, *or* she, was watching. | پاسْ مِيداشْتَنْدْ | They were watching. |

### PLUPERFECT TENSE.

| | | | |
|---|---|---|---|
| پاسْ داشْتَهْ بُودَمْ | I had watched. | پاسْ داشْتَهْ بُودِيمْ | We had watched. |
| پاسْ داشْتَهْ بُودِي | Thou hadst watched. | پاسْ داشْتَهْ بُودِيدْ | You had watched. |
| پاسْ داشْتَهْ بُودْ | He, *or* she, had watched. | پاسْ داشْتَهْ بُودَنْدْ | They had watched. |

### FUTURE TENSE.

| | | | |
|---|---|---|---|
| پاسْ خواهَمْ داشْتْ | I will *or* shall watch. | پاسْ خواهِيمْ داشْتْ | We will *or* shall watch. |
| پاسْ خواهِي داشْتْ | Thou wilt *or* shalt watch. | پاسْ خواهِيدْ داشْتْ | You will *or* shall watch. |
| پاسْ خواهَدْ داشْتْ | He, *or* she, will *or* shall watch. | پاسْ خواهَنْدْ داشْتْ | They will *or* shall watch. |

### PAST PARTICIPLE.

پاسْ داشْتَهْ Having watched.

### PRESENT TENSE.

| | | | |
|---|---|---|---|
| پاسْ مِيدارَمْ | I watch. | پاسْ مِيدارِيمْ | We watch. |
| پاسْ مِيدارِي | Thou watchest. | پاسْ مِيدارِيدْ | You watch. |
| پاسْ مِيدارَدْ | He, *or* she, watches. | پاسْ مِيدارَنْدْ | They watch. |

### AORIST.

| | | | |
|---|---|---|---|
| پاسْ بِدارَمْ | I may watch. | پاسْ بِدارِيمْ | We may watch. |
| پاسْ بِدارِي | Thou mayst watch. | پاسْ بِدارِيدْ | You may watch. |
| پاسْ بِدارَدْ | He, *or* she, may watch. | پاسْ بِدارَنْدْ | They may watch. |

### PRESENT PARTICIPLE—SELDOM USED.

| SINGULAR. | | PLURAL. | |
|---|---|---|---|
| پاس دارانم | I am watching. | پاس دارانیم | We are watching. |
| پاس دارانی | Thou art watching. | پاس دارانید | You are watching. |
| پاس دارنت | He, *or* she, is watching. | پاس دارانند | They are watching. |

### PARTICIPLE ACTIVE.

| | | | |
|---|---|---|---|
| پاس دارنده ام | I am watch*er*. | پاس دارنده ایم | We are watch*ers*. |
| پاس دارندهٔ | Thou art watch*er*. | پاس دارندهٔ اید | You are watch*ers*. |
| پاس دارنده است | He, *or* she, is watch*er*. | پاس دارنده اند | They are watch*ers*. |

---

## The Verb شکار کردن "*To Hunt.*"

---

### SUBJUNCTIVE MOOD.

#### COMPOUND PRETERITE.

SINGULAR.

| | |
|---|---|
| شاید که شکار کرده باشم | Perhaps I may have hunted. |
| شاید که شکار کرده باشی | Perhaps thou mayst have hunted. |
| شاید که شکار کرده باشد | Perhaps he, *or* she, may have hunted. |

PLURAL.

| | |
|---|---|
| شاید که شکار کرده باشیم | Perhaps we may have hunted. |
| شاید که شکار کرده باشید | Perhaps you may have hunted. |
| شاید که شکار کرده باشند | Perhaps they may have hunted. |

### PRETERITE IMPERFECT.

SINGULAR.

| | |
|---|---|
| باشد که شکار میکردم | I may have been hunting. |
| باشد که شکار میکردي | Thou mayst have been hunting. |
| باشد که شکار میکرد | He, *or* she, may have been hunting. |

PLURAL.

| | |
|---|---|
| باشد که شکار میکردیم | We may have been hunting. |
| باشد که شکار میکردید | You may have been hunting. |
| باشد که شکار میکردند | They may have been hunting. |

### PRETERITE PLUPERFECT.

SINGULAR.

| | |
|---|---|
| اگر شکار کرده بودم | Had I, *or* if I had hunted. |
| اگر شکار کرده بودي | Hadst thou, *or* if thou hadst, hunted. |
| اگر شکار کرده بود | Had he, *or* she, *or* if he *or* she, had hunted. |

PLURAL.

| | |
|---|---|
| اگر شکار کرده بودیم | Had we, *or* if we had hunted. |
| اگر شکار کرده بودید | Had you, *or* if you had hunted. |
| اگر شکار کرده بودند | Had they, *or* if they had hunted. |

### FUTURE TENSE.

SINGULAR.

| | |
|---|---|
| اگرچه شکار خواهم کرد | Although I would *or* should hunt. |
| اگرچه شکار خواهي کرد | Although thou wouldst *or* shouldst hunt. |
| اگرچه شکار خواهد کرد | Although he, *or* she, would *or* should hunt. |

PLURAL.

اَگرچه شِکار خواهیم کَرد — Although we would *or* should hunt.

اَگرچه شِکار خواهید کَرد — Although you would *or* should hunt.

اَگرچه شِکار خواهَند کَرد — Although they would *or* should hunt.

PAST PARTICIPLE.

اَگرچه شِکار کَردَه شُدَه — Although having been hunted.

PRESENT TENSE.

SINGULAR.

اَگر شِکار میکُنَم — If I do hunt.

اَگر شِکار میکُنی — If thou dost hunt.

اَگر شِکار میکُنَد — If he, *or* she, does hunt.

PLURAL.

اَگر شِکار میکُنیم — If we do hunt.

اَگر شِکار میکُنید — If you do hunt.

اَگر شِکار میکُنَند — If they do hunt.

AORIST.

SINGULAR.

تا شِکار بِکُنَم — That I may hunt.

تا شِکار بِکُنی — That thou mayst hunt.

تا شِکار بِکُنَد — That he, *or* she, may hunt.

PLURAL.

تا شِکار بِکُنیم — That we may hunt.

تا شِکار بِکُنید — That you may hunt.

تا شِکار بِکُنَند — That they may hunt.

### PRESENT PARTICIPLE.

SINGULAR.

| | |
|---|---|
| شِکارْکُنانْ باشَمْ | I should, *or* may be hunting. |
| شِکارْکُنانْ باشي | Thou shouldst, *or* mayst be hunting. |
| شِکارْکُنانْ باشَدْ | He, *or* she, should, *or* may be hunting. |

PLURAL.

| | |
|---|---|
| شِکارْکُنانْ باشِيمْ | We should, *or* may be hunting. |
| شِکارْکُنانْ باشِيدْ | You should, *or* may be hunting. |
| شِکارْکُنانْ باشَنْدْ | They should, *or* may be hunting. |

### PARTICIPLE ACTIVE.

SINGULAR.

| | |
|---|---|
| شِکارْکُنَنْدَهْ شَوَمْ | I may become a hunt*er*. |
| شِکارْکُنَنْدَهْ شَوِي | Thou mayst become a hunt*er*. |
| شِکارْکُنَنْدَهْ شَوَدْ | He, *or* she, may become a hunt*er*. |

PLURAL.

| | |
|---|---|
| شِکارْکُنَنْدَهْ شَوِيمْ | We may become hunt*ers*. |
| شِکارْکُنَنْدَهْ شَوِيدْ | You may become hunt*ers*. |
| شِکارْکُنَنْدَهْ شَوَنْدْ | They may become hunt*ers*. |

---

## The Verb نامَهْ نِوِشْتَنْ "*To write a Letter.*"

### POTENTIAL MOOD.

SIMPLE PRETERITE.

SINGULAR.

| | |
|---|---|
| نامَهْ تَوانِسْتَمْ نِوِشْتْ | I could *or* might write a letter. |
| نامَهْ تَوانِسْتي نِوِشْتْ | Thou couldst *or* might write a letter. |
| نامَهْ تَوانِسْتْ نِوِشْتْ | He, *or* she, could *or* might write a letter. |

PLURAL.

| | |
|---|---|
| نامَهْ تَوانِسْتِيمْ نِوِشْتْ | We could *or* might write a letter. |
| نامَهْ تَوانِسْتِيدْ نِوِشْتْ | You could *or* might write a letter. |
| نامَهْ تَوانِسْتَنْدْ نِوِشْتْ | They could *or* might write a letter. |

### COMPOUND PRETERITE.

SINGULAR.

| | |
|---|---|
| نامَهْ تَوانِسْتَه اَمْ نِوِشْتْ | I have been able to write a letter. |
| نامَهْ تَوانِسْتَهٔ نِوِشْتْ | Thou hast been able to write a letter. |
| نامَهْ تَوانِسْتَه اَسْت نِوِشْتْ | He, *or* she, has been able to write a letter. |

PLURAL.

| | |
|---|---|
| نامَهْ تَوانِسْتَه ايمْ نِوِشْتْ | We have been able to write a letter. |
| نامَهْ تَوانِسْتَه ايدْ نِوِشْتْ | You have been able to write a letter. |
| نامَهْ تَوانِسْتَه اَنْدْ نِوِشْتْ | They have been able to write a letter. |

### PRETERITE IMPERFECT.

SINGULAR.

| | |
|---|---|
| نامَهْ مِيتَوانِسْتَمْ نِوِشْتْ | I could have written, *or* might be writing, a letter. |
| نامَهْ مِيتَوانِسْتِي نِوِشْتْ | Thou couldst have written, *or* might be writing, a letter. |
| نامَهْ مِيتَوانِسْتْ نِوِشْتْ | He, *or* she, could have written, *or* might be writing, a letter. |

PLURAL.

| | |
|---|---|
| نامَهْ مِيتَوانِسْتِيمْ نِوِشْتْ | We could have written, *or* might be writing, a letter. |
| نامَهْ مِيتَوانِسْتِيدْ نِوِشْتْ | You could have written, *or* might be writing, a letter. |
| نامَهْ مِيتَوانِسْتَنْدْ نِوِشْتْ | They could have written, *or* might be writing, a letter. |

### PRETERITE PLUPERFECT.

SINGULAR.

| | |
|---|---|
| نامَهْ تَوانِسْتَمْ نِوِشْتَهْ بُودْ | I could, *or* might, have had written a letter. |
| نامَهْ تَوانِسْتِي نِوِشْتَهْ بُودْ | Thou couldst, *or* might, have had written a letter. |
| نامَهْ تَوانِسْتْ نِوِشْتَهْ بُودْ | He, *or* she, could, *or* might, have had written a letter. |

PLURAL.

| | |
|---|---|
| نامَهْ تَوانِسْتِيمْ نِوِشْتَهْ بُودْ | We could, *or* might, have had written a letter. |
| نامَهْ تَوانِسْتِيدْ نِوِشْتَهْ بُودْ | You could, *or* might, have had written a letter. |
| نامَهْ تَوانِسْتَنْدْ نِوِشْتَهْ بُودْ | They could, *or* might, have had written a letter. |

### FUTURE TENSE.

SINGULAR.

| | |
|---|---|
| نامَهْ خواهَمْ تَوانِسْتْ نِوِشْتْ | I shall be able to write a letter. |
| نامَهْ خواهِي تَوانِسْتْ نِوِشْتْ | Thou wilt be able to write a letter. |
| نامَهْ خواهَدْ تَوانِسْتْ نِوِشْتْ | He, *or* she, will be able to write a letter. |

PLURAL.

| | |
|---|---|
| نامَهْ خواهِيمْ تَوانِسْتْ نِوِشْتْ | We shall be able to write a letter. |
| نامَهْ خواهِيدْ تَوانِسْتْ نِوِشْتْ | You will be able to write a letter. |
| نامَهْ خواهَنْدْ تَوانِسْتْ نِوِشْتْ | They will be able to write a letter. |

### PRESENT TENSE.

SINGULAR.

| | |
|---|---|
| نامَهْ مِيتَوانَمْ نِوِشْتْ | I can write, *or* am able to write, a letter. |
| نامَهْ مِيتَوانِي نِوِشْتْ | Thou canst write, *or* art able to write, a letter. |
| نامَهْ مِيتَوانَدْ نِوِشْتْ | He, *or* she, can write, *or* is able to write, a letter. |

PLURAL.

| | |
|---|---|
| نامَهْ مِيتَوانيم نِوِشْت | We can write, *or* are able to write a letter. |
| نامَهْ مِيتَوانيد نِوِشْت | You can write, *or* are able to write a letter. |
| نامَهْ مِيتَوانَند نِوِشْت | They can write, *or* are able to write a letter. |

AORIST, POTENTIAL.

SINGULAR.

| | |
|---|---|
| نامَهْ بايَدْ بِنِوِيسَم | I must, *or* ought to write a letter. |
| نامَهْ بايَدْ بِنِوِيسي | Thou must, *or* oughtst to write a letter. |
| نامَهْ بايَدْ بِنِوِيسَد | He, *or* she, must, *or* ought to write a letter. |

PLURAL.

| | |
|---|---|
| نامَهْ تَوانيم نِوِشْت | We may be able to write a letter. |
| نامَهْ تَوانيد نِوِشْت | You may be able to write a letter. |
| نامَهْ تَوانَنْد نِوِشْت | They may be able to write a letter. |

PRESENT PARTICIPLE.

SINGULAR.

| | |
|---|---|
| بايَدْ نامَهْ نِوِيسانْ باشَم | I must *or* should be writing a letter. |
| بايَدْ نامَهْ نِوِيسانْ باشي | Thou must, *or* shouldst, be writing a letter. |
| بايَدْ نامَهْ نِوِيسانْ باشَد | He, *or* she, must *or* should be writing a letter. |

PLURAL.

| | |
|---|---|
| نامَهْ نِوِيسانْ تَوانيم شُد | We could be writing a letter. |
| نامَهْ نِوِيسانْ تَوانيد شُد | You could be writing a letter. |
| نامَهْ نِوِيسانْ تَوانَنْد شُد | They could be writing a letter. |

### ACTIVE PARTICIPLE.

SINGULAR.

| | |
|---|---|
| مَن بايَد نويسَندَه اين نامَه باشَم | I must be the writer of this letter. |
| تو بايَد نويسَندَه اين نامَه باشي | Thou must be the writer of this letter. |
| أو بايَد نويسَندَه اين نامَه باشَد | He, *or* she, must be the writer of this letter |

PLURAL.

| | |
|---|---|
| ما بايِست نويسَندَه اين نامَه باشيم | We should, *or* ought to have been the writers of this letter. |
| شُما بايِست نويسَندَه اين نامَه باشيد | You should, *or* ought to have been the writers of this letter. |
| ايشان بايِست نويسَندَه اين نامَه باشَند | They should, *or* ought to have been the writers of this letter. |

---

## The Verb رَشك بُردَن "*To Envy.*"

---

### PASSIVE VOICE.

رَشك بُردَه شُدَن To be, *or* to become, envied.

### INDICATIVE MOOD.

SIMPLE PRETERITE.

| SINGULAR. | | PLURAL. | |
|---|---|---|---|
| رَشك بُردَه شُدَم | I was envied. | رَشك بُردَه شُديم | We were envied. |
| رَشك بُردَه شُدي | Thou wast envied. | رَشك بُردَه شُديد | You were envied. |
| رَشك بُردَه شُد | He, *or* she, was envied. | رَشك بُردَه شُدَند | They were envied. |

COMPOUND PRETERITE.

| | | | |
|---|---|---|---|
| رَشك بُردَه شُدَه أم | I have been envied. | رَشكبُردَه شُدَه ايم | We have been envied. |
| رَشكبُردَه شُدَه | Thou hast been envied. | رَشكبُردَه شُدَه ايد | You have been envied. |
| رَشكبُردَه شُدَه أست | He, *or* she, has been envied. | رَشكبُردَه شُدَه أند | They have been envied. |

### IMPERFECT TENSE.

| SINGULAR. | | PLURAL. | |
|---|---|---|---|
| رشکبرده میشدم | I was being envied. | رشکبرده میشدیم | We were being envied. |
| رشکبرده میشدي | Thou wast being envied. | رشکبرده میشدید | You were being envied. |
| رشکبرده میشد | He, *or* she, was being envied. | رشکبرده میشدند | They were being envied. |

### PRETERITE PLUPERFECT.

| | | | |
|---|---|---|---|
| رشکبرده شده بودم | I had been envied. | رشکبرده شده بودیم | We had been envied. |
| رشکبرده شده بودي | Thou hadst been envied. | رشکبرده شده بودید | You had been envied. |
| رشکبرده شده بود | He, *or* she, had been envied. | رشکبرده شده بودند | They had been envied. |

### FUTURE TENSE.

| | | | |
|---|---|---|---|
| رشکبرده خواهم شد | I shall be envied. | رشکبرده خواهیم شد | We shall be envied. |
| رشکبرده خواهي شد | Thou wilt be envied. | رشکبرده خواهید شد | You will be envied. |
| رشکبرده خواهد شد | He, *or* she, will be envied. | رشکبرده خواهند شد | They will be envied. |

### PRESENT TENSE.

| | | | |
|---|---|---|---|
| رشکبرده میشوم | I am being envied. | رشکبرده میشویم | We are being envied. |
| رشکبرده میشوي | Thou art being envied. | رشکبرده میشوید | You are being envied. |
| رشکبرده میشود | He, *or* she, is being envied. | رشکبرده میشوند | They are being envied. |

### AORIST.

| | | | |
|---|---|---|---|
| رشکبرده شوم | I may become envied. | رشکبرده شویم | We may become envied. |
| رشکبرده شوي | Thou mayst become envied. | رشکبرده شوید | You may become envied. |
| رشکبرده شود | He, *or* she, may become envied. | رشکبرده شوند | They may become envied. |

### PAST PARTICIPLE.

رشک برده شده Having been envied.

## SUBJUNCTIVE MOOD.

| SINGULAR. | | PLURAL. | |
|---|---|---|---|
| شاید رشکبرده شدم | Perhaps I was envied. | شاید رشکبرده بشویم | We may perhaps become envied. |
| شاید رشکبرده شدي | Perhaps thou wast envied. | شاید رشکبرده بشوید | You may perhaps become envied. |
| شاید رشکبرده شد | Perhaps he, *or* she, was envied. | شاید رشکبرده بشوند | They may perhaps become envied. |
| شاید رشکبرده میشدم | Perhaps I was being envied. | اگر رشکبرده میشویم | If we are being envied. |
| شاید رشکبرده میشدي | Perhaps thou wast being envied. | اگر رشکبرده میشوید | If you are being envied. |
| شاید رشکبرده میشد | Perhaps he, *or* she, was being envied. | اگر رشکبرده میشوند | If they are being envied. |

&c. &c. &c.

The reader will have now no difficulty, according to the models before him, in forming any Compound, whether of Arabic extraction or otherwise, as he pleases.

### 132. AN ALPHABETICAL SERIES OF VERBAL NOUNS, OR SIMPLE PERSIAN INFINITIVES, WITH THEIR RESPECTIVE IMPERATIVES.

| INFINITIVE. | | IMPERATIVE. | INFINITIVE. | | IMPERATIVE. |
|---|---|---|---|---|---|
| آجیدن | To stitch | آجین | آفریدن | To create | آفرین |
| آزردن | To offend | آزار | آگاهانیدن | To warn | آگاهان |
| آسودن | To repose | آساي | آکندن | To stuff | آکند |
| آشفتن | To disturb | آشوب | آلودن | To stain | آلاي |
| آغالیدن | To excite | آغال | آمدن | To come | آي |
| آغشتن | To steep | آلاي | آموختن | To learn | آموز |

| INFINITIVE. | | IMPERATIVE. |
|---|---|---|
| آمیختن | To mingle | آمیز |
| آویختن | To suspend | آویز |
| ارزیدن | To be worth | ارز |
| افتادن | To fall | افت |
| افراختن | To elevate | افراز |
| افراشتن | To hoist | افراز |
| افزودن | To increase | افزاي |
| افشردن | To squeeze | افشار |
| افکندن | To fling | افکن |
| انباشتن | To store | انباز |
| انداختن | To throw | انداز |
| اندوختن | To treasure | اندوز |
| انگاشتن | To suppose | انگار |
| ایستادن | To stand | ایست |
| باختن | To play | باز |
| باریدن | To rain | بار |
| بافتن | To weave | باف |
| بالیدن | To exult | بال |
| بردن | To carry | بر |
| بریدن | To cut | بر |
| بستن | To bind | بند |
| بوئیدن | To smell | بوي |

| INFINITIVE. | | IMPERATIVE |
|---|---|---|
| بیختن | To sift | بیز |
| پاشیدن | To scatter | پاش |
| پائیدن | To guard | پاي |
| پالودن | To strain | پالاي |
| پختن | To cook | پز |
| پرستیدن | To worship | پرست |
| پرسیدن | To ask | پرس |
| پریدن | To fly | پر |
| پژوهیدن | To investigate | پژوه |
| پوسیدن | To rot | پوس |
| پذیرفتن | To accept | پذیر |
| پیوستن | To join | پیوند |
| پیمودن | To measure | پیماي |
| تابیدن | To twist | تاب |
| تاختن | To gallop | تاز |
| تازیدن | To run | تاز |
| تافتن | To shine | تاب |
| تپیدن | To palpitate | تپ |
| ترسیدن | To fear | ترس |
| ترسانیدن | To frighten | ترسان |
| جائیدن | To masticate | جاو |
| جستن | To leap | جه |

| INFINITIVE. | | IMPERATIVE. |
|---|---|---|
| جستن | To search | جوي |
| جنبیدن | To shake | جنب |
| جنبانیدن | To stir | جنبان |
| جهانیدن | To urge to leap | جهان |
| جوئیدن | To search | جوي |
| چریدن | To graze | چر |
| چرانیدن | To cause to graze | چران |
| چسبیدن | To stick | چسب |
| چسبانیدن | To glue | چسبان |
| خلیدن | To prick | خل |
| خمیدن | To bend | خم |
| خمانیدن | To double down | خمان |
| چشیدن | To taste | چش |
| چشانیدن | To cause to taste | چشان |
| چکیدن | To drop | چك |
| چکانیدن | To cause to drop | چکان |
| چمیدن | To walk proudly | چم |
| چیدن | To pick *or* select | چین |
| خاستن | To rise | خیز |
| خاریدن | To itch | خار |
| خارانیدن | To scratch | خاران |
| خائیدن | To bite | خاي |

| INFINITIVE. | | IMPERATIVE. |
|---|---|---|
| خوابیدن | To sleep | خواب |
| خوابانیدن | To cause to sleep | خوابان |
| خواستن | To desire | خواه |
| خریدن | To purchase | خر |
| خزیدن | To creep | خز |
| خسبیدن | To reposc | خسب |
| خلیدن | To prick | خل |
| خندیدن | To laugh | خند |
| خندانیدن | To cause to laugh | خندان |
| دادن | To give | ده |
| داشتن | To have | دار |
| دانستن | To know | دان |
| درودن | To reap | درو |
| دریدن | To rend | در |
| دزدیدن | To steal | دزد |
| دمیدن | To blow | دم |
| دوختن | To sew | دوز |
| دوشیدن | To milk | دوش |
| دویدن | To run | دو |
| دیدن | To see | بین |
| راندن | To drive | ران |
| رخشیدن | To shine | رخش |

| INFINITIVE. | | IMPERATIVE. | INFINITIVE. | | IMPERATIVE. |
|---|---|---|---|---|---|
| رستن | To grow | روي | سرودن | To sing | سراي |
| رستن | To scape | ره | سفتن | To bore | سنب |
| رسيدن | To arrive | رس | سگاليدن | To think | سگال |
| رشتن | To spin | ريس | سودن | To pound | ساي |
| رفتن | To go | رو | شدن | To become | شو |
| رفتن | To sweep | روب | شكستن | To break | شكن |
| رميدن | To startle | رم | شكافتن | To cleave | شكاف |
| رمانيدن | To scare | رمان | شكفتن | To bloom | شكفت |
| ريشتن | To spin | ريس | شناختن | To recognise | شناس |
| زادن | To bring forth | زا | شمردن | To count | شمار |
| زائيدن | To bear young | زاي | غنجيدن | To rejoice | غنج |
| زاريدن | To lament | زار | فروختن | To sell | فروش |
| زدودن | To rub off | زداي | فزودن | To increase | فزاي |
| زيستن | To live | زي | فريفتن | To deceive | فريب |
| سائيدن | To rub | ساي | فشردن | To squeeze | فشار |
| سپردن | To commit | سپار | فهميدن | To understand | فهم |
| ساختن | To make | ساز | كاشتن | To plant | كار |
| سپوختن | To stuff | سپوز | كاويدن | To hollow out | كاو |
| ستاندن | To take | ستان | كاهيدن | To decrease | كاه |
| ستودن | To praise | ستاي | كردن | To do | كن |
| سرشتن | To mix | سريش | گشتن | To become | گرد |
| سرائيدن | To chant | سراي | گرديدن | To turn round | گرد |

| INFINITIVE. | | IMPERATIVE. |
|---|---|---|
| كِشْتَن | To sow | كار |
| كُشْتَن | To kill | كُش |
| كَشِيدَن | To draw | كَش |
| گَنْدِيدَن | To stink | گَنْد |
| كَنْدَن | To dig | كَن |
| كُوفْتَن | To beat | كُوب |
| كُوشِيدَن | To strive | كُوش |
| گَزِيدَن | To sting *or* bite | گَز |
| گُزِيدَن | To chose | گُزِين |
| گُسِيخْتَن | To snap | گُسِل |
| گُشادَن / گُشُودَن | To loose | گُشاي |
| گُفْتَن | To speak | گُوي |
| لافِيدَن | To boast | لاف |
| لَرزِيدَن | To tremble | لَرز |
| لَغزِيدَن | To slip | لَغز |
| لَنگِيدَن | To limp | لَنگ |
| مالِيدَن | To rub | مال |
| ماندَن | To remain | مان |
| مُردَن | To die | مِير |
| مَكِيدَن | To suck | مَك |
| نازِيدَن | To coquet | ناز |
| نالِيدَن | To complain | نال |
| نامِيدَن | To name | نام |
| نِشاندَن | To place | نِشان |
| نِشَستَن | To sit down | نِشِين |
| نِكُوهِيدَن | To reproach | نِكُوه |
| نِمُودَن | To show | نِماي |
| نَوردِيدَن | To roll | نَورد |
| نِوِشْتَن | To write | نِوِيس |
| نِهادَن | To place | نِه |
| نِهُفْتَن | To conceal | نِهُفت |
| وَرزِيدَن | To exercise | وَرز |
| وَزِيدَن | To blow | وَز |
| هِشْتَن | To let down | هِل |
| يازِيدَن | To long for | ياز |
| يافْتَن | To find | ياب |
| يالِيدَن | To be proud | يال |

## COMPOUND ADJECTIVES,
AND
THE NATURE OF THEIR COMPOSITION.

133. This is a very extensive and useful class of Compounds in Persian. They are formed in three ways: By placing a Substantive before a Contracted Participle (Active or Passive); as, جُهانْ آفَرِينْ "world-creating"; آفَرِينْ being a contraction of آفَرِينَنْدَه, "Creator," the Active Participle of آفَرِيدَنْ "To create." By prefixing an Adjective to a Substantive; as, شِيرِينْ‌زَبانْ "sweet-tongued": or, By adding one Noun Substantive to another; as, پَرِي پَيكَرْ "fairy-formed."

134. However susceptible these Compounds may appear of unlimited extent, they must still be restricted within certain bounds. We must not attempt to form new and arbitrary Compounds; but be content with the use of such only as are already to be found in the works of writers of authority (who are, after all, our best guides in all languages), or with those which are in common use among the educated Natives of Persia.

135. It is a mistake, to suppose "that these Compounds may *be multiplied without end,* according to the pleasure and taste of the writer." Those who hold this opinion have, indeed, attempted many new formations, of which they have given long lists in their works; but the beginner must be very cautious how he adopts any of them, for they cannot safely be relied on. Even in the selection of Compounds unquestionably legitimate, some judgment is required in their adaptation to different occasions. Many of them, though composed of different words, imply the same meaning; and the

writer's *taste*, certainly, must here be judiciously exercised. For instance, شیرین زبان شیرین گفتار شیرین سخن نوش لب شکرخا شکردهان &c. &c., are all Compound Adjectives, employed to express sweetness of mouth, the beauty and the elegance of manner in which an admired object joins in discourse; but they are not all indiscriminately and equally applicable to every occasion: study and experience can alone guide the selection.

136. These Compounds may be formed with two Persian words, two Arabic words, or one Persian and one Arabic word. Of the last-mentioned kind, are all those that are composed of an Arabic Noun and a Contracted Participle; for the Participle must always be Persian: and for distinction sake, we call these "Compound Epithets," of which the following afford a few Examples:—they are by far the most extensive class of Compounds in the Persian language.

137. COMPOUND EPITHETS.

| | | | |
|---|---|---|---|
| جهانگیر | World-conquering. | مجلس آرا | Assembly-adorning. |
| عدوبند | Enemy-enslaving. | روح آسا | Soul-refreshing. |
| درافشان | Pearl-scattering. | دلارام | Heart-soothing. |
| عنبرآگین | Amber-scented. | خطا بخش | Fault-forgiving. |
| مرد افکن | Hero-overthrowing. | بهجت افزا | Delight-increasing. |
| دل آزار | Heart-afflicting. | شهرآشوب | Town-disturbing. |
| گل افشان | Rose-scattering. | غبار آلود | Being covered with dust. |
| خجلت زده | Shame-stricken. | خونریز | Blood-shedding. |

شَهد آميز Being mixed with honey.

گيتي اَفروز World-illuminating.

وَحشَت اَفزا Fear-increasing.

دهشَت اَنگيز Dread-inspiring.

جَنگجوي Battle-seeking.

سَحَرخيز Early-rising.

تَن پرور Self-indulging.

ضيا گُستَر Light-spreading.

غَريب نِواز Stranger-cherishing.

دِل گُشا Heart-expanding.

عِطر بيز Perfume-diffusing.

جان آفرين Soul-creating.

خوش خوان Sweet-singer.

عالَمتاب World-brightening.

ظُلمَت زدا Darkness-dispelling.

صَف شِكَن Rank (of battle)-breaking.

غَمزَداي Grief-dispersing.

&c. &c. &c.

## COMPOUND ADJECTIVES.

38. Adjectives compounded of two Nouns-Substantive, both Arabic, both Persian, or one of each; thus:

پَري رُخسار Fairy-faced.

مَلَك اَخلاق Angelic-disposition.

شير دِل Lion-hearted.

كَريم طَبع Generous-disposition.

غُنچه دَهان Rose-bud mouthed.

ياقوت لَب Ruby-lipp'd.

اَنجُم سِپاه Army numerous as stars.

شَريف نِهاد Of noble birth.

سَلطَنَت دَستگاه Kingly-pomp.

عَدالَت آئين Justly-disposed.

مَحزون خاطِر Melancholy-minded.

سَمَن بوي Jessamine-scented.

فَصيح كَلام Perspicuous in speech.

دَريا مِثال Resembling the sea.

بَليغ خِطاب Eloquent in discourse. &c. &c. &c.

139. Adjectives and Substantives together forming Compound Adjectives:—

| | | | |
|---|---|---|---|
| خُوبْ رُويْ | Handsome-faced. | شِيرِينْ زَبَانْ | Sweet-tongued. |
| صَافْ دِلْ | Pure-hearted. | سُرْخْ رُويْ | Red-faced. |
| سَلِيمْ قَلْبْ | Simple-minded. | سَفِيدْ مُويْ | Grey-haired. |
| پَاكِيزَهْ خُويْ | Well-disposed. | كَجْ خُلْقْ | Ill- (*lit.* crooked-) -tempered. |
| نِيكْ مَحْضَرْ | Right-minded (benevolent). | تَلْخْ گُفْتَارْ | Bitter in speech. |
| خُوشْ اَلْحَانْ | Pleasant-chanting (warbling). | تِيزْ فَهْمْ | Sharp-witted. |
| زِشْتْ رُويْ | Ugly-faced. | سَبُكْ سَيْرْ | Swift-footed. |
| سَنْگِينْ دِلْ | Hard-hearted. | بَدْرَوِشْ | Ill-mannered. |
| تُرُشْ اَبْرُو | Sour-browed. | پَاكْ طَبِيعَتْ | Pure-natured. |
| صَافِي ضَمِيرْ | Pure-minded. | نِيكْ اَخْلَاقْ | Of good-morals. |
| پَاكْ طِينَتْ | Good- (*lit.* pure-) -natured. | رُوشَنْ عَقْلْ | Clear in judgment. |
| سِيَاهْ چَشْمْ | Black-eyed. | شِكَسْتَهْ بَالْ | Broken-hearted. |

&c. &c. &c.

140. The vast number of Epithets and Adjectives which are capable of being combined after these three forms,—and which are often used, especially in the Plural Number, as Substantives, without any Noun being expressed,—renders the Persian language exceedingly rich, and particularly adapted to poetical writings.

## NOUNS COMPOUNDED WITH PARTICLES.

141. There are several significant Particles in Persian, which, when prefixed or added to Nouns, form another extensive class of Compounds.

(1) The Particle هَم "together," or "with," prefixed to Nouns, implies "society," "intimacy," "sympathy," "fellowship," &c. &c.; as,

| | |
|---|---|
| هَمخانَه | Being in the same house, *or* fellow-lodgers. |
| هَم صُحبَت | Being associates. |
| هَمدَم | (*lit.*) Breathing together, *i. e.* being intimate. |
| هَمدَرد | Sympathizing; (*lit.*) Feeling the same pain. |
| هَم مَكتَب | Being in the same school together, *i.e.* school-fellows. |
| هَمراز | Having the same secret, *or* being confidants. |
| هَمبِستَر | Lying on the same pillow, *i.e.* being bed-fellows. |

&c. &c. &c.

(2) The Particles نا "not," بي "without," and كَم "little," are placed before Nouns to denote scarcity or privation; as,

| | | | |
|---|---|---|---|
| نادان | Ignorant. | بي دين | Irreligious. |
| نامَرد | Unmanly. | بي باك | Careless. |
| ناپاك | Unclean. | كَم تَجرِبَه | With little experience. |
| بي خِرَد | Senseless. | كَم بُها | Of little value. |
| بي تَميز | Without discrimination. | كَم ريش | Thin-bearded. |
| بي مَصرَف | Useless. | كَم مايَه | Of little resource. |

&c. &c. &c.

## NAMES OF AGENTS.

142. The modern Persians have very extensively taken their names of Agents from the Arabic in precisely the same form as is used by the Arabs, of which several instances are to be found in the list of the *simple significant words* at the beginning of this work*: but the Persian names of Agents are properly formed by prefixing Nouns to Contracted Participles Active; as, گُلفروش "a seller of roses"; آش پَز "a cooker of broth"; کَفش دوز "a shoemaker"; کُلاه‌دوز "a cap-maker" or "a hatter"; زین‌ساز "a saddler"; &c. &c.

143. These Contracted Participles are sometimes corrupted; for instance: بان, a corruption of مان, contracted from مانَندَه "a remainer with," or "waiter upon," is added to many Nouns; as, باغبان "a gardener"; دَربان "a porter"; زِندان بان "a jailor." In the same manner is گَر "both," corrupted and contracted from کار; which itself is here a part, or contraction (as it were), of the Compound Participle Active کارکُنَندَه "a worker," and is thus added to Nouns; as, زرگر "a goldsmith"; آهنگر "an iron," or "blacksmith"; کوزه‌گر "a potter"; &c. &c.

## NOUNS OF PLACE.

144. The Persians have also adopted this Noun from the Arabic; as, مَسجِد "a mosque" or "place of worship"; مَنزِل "a station," or "place of descent"; مَعبَر "a ford over a river," &c.: but still the genuine Persian form is

---

* See p. 21.

frequently used; which is, to add گاه, meaning both *time* and *place*, to the Noun; as, خوابگاه "a bed" or "place of sleep"; مَنزِلگاه "a resting-place"; تَخت گاه "a throne-chamber," and sometimes the "capital of the empire," for the throne rests there; شامگاه "the evening," or "the night-time"; بیگاه "untimely," or "out of time"; &c. &c.

145. In like manner, سِتان, زار, کَدَه, دان, سار, لاخ, added to Nouns, all denote the places of any thing of which the Nouns bear the name; as,

| | | | |
|---|---|---|---|
| گُلستان | A rose-garden. | قَلَمدان | A penholder, *or* inkstand. |
| خارِستان | A thorny place. | شَمعدان | A candlestick. |
| شورَه زار *or* نَمَك زار | A salt-desert, *or* a salt-mine. | کُوهسار | A mountainous country. |
| بُتکَدَه | An idol-temple. | سَنگ لاخ | A rough stony place. |
| آتَشکَدَه | A fire-temple. | دیو لاخ | A place haunted by evil spirits. |

&c. &c. &c.

146. Adjectives implying possession, plenty, mixture, or colour, are formed by prefixing the Nouns to the Particles گین, آگین, وار, وَر, مَند, ناك, سار, ین, فام, گون; as,

| | | | |
|---|---|---|---|
| غَمگین | Sorrowful. | خَوف ناك | Fearful. |
| شرم آگین | Bashful. | شَرمسار | Ashamed. |
| اُمیدوار | Hopeful. | زُمُرّدین | Emerald-coloured. |
| دانش وَر | Learned. | سِیَه فام | Black-coloured. |
| خِرَد مَند | Wise. | گُلگون | Rose-coloured. |
| زَهرناك | Poisonous. | | |

&c. &c. &c.

147. Adjectives denoting *similitude*, or *fitness*, are formed by placing the Nouns before وارْ, سانْ, آنَهْ, وَش, آسا, سا &c. &c.; as,

| | | | |
|---|---|---|---|
| سِحْرسا | Like magic. | زَنانَهْ | Fit for women. |
| عَنْبَرآسا | Like ambergris. | دِيْوسانْ | Demon-like. |
| ماهْ وَش | Resembling the moon. | خُورْشِيْدْ سانْ | Resembling the sun. |
| مَردانَهْ | Manly; *and also*, Fit for men. | شاهْ وارْ | Prince-like, *or* Fit for kings. |

148. Some Adjectives, when intended to express *fulness*, *entireness*, *completeness*, or *variety*, are repeated, having the letter (ا) *Alĕf* interposed between them; as لَبالَبْ "brimful"; سَراسَرْ "entirely," or "from one end to the other"; گُوناگُونْ "of various colours"; &c. But the instances of these two or three classes of Adjectives are very few,—almost confined, indeed, to those above stated.

149. From the Compounds above mentioned, or any other Adjectives Compound or Simple, Abstract Substantives may be formed, by adding the Particle ي; subject to the same conditions as already stated, when speaking of *Definite and Indefinite Nouns**.

150. Another class of these Abstracts is formed by placing the Third Person Singular of the Simple Preterite of a Verb before the Imperative of the same Verb; or before the Third Person Singular of the Simple Preterite of the same, or of another Verb.

* See the Rules on Definite and Indefinite Nouns, p. 32.

The Conjunction و is sometimes placed between them; which is, however, never fully pronounced, but only serves as a (ُ) Peesh on the last letter of the preceding word; as, گُفتُ وگوي or گُفتُگو "conversation"; جُستُجو "search"; خَرِيدُوفروخت or خَرِيدُوفروش "buying and selling;" آمَدُوشُد or آمَدُورفت "coming and going," *or* "frequenting"; &c. &c.

151. Others are made, again, by adding آر to the Third Person Singular of the Simple Preterite of a Verb; as, گُفتار "speech"; رَفتار "motion" *or* "behaviour"; &c. &c.

## OF PREPOSITIONS.

152. Prepositions serve to connect words one with another, and to shew the relation between them. They are, for the most part, set before Nouns and Pronouns; as,

پِدَرِمَن اَزخانَه بِبازاررَفت "My father went *from* home *to* the market."

مَن اين كِتابرِااباوُدادَم "I gave this book *to* him.

153. Prepositions are of great use in all languages; but in one particular they are of greater use in Persian than in any other language not similarly constituted; inasmuch as, in Persian, they express all those relations which, in some languages, are chiefly marked by Cases, or the different endings of Nouns.

154. Prepositions are Separable or Inseparable. The Separable Prepositions are those which may be used separated

from other words.; as, بالا "upon," or "atop," "aloft"; پائین "down"; زبر , فراز "above"; زیر "below," or "beneath"; فرود , نشیب "down"; پیش "before," or "in front"; پس "after," or "behind"; سوی "towards," "side of"; میان "between"; پهلو "by the side"; نزدیک , نزد "near"; نزدیکی , "vicinity," "neighbourhood"; برای , بهر "for," "on account of"; بیرون "out"; اندرون "in." To which may be added these four, borrowed from the Arabs; قبل "before"; بعد "after"; جهت "toward"; جانب "side."

155. The Inseparable Prepositions are those which cannot be used separately; as, ز , از "from," "by," "of"; بر , ابر "on," "upon"; ب , بِهِ "to"; با "with"; در "in"; را "for," "to," "of." Some of these are often used two together, so as to form Compound Prepositions; as, ازبالا , اززبر "from above," or "from top"; ازفراز "from the height"; ازپائین , اززیر , ازنشیب "from below," "from beneath," "from under"; ازپس "from behind"; پس از , or سپس "then," or "afterwards"; ازپیش "from before"; ازسوی "from"; ازمیان "from the middle," "from the midst," "from amongst"; ازپهلو "from the side"; ازنزدیک "from near"; ازجانب , ازنزد , ازجهت "from"; ازبرای , ازبهر "for," "because of," "on account of"; ازبیرون "from without"; ازاندرون "from within"; قبل از "before"; بعد از "after." Taking از away, ب (to), may be prefixed to all the foregoing Prepositions, except سپس , برای , بهر , قبل and بعد. بدر is very often used to signify "out-and-out," "clear-out," "quite out." ز is no more than از contracted, and therefore

may be used instead of it, but must always be prefixed to the Preposition: the use of it is, however, chiefly, if not wholly, confined to poetry.

## OF CONJUNCTIONS.

156. There are, in Persian, Simple as well as Compound Conjunctions. The following are the Simple Conjunctions: وَ* "and"; نیز , هَم "also," "likewise"; اَگَر *or* گَر "if"; یا "or," "either"; جُز "except"; مَگَر "unless," "rather"; کِه , چِه "for," "because," or "whether."

157. Compound Conjunctions are of various sorts. One sort is composed of two Conjunctions; as, وَاَگَر *or* وَگَر "and if"; وَیا "and or"; وَلیکن , وَاَمّا which latter is also abbreviated, thus وَلیک , وَلي "and but," "nevertheless"; بَلکِه "but rather," *or* "perhaps"; اَگَرچِه , گَرچِه , وَاَگَرچِه , وَگَرچِه "although," "and although," &c. Another sort is compounded of a

* This Conjunction is borrowed from the Arabs, and is pronounced وَ *va*; but it is not always distinctly articulated in Persian. Very often, when coming between two words, especially when such words have a natural affinity or any other relation one to another, the و is used as a vowel; and it serves only as پیش (ُ), or the vowel *ū* in English, as if placed on the last letter of the first of the two words; as, پدرو مادر "the father and mother"; روزوشب "day and night"; گرم وسرد "warm and cold," &c.; which are not usually pronounced "Pedar *va* mandar," "Rooz *va* shab," "Garm *va* sard"; but, "Pedarū mandar," "Roozū shab," "Garmū sard," &c. &c. The following Conjunctions are also borrowed from the Arabs: لیکن , بَل , اَمّا "but"; بَل "rather."

Conjunction and a Preposition ; as, بِجُز "excepting"; بِهَم, باهَم, "together"; &c. &c.

158. Other Compound Conjunctions are formed by the union of Adjectives, Prepositions, Adverbs, Pronouns, and Conjunctions ; as, هَرچَند, هَرچَندکِه, وَهَرچَند, وَهَرچَندکِه "although," "notwithstanding," &c. ; زیراکِه, زیرا, بِنابَراین, ازاین سَبَب, زینرو, ازاین جِهَت "because," "therefore," &c.

159. A Preposition alone is sometimes used as a Conjunction ; as, پَس "then"; بِی "without": and sometimes a Noun also ; as, خواه "whether"; &c. &c.

160. Conjunctions and Prepositions being equally essential to discourse, since they form that class of words called *Connectives*, without which there could be no language ; some further remarks, joined with a few examples on the nature and the use of Conjunctions, may not be unacceptable to the learner.

161. Conjunctions are principally divided into two sorts, the Copulative and Disjunctive.

The Conjunction-Copulative serves to connect or to continue words or sentences, by expressing an addition, a supposition, a cause, &c. ; as,

| | |
|---|---|
| اُو وَبِرادَرَش دَرلَندَن مِیباشَند | He *and* his brother reside in London. |
| مَن خواهَم رَفت اَگَراُومَرا رُخصَت دَهَد | I will go, *if* he would give me permission. |
| مَن نَرَفتَم زیراکِه مِیتَرسیدَم | I did not go, *because* I was afraid. |

&c. &c. &c.

162. The Conjunction-Disjunctive serves also to connect or to continue words or sentences: but instead of connecting their meanings, as the Conjunctives do, they disjoin them, or set them, as it were, in opposition; as,

| | |
|---|---|
| یَكْ فِنْجانْ چایْ بِی شیرْ بِمَنْ بِدِهْ | Give me a cup of tea, *without* milk. |
| اَزْ هَمَهْ كَسْ پُرْسیدْ مَگَرْ اَزْ مَنْ | He asked every body, *except* me. |
| خادِمِ مَنْ رَفْتْ اَمّا بَرْنَگَشْت | My servant went, *but* he did not return. |

163. These two kinds of Conjunctions may further be subdivided in the following manner.

Conjunctions that unite both sentences and their meanings: they are either *Copulatives* or *Continuatives*.

The former may join all sentences, however incongruous in signification; as,

سَعْدیْ شاعِرِ خُوبی بُودْ وَهِنْدْ بِسْیارْ گَرْمَسْت

Sādy was a fine Poet, and India is very hot.

The latter join those sentences only which have a natural connection; as,

سَبْزَهْ دَرْ صَحْرا یافْتْ نَمیشَوَدْ بِجِهَتِ اینكه بارانْ نَیامَدَه اَسْت

No verdure is found in the fields, *because* there has been (come) no rain.

پَنْدِ پِدَرْ تُرا بِشْنَوْ چه اُوْ خَیْرْ خواهِ تُسْت

Listen to the advice of thy father, *for* he is thy well-wisher.

164. Continuatives are also of two sorts, *Suppositive* and *Positive*.

The former denote connexion, but not actual existence; as,

آفْتابْ تُرا خواهَدْ سُوخْتْ اَگَرْ بِیرُونْ بِرَوِی

The Sun will scorch thee, *if* thou goest abroad.

The latter imply connexion and actual existence at the same time; as,

تُوخُدا تَرسِي زِيرَاكِهِ پِدَرُومَادَرتَرا عَزِيز مِيدَارِي

Thou art a God-fearing man, *since* thou lovest thy parents.

165. Again, Positive Continuatives are either Causal or Collective. The former subjoin causes to effects; as,

اَز دِرَخت اُفتَادچِه شَاخَه تَاب نَيَاوَرد He fell from the tree *because* the branch could not bear (him).

The latter subjoin effects to causes; as,

اُو اَبلَه اَست زِينرو نَمِيفَهمَد He is a fool, *therefore*, he does not understand.

&c. &c. &c.

166. Disjunctive Conjunctions, which unite sentences, while they disjoin their meanings, are either Simple, which merely disjoin; as, آن يا اَسب اَست يا خَر "That is *either* a horse or an ass"; or Adversative, which both disjoin and mark an opposition; as, آن اَسب نيست بَلكِه خَرَاَست "That is not a horse, *but* it is an ass"; &c. &c.

167. Adversative Disjunctives are divided into *Absolute* and *Comparative*:—Absolute, as when I say, مَن بيدار بُودَم اَمّا تُو نَبُودِي "I was awake, *but* thou wast not." Comparative, as in this example: اين اَسب رَوانتَر اَز آنست "This horse is swifter *than* that"; &c. &c.

168. Adversative Disjunctives are further divided into *Adequate* and *Inadequate*:—Adequate, as when it is said, اُو خواهَد آمَد مَگَر بيمار باشَد "He will come, *unless* he be sick"; that is, his sickness only will be an adequate cause to prevent his coming. Inadequate, as in this sentence, اُو قَبول نَخواهَد كَرد اَگَرچِه مِسكين باشَد "He will not accept (it), *although* he be poor;" that is, his poverty will not be a sufficient or adequate cause to make him accept it; &c. &c.

## OF INTERJECTIONS AND EXCLAMATIONS.

169. Interjections are words thrown in between the parts of a sentence to express the passions or emotions of a speaker. They may, however, be termed Exclamations when they occur at the beginning of a sentence; that is, when the speaker begins his speech by uttering one of these words first; as, از شدت بیماری افسوس که قوت حرکت ندارم "From extreme illness, *alas!* that I have not the power of moving." or, افسوس که مرگ اورا امان نداد "*Alas!* that death gave him no quarter!" &c. &c.

170. The Persians have borrowed most of their Interjections from Arabic; in which latter language they are pretty numerous. They are not, however, a set of words without definite meanings in themselves; as, "oh!" "ah!" "hem!" "ho!" &c.: but, on the contrary, they are all of them significant words, and some even short sentences, used as Interjections; because their very meanings express the passions or emotions which the speaker intends to express. Nor are their uses always confined to these modes of expression; but are otherwise employed as Adjectives, as Substantives, as Verbs Simple or Compound, just as they happen to be. Similar instances are numerous, even in English. What are, for instance, "O misery!" "Death!" "Shame!" &c. but significant words, used as Interjections, as well as otherwise?

171. The following is a list of the principal Interjections used in Persian; which are, with the exception of those marked P., all Arabic:—

172. Interjections expressing regret or sorrow are, اَفسوس P. دِرِيغ P. "Alas!" حَيْف "Pity!" آهْ P. "a sigh."

173. Those which intimate grief, distress, or want of help, are, اَمانْ , دَخيل "O quarter!" فَريادْ P. "Cry!" بيدادْ P. "Injustice!" "Tyranny!" يارَبْ "O Lord!"

174. Such as are expressive of admiration, both real and ironical, are آفرين P. "create!" (that is, O Lord, let us have more!) مَرحَبا "Welcome!" تبارَكَ اللّٰه , بارَكَ اللّٰه "God is mighty!" ماشآءَ اللّٰه "God has willed!" واهْ واهْ , بَهْ بَهْ , وَهْ وَهْ "Heigh-ho!" or "Bravo!" &c. &c.

175. Of aversion, or disgust: مَبادا P. "May it never be *or* come to pass!" نَعوذُ بِاللّٰه , عَياذاً بِاللّٰه "God protect us!" اَستَغفِرُ اللّٰه "God forgive me!" &c. &c.

176. Of lamentation, mourning, &c.: اَفغانْ P. فُغانْ P. "Lament!" "Oh!" "Alas!" واوَيلا , واي "O misery!" واحَسرَتا "O loss!" "O pity!" &c. &c.

177. Of hatred and contempt: اُفّ "Fie!" &c. &c.

178. Of a call of the attention: اينَكْ P. هانْ P. هين P. "Lo!" "Behold!" "Hark!" to all of which اَيْ "O!" also may be prefixed.

179. We may now give a few examples of the introduction of the above into sentences.

| | |
|---|---|
| فَرْدا اِنْشاءَ اللّٰه بِدِيدَنِ شُما خواهَمْ آمَدْ | To-morrow, please God! I will come to see you. |
| اَسْبِ شُما دِيرُوزْ ماشاءَ اللّٰه چِه خُوبْ دَوِيدْ | How well, as God willed yesterday, did your horse run? |
| بِرادَرِ مَنْ اَفْسُوسْ كِه بِشِدَّتْ بِيمارْ اَسْتْ | My brother, I regret, is very seriously ill. |
| آهْ اَزْ آن هَمَه مِهْرْبانيهاكِه اُوْ باتُو كَرْدْ | Alas! for all those kindnesses which he exercised towards thee! |
| مَرْحَبا اِيْنْ صَفْحَه‌را بِسْيارْ خُوبْ نِوِشْتَه | Bless thee! thou hast written this page very well. |
| اُفْ چِه قَدَرْ زَحْمَتِ بِيفايِدَه مِيدِهِي | Fie! how much useless trouble thou givest! |
| اَيْ وايْ كِه مَرْدُمِ اِينْ شَهْر ازْ كُرِسْنَكِي مُرْدَنْد | O misery! the people of this city all died of hunger! |

&c. &c. &c.

## OF ADVERBS.

180. Adverbs being parts of speech which express some quality or circumstance respecting what are called Verbs, are, in Persian, chiefly Nouns, Participles, and Prepositions; or are derived from, or made up of, different combinations of these parts of speech, with or without Particles, in the following manner:—

(1) Of Number: as, باري, or يَكْبارْ "once"; دُوبارْ "twice"; سِهْ بارْ "thrice"; &c. &c.

(2) Of Order: as, نخستین, اوّلا, اوّل مرتبه, or اوّلین, "first"; دومین, دوم, or ثانیا, "secondly"; سیوم, سوم, سیومین, سیوم مرتبه, or ثالثا, "thirdly"; چهارمین, چهارم, چهارم مرتبه, or رابعا "fourthly"; &c. &c.

(3) Of Place: as, اینجا "here"; اینسو, اینجانب, اینطرف, &c. "this way," "this direction," &c.; آنجا, آنسو, &c., "there," "that way"; &c. &c.

(4) Of Interrogation: as, کو "Where?" کجا, کدامجا, کدام طرف, &c., "What place?" "What way?" "What direction?" &c. چند "How many?" چگونه "In what manner?" چون "How?" چرا "Wherefore?" برائ چه, بچه سبب, ازچه‌رو, &c., "Why?" "On what account?" "For what cause?" چه قدر "How much?" "What quantity?" &c. &c.

(5) Of Time Present: as, اکنون, کنون, حالا, "now"; همیندم, این زمان, همین زمان, هم اکنون, &c., "just now," "this instant," "this very moment"; امروز "to day"; امشب "to night"; امسال "this year"; &c. &c.

(6) Of Time Past: as, پیش ازاین, قبل ازاین, "before this"; ازپیش, پیشتر, پیش, "previously": پیشین, قدیم "anciently"; دیروز "yesterday"; دیشب "last night"; پارین پارسال "last year."

(7) Of Time to Come: as, فردا "to-morrow"; دیگرروز, روزدیگر "the next day"; فرد اشب "to-morrow night"; شب دیگر "the next night"; پس فردا "the day after to-morrow"; پس فرد اشب "the night after to-morrow"; سال دیگر "the

next year"; ماهِ دِیگَر "the next month"; هَفتَهٔ دِیگَر "the next week"; *or* سالِ آیندَه, ماهِ آیندَه, هَفتَهٔ آیندَه "the coming *or* approaching week, month, and year." سِپَس, بَعد اَزاین, پَس اَزاین, آیندَه "henceforth," "in future," "hereafter," &c.; عَنقَرِیب, دَراین زُودِي "by-and-bye," "presently, &c.: فِي الفَور, فِي الحال, بِزُودِي "immediately," "instantly," "directly," &c.

(8) Of Time Indefinite: as, بِسیارِبار, بِسیار, مُکَرَّر, بارها "often," "many a time," "oftentimes"; گاهگاهِي "occasionally"; گاهِوَقتِي "sometimes"; زُود "soon"; کَمتَر "very seldom"; نادِر "rarely"; هَمیشَه, هَموارَه "always," "ever"; پَیوَستَه "constantly"; مُدام "continually"; هَرروز, یَومِیّه, رُوزانَه "every day," "daily"; هَرسالَه "every year"; سالِیانَه "yearly"; هَرماهَه "every month"; ماهِیانَه "monthly"; هَرهَفتَه "every week"; هَفتَگِي "weekly"; هَردَم "every moment"; دَمبَدَم "momentarily"; باز, دِیگَر, دِیگَربار "again"; &c. &c.

(9) Of Quantity: as, اَندَك "little"; بِسیار "much"; کَم "rare"; خَیلِي "greatly," "a great many"; وافِر, فَراوان "abundantly"; کافِي "sufficiently"; بَس "enough," "only"; هَمِین "even," "even this only."

### (10) OF MANNER OR QUALITY.

181. Adverbs of Quality are the most numerous: they are generally formed by adding the termination آنَه (which answers to the English "*ly*") to an Adjective, whether Simple or Compound; as, دِلیرانَه "bold-*ly*";

دانشورانه "learned-*ly*"; &c. Every Compound Epithet, therefore, with very few exceptions, can be thus used as an Adverb*.

182. Participles Present are also used as Adverbs: they may be Simple; as,

اُونالان بمن گفت He spoke to me lamentingly.

وي خندان ازمن پرسيد He asked me smilingly.

or Compound; as,

پرخاش جويان آمد He came contentiously, or in a manner evidently seeking contention, *i.e.* to pick a quarrel.

گريه كنان بردر سراي شاه رفت He went weeping to the gate of the palace of the king.

183. Compound Past Participles are likewise employed as Adverbs; as,

دلشكسته بازگشت He returned broken-hearted.

In fact, every Noun which describes a Quality, Manner, or Attribute, may be employed in Persian as an Adverb.

(11) Of Doubt; as, شايد "perhaps"; باشد "it may be" *or* "may happen"; تواند "possibly"; بوكه "peradventure"; &c.

(12) Of Affirmation; as, همانا , هرآينه "certainly"; البته "verily"; بيشك , لاشك , بلاشك , بيشبهه , "undoubtedly"; بيهمه چيز "without any doubt whatever"; بيساخته "without artifice."

* See the List of the Compounds, Adjectives and Epithets, p. 103, 4.

(13) Of Negation; as, هَرگز "never"; نَه "no," "not"; مُطلَقا, اَبَدا, "not at all"; هيچ "not any"; هيچ وَقت "at no time"; هيچ چيز "nothing whatever"; بِهيچوَجه "in no wise"; هيچ كُدام "none whatever"; هيچ كَس "no person"; هيچ باب "on no account;" &c. &c.

(14) Of Comparison; as, زِيادَت, بيشتَر, اَفزون, فزون, "more"; بِسيارتَر, كَمتَر "much-more"; بيشتَرين, اَغلَب, اَكثَر, "most"; اَقَل, "less"; كَمتَرين "least"; خُردتَر, كوچك, خُرد, "small"; كوچكتَر, "smaller"; مثِل "alike"; مُساوي "equal"; مُوازي "parallel"; روبِرو, مُقابِل, مُحاذي, "opposite," "face to face"; مُوازِن, هَموزن, "of the same weight."

184. Prepositions, or even Adjectives, singly, in some instances, become Adverbs, by their application merely, *without* suffering any change; as in these phrases:

| | |
|---|---|
| رَفتَنِ ما نَزديك اَست | (The time of) our departure is *near* (at hand). |
| پَس چرا اَز مَن شِكايَت مِيكُني | Why, *then*, dost thou complain of me? |

&c. &c. &c.

185. The following sentence will better explain the manner in which Adverbs are used in Persian:

| | |
|---|---|
| مَن يَكبار بِديَدَنش رَفتَم | I went to see him *once*. |

186. When the Adverb "once" is employed in English, it may mean indefinitely; namely, "*once upon a time.*"

In Persian, in such instances, the Indefinite Particle ي is added to the Adjective بار; as,

بارِي بِدِيدَنَش رَفت *Once upon a time,* he went to see him.

It may be used without any emphasis being intended; as, "Once I went to see him." Either of the two foregoing phrases, in Persian, may be employed here; when the context *will do the rest.*

187. It may, in English, mean "*one time only,*" *i.e.* neither "*more nor less.*" Now, in Persian, the Adjective-Adverb بَس "sufficient," or "only," must also be used with the other Adverbs in manner following:

مَنْ يكبارْ بِدِيدَنَش رَفتَمُ وبَس I went to see him, *only once.*

أُو دُوساعَت بامَنْ بُودُ وبَس He was *only two hours* with me.

يكي أَزْ ايشانْ خَنْدانْ بُودُ وبَس One of them was *smiling only.*

188. Sometimes the Adverb هَمين, the Adjective تَنها "alone," or the Adjective-Adverb تَنهائي "singly," are used with بَس, or employed instead of it; as,

هَمينْ يكبارْ أَزْ من پُرسيدُ وبَس He asked me only once, and no more.

مَنْ تَنْها اَز تُو شِكايَت مْيكُنَمُ وبَس I complain of thee alone, and only.

شُما هَمين تَنْها اَزْ مَنْ پُرسيديد You asked of me alone.

ايشانْ هَمينْ تَنها مْيگُفتَنْد وبَس They alone were speaking, and no one else.

اَكنُون اَزْ مَنْ بِشنَو Listen to me now!

| | |
|---|---|
| اَزْچندین جِهَتْ مَنْ اینْ اَسْبرا نَخَرِیدَمْ | I did not buy this horse, for several reasons. |
| اَوّلا اینْکهْ پِیراَسْت | *First*, that it is old. |
| ثانیا اینِکه لَنْگَسْت or دُوُمْ | *Secondly*, that it is lame. |
| ثالثا or سِیُمْ اینِکهْ بَدْرَنْگَسْت | *Thirdly*, that it is of a bad colour. |

&c. &c. &c.

| | |
|---|---|
| دیرُوزْ کُجارَفْتَهْ بُودي | *Where* hadst thou gone *yesterday?* |
| چرامیْپُرسي | *Why* dost thou ask? |
| اَزْ انیکهْ دُوبارْ دَرْزَدَمْ وَکَسِي جَوابْ نَدادْ | Because I knocked at the door *twice*, and no one gave me an answer. |
| چِه وَقْتْ بُودْ | *What* time was it? |
| دُرُسْتْ خاطِرَمْ نیسْتْ میتَوانِسْتَ که ظُهْرْ باشَد | I do not *exactly* recollect (it is not exactly in my recollection): it might have been *mid-day*. |

189. The learner will observe, that the Adjective دُرُسْت "perfect" has here been employed as the Adverb "exactly," without having suffered any change of form: so he may also remark with regard to the Adjective خوب "good," or "well," in the following sentence:

| | |
|---|---|
| خُوب تَاَمُّلْ بِکُنْ شایَدْ خاطِرَت بِیایَدْ | Think *well!* it may *perhaps* come into thy recollection. |
| حالا خاطِرَمْ آمَدْ یَکْساعَتْ بَعْد اَزْظُهْر بُودْ | *Now* I recollect (*or* it is just come into my recollection); it was *an hour after noon* (one o'clock). |

| | |
|---|---|
| اَزْ کُجا بِخاطِرَتْ آمَدْ | *Whence* came it into thy recollection? |
| اَزْ مُزْدُورانْ کِهْ اَغْلَبْ دَرْساعَتِ یَکْ بِچاشْتْ مِیرَوَنْدْ | From (seeing) the common labourers, who *mostly* go to (their) meals at *one o'clock.* |
| اِیْن چِهْ دَخْلْ بِدَرْزَدَنِ دِیرُوزِ شُما دارَدْ | What has this to do (what connection has this) with your knocking at the door *yesterday.* |
| چِراکِهْ چُونْ مَنْ مَحْرُومانَهْ اَزْ دَرِ خانَهٔ شُما بَرمِیگَشْتَمْ جَمْعِي اَزْ آنْها رادَرْ کُوچَهْ دِیدَمْ | *Why, because just as* I was returning, *disappointedly,* from the door of your house, I saw *a number* of them in the street. |
| اِیْن هَرْگِزْ دَلِیلْ نَمِیشَوَدْ بَراِیْنکِهْ شُما ساعَتِ یَکْ بِدَرِ خانَهٔ مَنْ آمَدِیدْ | This can *never* be considered (become) a proof that you came to the door of my house at one o'clock. |
| چِرا نَمِیشَوَدْ | Why not? |
| اَزْ اِیْنَ سَبَبْ کِهْ عَمَلَهْ هَمِیشَهْ وَهَرْرُوزْ دَرْساعَتِ یَکْ مُقَرَّراً بِچاشْتْ نَمِیرَوَنْدْ | For this reason, that the workmen do not *always,* and *every day,* go to (their) meals *exactly* at one o'clock. |
| چِهْ مَنْ بِسْیارْ دِیدَهْاَمْ کِهْ اِیشانْ دَرْ ساعَتِ دُوْ غَذا مِیخُورَدَنْدْ | For I have *often* seen them eating their food at *two o'clock.* |
| وَدِیگَرْ آنْکِهْ جَمْعِي عَمَلَهْ راتَنْها دَرْکُوچَهْ دِیدَنْ اَبَداً دَلِیلْ نِیسْتْ کِهْ اَلْبَتَّهْ اِیشانْ بِخُورْدَنْ مِیرَوَنْدْ | And *again,* to see *merely* (تَنْها) a number of workmen in the street, is by *no means* a proof that, *positively,* they are going to eat. |
| حالابَسْ اَسْتْ شُما خَیْلِي خُوبْ مَنْطِقِيْ هَسْتِیدْ | It is *enough, now:* you are a *very good* [ironically used] logician. |

| | |
|---|---|
| اَمّا راسْتْ بِگُوفَرْدا خانَهْ خواهِي بُودْ يانَهْ | But tell me (speak), *Really*, wilt thou be at home *to-morrow*, or not? |
| خُدا مِيْدانَدْ وبَسْ | God *only* knows. |
| مَگَرْ انيكِهْ بِگُوئِي كَيْ خواهِي آمَدْوَاَلْبَتّه بِيائِي | Unless thou shouldst say *when* thou wilt come, and dost come *accordingly*. |
| يَكْساعَتْ پِيْشْ اَزْ ظُهْرْ بِي شَكْ وَعْدَهْ مِيكُنَمْ كِهْ بِيايَمْ | I promise that I will come, *without fail, an hour before* noon. |
| بِسْيارْ خُوبْ اَگَرْ ميتَوانِي زُودْتَرْ هَمْ بِيائِي باكْ نِيسْت | Very well: if thou canst, come *earlier* even: there is no objection (*lit.* harm). |

## OF DIMINUTIVE NOUNS.

190. This class of Nouns has a very extensive and peculiar application. With a complete knowledge of the properties of a Persian Noun, and of the changes which it undergoes by grammatical inflection, the mode of imparting to them a diminutive signification would appear to be simple and obvious, and scarcely of sufficient importance to require separate illustration; especially when we consider the vast power of expression, and the unlimited variety of epithets existing in the Numbers of the Persian Adjectives, and their susceptibility of almost infinite combinations with other Parts of Speech.

The fact, however, is, that, in the Persian Language, these Nouns constitute quite a separate class, and their forms are of a very perplexing nature; contrary to that general uniformity and simplicity which characterizes the grammar of this Language. One cause of this peculiarity, perhaps, is, that the Affixes (four in number, كْ, كَهْ, چَهْ, هْ) which—being added to a Noun—at one time express simply *smallness of size*, at other times impart to it other meanings; such as, *tenderness, pity, contempt, artificial* things in imitation of nature, *nicknames*, &c. &c.

Hence these Particles are not exclusively appropriated to one particular purpose, but vary their office when added to different classes of Nouns; and a foreigner may experience some difficulty in duly comprehending the use and application of these Affixes.

The difficulty, however, will in general be experienced by the Student only in writing Persian; for in reading any respectable Persian book, he will always find the context so clear, that, if he understands what he reads at all, he will readily comprehend what a Noun, having any of these Affixes, is intended to express: but in *writing*, if he cannot trust to his knowledge of the idiom, he need not make use of them to express any of the different meanings above mentioned. Some Adjectives, Adverbs, Epithets, &c., may equally be, and are, by the Persians, universally employed for that purpose, as already stated.

191. I will now proceed to explain, as clearly as I can, how Diminutive Nouns of various kinds are formed in Persian, by the aid of the four Particles above specified.

## 192. OF THE DIMINUTIVE PARTICLES, WHEN ADDED TO THE NAMES OF RATIONAL BEINGS.

(1) The Particle کْ, when added to the names of Rational Beings, may simply denote Diminutiveness; as, مَرْدَکْ "a *small* man"; زَنَکْ "a *small* woman"; پِسَرَکْ "a *small* boy"; دُخْتَرَکْ "a *small* girl." In this sense, however, unless jestingly, it is seldom used.

(2) When added to a Noun of this class, and not intended simply to express Diminutiveness, an Adjective must be added, to define the meaning, which, in this case, however, is not always of a favourable nature; as, مَرْدَکِ پارْسا "a good holy man"; مَرْدَکِ شَرِیرْ "a wicked man"; &c. &c.

(3) It may be used in an endearing sense, to imply Pity, Affection, Regret, &c.; as, طِفْلَکِ مَنْ بِیمارَسْت "My *poor dear* child is sick"; &c. &c.

(4) With the letter ہْ added to the کْ, so as to make it کَہْ, it may imply "*contempt*," with or without an Adjective; as, اَیْ مَرْدَکَہْ "O thou *fellow!*" اِینْ زَنَکَہْ "Why, this woman"; &c. &c. But this is restricted to Grown-up persons; for in the case of a Boy or a Girl, the ہْ alone (also, with or without an Adjective) is quite sufficient to imply the contemptuous sense; as, پِسَرَہْ "a naughty boy"; دُخْتَرَہْ "a good-for-nothing girl": or, پِسَرَہْ ہَرْزَہْ "a profligate boy *or* youth"; دُخْتَرَہْ بِی حَیا "a shameless girl"; &c. &c.

193. The Particle چَہْ is never added to the names of Rational Beings.

## 194. OF DIMINUTIVE PARTICLES, WHEN ADDED TO THE NAMES OF IRRATIONAL BEINGS.

In Persian, we may say أَسْبَكْ, خَرَكْ, &c., signifying "a small horse," "a *small* ass," &c. &c.; and the Adjectives كُوچِكْ *or* خُرْدْ "little" *or* "small" may at the same time be used; as, أَسْبَكِ كُوچِكْ "a little horse"; خَرَكِ خُرْدْ "a small ass"; &c. &c.

195. It may also be added to this class of Nouns, to imply *pity* or *compassion*, &c.; but in this meaning it is generally accompanied *with* an Adjective; as, خَرَكِ مِسْكِين "*the poor wretched* ass"; گاوَكِ خَسْتَهْ "the poor tired ox"; &c. In both these senses, however, it is more usual to add the Particle كْ, *with* or *without* an Adjective, to the Generic Noun, حَيْوانْ or جانْوَرْ "Animal," for Beasts of all kinds; and to مُرْغْ "Bird," for Fowls of all descriptions; as, حَيْوانَكْ "poor little creature," or merely "little creature"; مرغَكْ "poor little bird"; &c.; or حَيْوانَكِ خَسْتَهْ "the poor jaded beast"; جانْورَكِ ضَعِيفْ "the weak miserable animal"; &c. &c.

196. It is at the same time to be observed, that حَيْوانْ is chiefly to be used for Domestic Animals, Quadrupeds, and Fish; while جانْوَرْ applies to Wild Beasts, Reptiles, and Vermin of all kinds.

197. The Particles كَهْ, چَهْ, and ةْ, are never added to this class of Nouns.

## 198. OF DIMINUTIVE PARTICLES, ADDED TO INANIMATE THINGS.

---

The Particles كَ and چَه are most extensively used, in Persian, with this class of Nouns:

(1) To indicate Smallness of Size; as, حَوْضَكْ "a little pond"; باغْچَه "a small garden." But in this sense the affix چَه is mostly employed.

(2) To imply things made in imitation of nature, or other works of art: and under these heads are to be included toys, and all those things which are made for pastime, resembling, or having a connexion with any thing really useful or important.

199. The Particle كَ is, however, most commonly employed in senses such as these; *i. e.* آدَمَكْ "a little image" (from آدَمْ "a man"); صُورَتَكْ "a little insignificant picture," scratched, as it were, upon a piece of paper, or daubed upon a wall; (تَصْوِير being the proper word for a regular "picture," and both derived from the primitive Arabic Substantive صُورَة "a form" or "a likeness.") In like manner, كاغَذَكْ means a "kite" ('a fictitious bird,' as Dr. Johnson terms it, 'made of paper'); كاغَذْ being the Persian for "paper"; &c. &c.

(3) The Particle كَ is again added to the Noun, when the intention is to express the application of it to the performance of an action out of its ordinary use; as, چَشْمَكْ "a significant *wink* of the eye"; دَسْتَكْ clapping the

*hands* for mirth or applause ; گُوشَكْ *listening,* by *stealth,* to what is going on ; پُشْتَكْ making a somerset, so as to fall upon the back ; &c. &c. (دَسْت, گُوش, and پُشْت, meaning the *hand,* the *ear,* and the *back,* respectively).

200. Many additional instances of the use of these (so-called) Diminutive Particles, with still more numerous modifications of their meanings, might be cited ; but it will probably be thought that quite sufficient attention has already been bestowed upon this comparatively unimportant part of the Grammar. The reason of my having dwelt upon it at so much length, is, that the Persian Language, being constitutionally poetical, is usually very figurative ; and, notwithstanding its simplicity and regularity of its general construction, it still abounds in pithy and concisely subtle expressions, chiefly perhaps arising out of these *little things.* Now, unless a foreigner—for whom, after all, Grammars are written—obtains a competent knowledge of phrases and idioms of this nature (I speak from experience), he can never master any language. He may indeed go on reading ever so much, but he will never *satisfy himself;* or write ever so many books, but he will never *satisfy others.*

201. The following dialogue between two friends may, after all, perhaps give the best idea of the mode in which these Diminutive Particles are employed in Persian :—

| | |
|---|---|
| Who is that *fellow?* | 1. آن مَرْدَكَه كِيسْت |
| Of whom dost thou speak? | 2. كِرا مِيگُوئِي |
| Of that person, who, with the *small box* under his arm, is standing yonder. | 1. آنكه صَنْدُوقْچَه زِيرِبَغَل آنجا اِيستادَه اَسْت |

Knowest thou not Hasan, the goat-dancer? He is of *some celebrity* in this town.

2. حَسَنِ بُزبازرا نَمیشِناسي اُودَراین شَهر شُهرَتَکي دارَد

I had often heard of a "monkey-dancer"; but a "goat-dancer" must be *something altogether* new.

1. مَیمون باز مُکَرَّر شَنیدَه بُودَم اَمّا بُزباز بایَد کِه چیزَكِ تازَه باشَد

O, don't mention the name of the monkey! for it is a disgusting *creature*.

2. اِسمِ مَیمون مَبَر کِه جانوَرَكِ مُغَصّیست

Do not say so; for it is a wonderful little *mimic*.

1. مَگو کِه مُقَلِّدَكِ غَریبیست

The extent of which is, that it *grins*, or *winks*, or makes a *somerset*.

2. مُنتَهاش اینَست کِه نیشَك وامیکُنَد یاچَشمَك میزَنَد یاپُشتَك بَرمیدارَد

Perhaps this *wonderful goat* of yours, then, performs some magic?

1. مَگَر این بُزَكِ شُما سِحر میکُنَد

There is no magic in the case; but this *little animal* exhibits *several tricks* that are very surprising.

2. سِحر دَر کار نیست اَمّا این حَیوانَك بازیچَه چَند مي آرَد کِه بِسیار مُتَعَجِّبَند

Describe one of them: let us see.

1. یَکي اَز آنهارا تَعریف کُن بِه بینَیم

For instance: its master has several *little round pieces* of wood, all of the same size, and each about a span long. First, he places one of them on the top of that *box* upon the ground: the *little goat* jumps upon it. He then puts another on the top of that: again *the clever goat* jumps on the top of it: and so on, to the number of ten or twelve *bits of wood*: and the *goat*, standing on the uppermost of all;

2. مَثَلاً صاحِبَش چَند پارچَه چوب دارَد مُدَوَّر هَمَه بِیَك اَندازَه وهَریَك بِقَدرِ یَکوجَب اَوَّل یَکي را میگُذارَد بالاي آن صَندوقچَه روي زَمین بُزَه میجَهَد بالایَش آن وَقت یَکي دیگَر بالاي آن میگُذارَد بازبُزَه بَرمیجَهَد بالایَش وَهَمچِنین تادَه دَوازدَه پارچَه چوب وبُز بالاي هَمَه

| | |
|---|---|
| at one time moving *its beard*, and at other times shaking *its head*, in a manner to kill one with laughing. | ایستاده گاهی ریشکی میجنباند وگاهی سرکی حرکت میدهد بطوری که از خنده آدم را میکشد |
| Enough of goats and monkeys! Each, in such *sort of tricks*, is a perfect *little devil*. —Now tell me, How is thy boy to day? Is he any better? | 1. بس از بز ومیمون هریك دراین بازیچها شیطانك تمامیست حالا بگو پسرت امروز چه طوراست هیچ بهتراست |
| *Poor child!* his back is very painful: last night he could not sleep at all. | 2. طفلك پشتش خیلی پردرد است دیشب هیچ نخوابید |
| His pedagogue must be a strange *petty tyrant!* | 1. این ملا مکتبی باید ظالمك غریبی باشد |
| He himself is not so bad: his wife, too, is a *good sort of woman*: but as to that *vile assistant* of his, he is worse than any thing thou canst name! | 2. خودش انقدر بد نیست زنش هم زنك خوبیست اما آن نایبك نادرستش از هرچه بگوئی بدتر است |
| Why, this *wretched youth* must be insane, to behave thus to the children! | 1. این جوانك باید دیوانه باشد که باطفال همچو رفتار میکند |
| He is not quite so insane as you imagine, neither. Art thou aware of his *cunning contrivance*, by which he frightens the *little birds*, that they may not go near his *orchard*? | 2. همچوهم که شما خیال میکنید او دیوانه نیست از تمهیدك کش خبرداری که مرغکهای کوچکرا چه طورمیترساند که نزدیك باغچه اش نروند |
| I have never heard (of it). What does he do? | 1. هرگز نشنیده ام چکار میکند |

2. چندي از اين تصنيفكهاي هرزه به
بچهها ياد داده است وروزي چند بار
بيرونشان ميفرستند بباغچه وميگويد
يكيتان اين شعركهارا بلند بخواند وباقي
بهمان نوا دستك بزنيد ببين كه اين
اوباشك چه اخلاق رزيله بطفلكها مي
آموزد بعلاوه اينكه از درس مستمري
بازميدارد شان

He has taught the boys some of these *low vulgar songs:* and, several times daily, he sends them out into his *orchard,* saying, "Let one of you sing these *little verses* out loud, while the rest join in chorus, and *clap their hands.*" See what low morals this *dissolute fellow* teaches *the poor innocent children;* besides hindering them from (prosecuting) their regular studies!

1. اوباش هرچه بخواهي اما اين تدبير
پوچش هرگز دلالت نميكند براينكه او
زكاوتي دارد چه يكطفل با چوبكي كفايت
اين مطلب ميكند واگر اطفال هريك
بنوبت خود چوبك بزنند هيچكدام را
احتياج نيست كه از كتابچه اش
فراموش كند

Profligate (call him) as much as you will; but this clumsy contrivance of his can never prove that he possesses any cleverness; for one boy, with a *bird-clapper* (چوبك from چوب "wood"), would be sufficient for the purpose: and if the boys, each in his turn, [were to go and] shake the *bird-clapper,* there would be no occasion for any of them to neglect his *little book.*

2. آنچه شما ميگوئيد راست است اما شرير
براي يكطاسك آب اگر شهري بسوزد
پروا ندارد آن چوبك را بايد بخرد مييابي
يا نه

What you say is true; but a wicked wretch, for the sake of (saving) a *cup* of water, does not care if a whole city burns. — *That clapper* he must *buy!*—Dost thou understand me, or not?

Very well; but if the boys, at play-time, should fly (their) *kites* in the *garden*, no winged creature would dare to fly near that place: [thus the object would be gained] without any expense on the part of that *miserly fellow*.

1. بسیار خوب امّا اگر بچّها وقتِ بازی
دَرباغچهٔ کاغذك هوا کنند هیچ پرندهٔ
نزدیکِ آنجا نتواند پرید بی اِخراجاتی
از طرفِ آن مُمسِکك

This is also true; but [this scheme] also is not without *danger*.

2. این هم راست است امّا باز خالی از
تشویشکی نیست

Whence [arises] the danger?

1. تشویش از کجاست

Perhaps, when they are playing and running about, they may break some *young tree*, or trample upon some *little plant*: (or what is) worse than all, they may now and then finger a *little fig*, or *handle a small apple*, and so on: but when they are altogether, *clapping their hands*, they cannot attend to other *little practices*.

شاید وقتیکه بازی میکنند ومیدوند
نوچهٔ رابشکنند یابوتهکی را پامال
کنند از همه بدتر مبادا که گاه وقتی
انگشت بانجیرکی برند یادست
بسیبکی رسانند وهمچنین امّا وقتیکه
همه باهم دستك میزنند کارکی
دیگر نمیتوانند کرد

According to my notion (of justice), the punishment of this *worthless wretch* would be, that having tied him to a post, in the public gardens of the city, there they should leave him, in order that, at one and the same time, the birds may be frightened away, and other assistant schoolmasters may take warning.

2. باعتقادِ من سزای این مُلحِدك نابکار
اینست که اورا در باغ شهر بر عمودی
بسته بگذارند تاهم پرندگان بترسند
وهم نایب مکتبداران دیگر عبرت
گیرند

## OF SYNTAX.

202. It is usual with Grammarians, on finishing the explanation of the different Parts of Speech, to treat of what they have termed "Syntax," or that part of Grammar which "*shews the agreement and right disposition of words in a sentence.*" Syntax, then, according to this definition, is, obviously, one of the most important parts of a Grammar; inasmuch as without a correct knowledge of its rules no language could be written or spoken correctly.

But, to illustrate a living language, in which *idiom* contributes so essentially to the perfection of a sentence, Syntax must embrace, not only "a right disposition of words," but also a developement of *idiomatic phrases;* and, in this point of view, it becomes doubly useful, and indispensable.

203. The plan hitherto pursued (I now speak exclusively of the writers on Persian Grammar) for teaching this important part of the Grammar, has been, to propound general rules, and illustrate them by quotations from different authors.

Instructive, however, as this plan unquestionably is, I do not think (though I speak with great diffidence) that it is the best, or, at all events, the easiest mode of teaching a foreigner how to *speak* a language. To quote an isolated passage, or a verse, from a poet—who may, after all, have licentiously strained an expression, to answer some of his prosodiacal whims—or to cite from an ancient writer, whose diction may now be obsolete—is not the best method of giving a beginner a correct notion of the existing phraseology or idiom of a language.

204. Another, and perhaps still stronger objection to the ordinary scheme, is, that, in its manner, it is repulsive, and, consequently, seldom studied with requisite attention. The beginner, by the time he has arrived at this stage, is probably already wearied of a study proverbially dry and unattractive; and, as his eagerness to begin the grammar of a new language may have induced him, at the outset, to reject a long preface, his anxiety to get at something more interesting in it may equally prompt him to disregard what he may, however unjustly, consider an unnecessary appendage; namely, *a long series of minute and complicated rules*, under the denomination of "Syntax": thus losing the opportunity of making himself acquainted with a most useful and instructive portion of his grammar; namely, how to arrange his words in a sentence, so as to express himself correctly, and *according to idiom*.

With regard to the Persian Language, I am inclined to think that a different plan may be successfully adopted. In a series of Dialogues, in the shape of conversations on general subjects between different individuals, occasion may be taken to explain the Rules of Syntax in such a manner as to afford the learner an opportunity of making himself acquainted with the proper idiom, at the same time that he is instructed in the Persian Syntax: and as a literal translation of each individual speech, in these conversations, may be placed in juxta-position to the original Persian, the Student will possess also the advantage of having at once before him a multitude of idiomatic phrases and expressions, which, with a little judgment, he may arrange in various other ways, so as to express different ideas, and convey different meanings: and the practice of writing the Persian language will also be facilitated by means of these exercises.

205. I am aware that Dialogues of this description are generally *dull*, and uninteresting; but this, I fear, is an insuperable evil, to which a beginner of any language must necessarily submit. In adopting this plan, however, I have endeavoured, to the best of my ability, to make these Dialogues as *little tiresome* as possible, by diversifying them as much as is consistent with the principal object of works of this kind; in which, however, more regard must be had *to instruction* than to amusement.

206. Where any passage, phrase, or word, which may appear to me to require explanation, occurs the first time, such explanation will be given in a note at the bottom of the page; and the note will afterwards be referred to, wherever the same passage, phrase, or word, again occurs in the course of these Dialogues.

207. The English Student must not, nor can he reasonably, expect to find the English idiom and phraseology always strictly preserved in the translations of these Dialogues: the object being, to make him acquainted with the Persian idiom, by rendering it into English as literally as possible, consistently with the preservation of *the sense*, which would often be lost or perverted by too strictly verbal a translation. He should, therefore, be satisfied if the English translation is sufficiently clear and intelligible, although not such as an Englishman would use in expressing the same idea in his own language.

208. It is also proper to observe, that in the course of these Dialogues, excepting when absolutely necessary, I shall discontinue the use of the Pronouns "Thou" and "Thee," &c. &c., when addressing a Second Person Singular; as they sound too stiff and formal, and are never used in common conversation in English. Indeed, even in Persian, they are seldom used, except between familiar friends, or when a superior addresses one much inferior to, or dependent upon, himself.

209. In polite society in Persia, the rule for one person addressing another is briefly this:—Amongst persons moving in the same sphere of life, "You" is used instead of "Thou" and "Thee," &c. &c. Between intimate friends, either "You" or "Thou"; but the latter is more common. From a superior to an inferior, "Thou"; but if the inferior be not a dependent, say, a small tradesman, a poor neighbour, &c., it shews better breeding in a gentleman, in Persia, to say "You"; though he might, with propriety, say "Thou" and "Thee."

210. Kings are always addressed in the Third Person Singular; and "*His* Majesty" is uniformly applied to them; never "*Your* Majesty." Sovereigns, also, when speaking of themselves personally, even say "*His* Majesty," and never "*I*," or "*We*"; except in writing, when "*We*" is uniformly used.

211. Great personages also, unless upon intimate terms, address each other in the Third Person Singular; as, "*His* Lordship," "*His* Grace," &c. &c.: and so do their dependants, and persons inferior to them in rank, in addressing, or speaking of, them.

212. I do not know how it happens that Persian children are taught in schools always to speak of themselves in the First Person Plural; as, "*We*," "*Us*," &c. &c.; unless it be, that preceptors suppose "*I*" and "*me*" to be expressions of too *bold and decided* a character for a young scholar to use, and to savour too much of *egotism*.

213. Now, as to the plan of these *Dialogues*:—An English gentleman (A.), during his travels in Persia, becomes intimately acquainted with a gentleman (B.) of that country, who, having been in England some time, has acquired a tolerable knowledge of the English language. The English gentleman speaks Persian fluently; but not altogether free from occasional imperfections, as to the *idiom* and *grammar*. He has therefore begged his Persian friend to set him right, whenever he commits an error of that sort; promising never to be offended, except by "*injudicious pedantry in the presence of company*," when *such marks of affection* are, certainly, *not very agreeable*.

## DIALOGUE I.

| | |
|---|---|
| B. | ( ب ) |
| To-day, the air is very pure and soft: do not you wish we should ride? | امروز هوا بسیار لطیف وملایمست نمیخواهید سوار شویم [1] |
| A. | ( ا ) |
| Why (not)? I wish (it) very much. At what time shall we ride? | چرا من خیلي میخواهم چه وقت سوار شویم |

(1) See the Compound Verbs, p. 85.

| | |
|---|---|
| B. | (ب) |
| Whatever time *you* think proper. | هَرْوَقْت شُما صَلاح بِدانِید [2] |
| A. | (ا) |
| Two hours after noon (two o'clock)? | دُوساعَت بَعْد اَزْ ظُهر |
| B. | (ب) |
| Very good: in the mean while, I will go as far as the College, and return. | بِسْیار خُوب دَراین بَین مَن تامَدْرَسَه میروم وبَر میگَرْدَم |
| A. | (ا) |
| I have also two or three letters to write: I shall write till you come: but when *the horses are* ready, do you inform me. | مَنْهَم دُوسِه تا [3] کاغَذْ دارَم بِنْوِیسَم تا آمَدَنِ شُما مینویسَم اَمّا وَقْتیکه اَسْبها آمادَه اَنْد شُما مَرا خَبَر کُنید |
| B. | (ب) |
| O, certainly! But if you had said, "*when Horse is ready*," it would have been *nearer the idiom.* | اَلْبَتَّه اَمّا اَگَرفَرمودَه بودید [4] وَقْتیکه اَسْب آمادَه اَسْت بِمُحاوَرَه نَزدیکْتَر بود |

---

(²) From دانستن, properly, "To know." But this Verb is frequently used, also, for "To think," "To deem," "To believe," &c.

(³) This تا, which may be termed *expletive*, is frequently used with the Numerals: it implies *unity*, or *individuality*: so, the literal meaning of the expression دوسه تا کاغذ is, "two or three *individual* letters."

(⁴) فرمودن literally, signifies "To command"; but in polite conversation, as in writing, it is often employed metaphorically, to signify "To speak," "To honour," "To regard," "To condescend," &c.—See the Compound Verbs, p. 85.

**A.** (ا)

Is not the word "horse" singular?

[5] مگر لفظ اسب مفرد نیست

**B.** (ب)

Doubtless: but a word in the singular number does not always imply merely "unity."

بلاشك اما لفظ مفرد همیشه دلالت بر وحدت تنها نمیکند

**A.** (ا)

Nevertheless, what I said cannot be (altogether) wrong; for we, at least, have occasion *for two horses.*

اما آنچه من گفتم غلط نمیتواند باشد چرا که اقلاً دو اسبها را ضرور داریم

**B.** (ب)

Yours "is an apology worse than the fault." [Persian proverb.] What you first said was only out of idiom; but دو اسبها, which you now say, is, moreover, wrong, even according to (the rules of) Syntax.

عذر شما بدتر از گناه هست [6] آنچه اول فرمودید همین از محاورت بیرون بود اما دو اسبها * که حالا میفرمائید بعلاوه موافق نحو هم غلط است

**A.** (ا)

If you will do (me) the kindness to explain this point distinctly, I shall be very much obliged to you.

اگر محبت بفرمائید واین معنی را بتفصیل بیان کنید من از شما بسیار ممنون خواهم شد

---

([5]) The proper meaning of this word is "unless": it may also mean "perhaps," "rather," &c.: it is likewise employed very often to express a Verb interrogatively. See the Interrogative Verbs, p. 81; and also the Adversative Disjunctives, p. 116.

([6]) This proverbial expression, in Persian, implies that the *excuse* is unsatisfactory; and, in fact, it puts *the pleader* still more in the wrong.

* See the Adjectives, p. 29.

| B. | ( ب ) |
|---|---|
| Most willingly: but we have no leisure just now: when we are riding together (*literally,* go riding), if you wish it, we will converse on this topic. | بَچَشْم [7] اَمّا حالا فُرْصَتْ نَدارِيم وَقْتيكه سَوارَه باهَمْ مِيرَوِيم اَگَر مِيخواهِي دَراِين باب گُفْتگو [8] خواهِيم كَرْد |
| A. | ( ا ) |
| You (have) said well (well said): be it so. | خُوبْ گُفْتِي هَمْچُو باشَدْ |

### DIALOGUE II.

| A. | ( ا ) |
|---|---|
| You have not forgotten (your) forenoon's promise. | اَزْ وَعْدَهٔ پيش اَزْ ظُهر فَراموش نَكَرْدَه ايد |
| B. | ( ب ) |
| A promise, made to a friend like you, can never be forgotten. | وَعْدَهٔ كِه بِدُوسْتِي مِثْلِ شُما شَوَدْ هَرگِز فَرامُوش نَمِيتَوانَدْ شَد |
| A. | ( ا ) |
| We were talking of "Horse, and Horses." | اَزْ اَسْبْ وَاَسْبها گُفْتگو [1] مِيكَرْدِيم |
| B. | ( ب ) |
| It is well in my remembrance. Now, listen to the conclusion. | خُوبْ دَرْخاطِرَمْ اَسْتْ حالا تَتِمّهرا بِشْنَو |

---

(7) بَچَشْم literally, means "on the eye," or, "on my eye"; a metaphor frequently employed in Persian to express extreme willingness; as are also بِجانِ مِنَّت "with gratitude on my soul"; بِجانُ وِدِلْ "with (all) my heart and soul"; بِسَرِ چَشْم "on the top of my eye"; بَرسَرو بَرچَشْم "upon my head, and upon my eye"; &c. &c.

(8) This word, as well as several other Compounds of the same class, have already been fully explained.—See the Compound Nouns, pp. 110, 111.

(1) See Note 8. Dialogue 1.

| | |
|---|---|
| In the first place, you know what part of speech the word "Horse" is. | اَوّلاً[2] شُما مِیدانِید کِه لَفظِ اَسب چِه جُزء اَز کَلام اَست |
| A. | (١) |
| Yes; it is a Substantive: but if you will do (me) the kindness to explain (the matter) in English, I shall understand it better. | بَلی اِسم اَست اَمّا اَگَر لُطف فَرما ئِید و دَر اِنگلیسی بَیان کُنید مَن بِهتَر تَوانَم فَهمِید |

B.

Nouns Substantive, in Persian, of any denomination, whether Simple or Compound, may be classed under three heads—Specific, Generic, and Nouns of Multitude.

Specific Nouns always imply unity, or individuality, in their significations; and are, in themselves, definite as to the things or beings they represent. Under the first of these heads are considered to come all proper names of persons, places, seasons, countries, &c.; as, اَحمَد the proper name of a person; هِند of an empire; کَلکَتَّه of a city; بَهار (spring) "of a season," &c. &c. Nouns of this class may, however, be rendered unspecific, or vague, in their application, if used for the purpose of expressing the character or quality of some person or thing. For instance: when رُستَم (the Eastern Hercules), the proper name of a hero, is metaphorically used to imply *bravery*; or, بَهار "spring," to signify *freshness* or *cheerfulness*. The Verbs, of which Nouns of this description become the agents, must strictly agree with them in number; as, اَحمَد آمَد "Ahmad *came*";

(²) See Adverbs of Order, p. 122; and also the Examples, p. 125.

حَسَنْ رَفْتْ "Hassan *went*"; اَحْمَدْ وحَسَنْ ميرَوَنْدْ "Ahmad and Hassan *are* going"; &c. &c.

Nouns of Multitude always imply plurality in their significations; as, لَشْكَرْ "an army"; گَلَهْ "a flock"; &c. The Verbs belonging to this class of Nouns are better always to be in the Singular Number; excepting when the Nouns themselves are used in the Plural Number, in which case the Verbs of course must agree with them; as, لَشْكَرْ ميْ آيَدْ "the army *is* coming"; هَرْدُو لَشْكَرْ ميرَوَنْدْ "both the armies are going"; &c. In other respects, they are to be considered as Generic Nouns.

Generic Nouns are those which designate whole genera, species, classes, or the like, of beings, things, or events; as, اَسْبْ "horse"; آدَمْ "man"; دِرَخْتْ "tree"; مِهْمانِي "entertainment"; &c. They may be considered as definite, so far as they distinguish the genera, &c. But they may further be defined, rendered vague, or indefinite, as the circumstances of Case, Number, or any other grammatical construction, may decide; for instance, اَسْبْ "horse," has an abstract meaning when used merely as a Generic Noun: it implies that *species* of animal, without reference to any number, or any circumstance under which the animal may appear. If we would express the idea of *any*, or *one*, in an indefinite sense, we must use the ياءِ وَحْدَتْ or تَنْكير; as, اسبي "a certain horse," or "any horse." Any particular number expressed before a Generic Noun will make it definite; as,

| | |
|---|---|
| In my stable there are *two horses.* | دَرْ طَوِيلَهٔ مَنْ دُو اَسْبْ مْيباشَنْدْ |
| In his service there used to be *three servants.* | دَرْ خِدْمَتِ اُوسِهْ نَوْكَرْ ميبُودَنْدْ |

The various Cases in which a Substantive is declined will render a Generic Noun definite, as well as when used in the Plural Number *.

In the following expressions you will observe how a Generic Noun (beginning with its abstract meaning) may be rendered definite in various ways.

(A) *horse* cannot pass over the *sea*. اَسْب اَزْ دَرْیا نَمیتَوانَدْ گُذَشْت

Both horse and sea are here used in the abstract.

Once upon *a time*, a *horse* fell into the sea. وَقْتی اَسْبی بِدَرْیائی اُفْتادْ

All three, دَرْیا, اَسْب, and وَقْت, are here used indefinitely.

My *horse to-day forded this river*. اَسْبِ مَنْ اِمْرُوزْ اَزاینْ رُودْ خانَه گُذَشْت

Here all three, رُودْخانَه, رُوز, and اَسْب, are expressed definitely by the modification of the several *Cases* in which these *Generic* Nouns respectively appear; the first, اَسْب, being in a state of construction with the Personal Pronoun مَن, and at the same time Nominative to the Verb گُذَشْت; though either circumstance would have been sufficient to have made it definite: and the second and the third, رُودْخانَه and رُوز, are also each doubly defined; the first, by the demonstrative اِمْ (this), as well as by its being an Adverb; and the second, by the Demonstrative اِینَ (this), as well as by the Ablative Particle اَز.

With regard to the agreement of this class of Nouns with their respective Verbs in point of *number*, all I can tell you,

---

* See the Declension of Nouns, p. 22.

as a general rule, is, that with Nouns of rational beings, the Verbs, whether in the Active or in the Passive Voice, must *strictly* agree in number. With other animate beings, this rule is occasionally relaxed when the Verb is in the Passive Voice: for instance, you may say, in Persian, چهار اسب کشته شد, "four horses *was* killed." However, this phraseology is an affected innovation of modern origin; and I would advise you always to say چهار اسب کشته شدند "four horses *were* killed." But if you happen to be speaking of two or more animals of *distinct* genera, the Verb must, under all circumstances, agree with the Noun; as,

| | |
|---|---|
| The horse and the ass *are* not of the same genus. | اسب و خر از یک جنس نیستند |
| A horse, an ass, and an ox *were* killed. | اسبی و خری و گاوی کشته شدند |

Respecting Nouns representing inanimate objects, except under certain circumstances (which experience alone can teach you), you may, if you prefer it, put the Verb in the Singular; though in putting it in the Plural, to agree with its Nominative, you will not be wrong grammatically, nor quite out of idiom. But in this particular you must closely attend to the general conversation of educated natives as well as to your books, and form your own judgment; for I can hardly point out any rule, on this point, which may not be subject to various exceptions. All I can say, however, is, that you are never obliged to use a Verb in the Singular when your Noun is in the Plural: at the same time, you must observe, that it is frequently done, both by eminent writers and by the most correct speakers amongst the natives of Persia, especially when the Verb is expressed in the Passive Voice: for instance, you may say, either, خانهای مردم

"The houses of the people, خَرابْ شُدْ, *was* destroyed," or, خَرابْ شُدَنْدْ "*were* destroyed": but in the *Active Voice*, you should always give the preference to the Plural, when the Noun is in that Number; as, خانَهایِ اِین شَهْرِ بِسْیار کُوچَکَنْدْ "The houses of this city *are* very small"; though some would say, بِسْیار کُوچَکَسْت "*is* very small." Although, in bringing together several Nouns of distinct classes so as to form the Nominative to a Verb, the Verb must then be in the Plural, as, آب وُآتَش وُخاك اَزْ اَضْدادَنْدْ "water, fire, and earth, *are* of opposite natures"; yet, when they partake of the same quality or class of things, the Verb may, with equal propriety, be put either in the Singular or Plural Number: for instance, you may either say, دَرباغِ ما اَنْگُور و اَنْجِیر وسِیبْ یافْتْ نَمِیشَوَدْ "In our garden, grapes, figs, and apples, *is* not to be found," or یافْتْ نَمِیشَوَنْدْ "*are* not to be found." In like manner, you may either say, دَرایِن مَوسَم بَرْف وباران وتَگَرْگ وَرَعْد وبَرق مُکَرَّر باهَم مِیْ آیَدْ "At this season, snow, rain, hail, thunder and lightning, frequently *comes* together," or باهَم مِیْ آیَنْدْ "*come* together." But if the Verb is governed by Substantives that have no tangible or bodily existence, such as, time, day, night, joy, grief, &c., &c., the Singular Number is commonly preferred; as, سالهاسْت کِه ماهَم مَکْتَبْ مِیبُودِیم "It is (now) many years since we were school-fellows"; غَم وشادِي ومَرگ و زِنْدَگِي هَمَه اَزْ خُدامِي آیَدْ "Grief, joy, death, and life, all *comes* from God"; جَوانْمَردِي ومُرُوَّت چِنِین اِقْتِضا مِیکُنَدْ "Manliness and generosity *makes* this demand," &c. &c. Now, grammatically incorrect as this idiom appears to be, it may still be defended, in some measure, by the following chain of reasoning. A Verb indicates an action; an action naturally implies either power or volition on the part of the agent, which power or volition is not possessed by inanimate objects; and therefore they cannot always be considered in the light of real agents of the Verb. To this may perhaps be ascribed the origin of the grammatical incongruity in the Persian phraseology, which I have been exemplifying, and its subsequent continuance.

As to the situation of the Verb with respect to its Nominative, the latter is uniformly placed before the former; as, مَنْ رَفْتَم "I went"; شُما آمَدِيد "You came"; اِيشانْ گُفْتَنْد "They said"; &c. &c. You must except poetry, of course, in which a poet often deviates from this rule, to adjust the measure of his verses; or in translations, from the Arabic, of the sacred writings, where a strictly literal translation, even as to the position of the words, is thought to be indispensable. The Arabs, uniformly in their language, place the Verb before the Nominative.

I have wandered too far from the point which led me into this long dissertation:—I resume it. Now, in the first place, I have to remind you that Generic Nouns, in Persian, may be rendered *strictly* definite, so as to represent *one*, or more than one, particular individual of the same genus, in various ways:—By declining the Noun, or adding any of the Particles which decide the case; as, أَسْبْ رادِيدِي "Did you see *the horse?*"—By expressing the Noun in the Plural Number; as, أَسْبْهارا پَسَنْدِيدِي "Did you approve of *the horses?*"—By bringing it into contact with any other part of speech with which it may form any grammatical connection; as, اسْبِ مَنْ بِهْتَرْ ازْ اَسْبِ شُماسْتْ "*My horse* is better than *your horse*":—or, By placing any of the cardinal numbers before it, so as express one, two, three, or more; as, چهار اَسب گارِیَشرا میکَشیدند "*Four horses* were drawing his carriage."

Now, when you first said to me وقتیکه اَسبها آماده اَند شُما مَرا خَبر کُنید, your expression meant "When *the horses* are ready" &c.; because you expressed the *generic* Noun in the Plural Number. But in Persian, they never say "the horse," or "the horses," unless it is intended to express some particular horse, or horses, respecting which there is some understanding between the parties who are talking on the subject.

You know that we were not speaking about any *particular* horses at the time; nor was there any understanding between us with respect to any horse, to which your expression might allude: we merely wanted to ride on horseback, *not* on the back of the *horses;* and, to convey this meaning, the generic Noun اَسب "horse," would have been quite sufficient. You were, therefore, out of idiom, in so far as you preferred a *definite* Noun when you ought to have preferred the *generic* one. But your expression, grammatically speaking, was perfectly correct in itself; and any person, not listening to our conversation at the time, would discover no defect, even of idiom, in it. But in your second expression, چراکِه ما اَقلّادو اَسبهارا ضرورداریم, you were wrong, both grammatically and idiomatically; for your expression (understood in connection with the preceding sentence), if translated literally into English, would run thus: "For, at *the fewest,* we have occasion for *the two horses.*"

You were incorrect as to idiom, for the reasons I have already explained respecting your first expression; that is, in having used the Noun definitely, by adding the Accusative Particle را: and you were also grammatically wrong, because, either the cardinal number دُو "two," *alone*, placed before the Noun as you used it, or putting only the Accusative Noun in the Plural Number, would have been quite sufficient (if necessary at all) to render the generic Noun definite: you made use of bad Grammar, therefore, in using both; that is, placing the cardinal number before an Accusative Noun already in the Plural.

| | |
|---|---|
| A. But in English we always use the cardinal number with a Plural word (Noun). | (۱) اَمّا مادَرْ اِنْگِلیسی هَمیشَه اِسْمِ عَدَدْرا بالَفْظِ جَمع اِسْتِعْمالْ میکُنیم |
| B. I am aware that in English they say *two horses*; but every tongue has a (its) peculiar idiom. It is now grown late. Come, let us go back. | (ب) مَن میدانَم کِه دَرْانگِلیسی میگُویَنْد دُواَسْبها اَمّا هَرزَبانی مُحاوَرَه دارَدْ حالا دیرْشُدَه اَسْت بِیاتا بَرگَرْدیم |

## DIALOGUE III.

| | |
|---|---|
| A. Peace be unto you! (Good morning to you!) | (۱) سَلامٌ عَلَیکُم |
| B. And upon you be peace, and the blessing of God! | (ب) وَعَلَیکُمُ السَّلامُ وَرَحْمَةُ اللّه |
| A. I was dreaming strangely last night. | (۱) دیشَب غَریبْ خوابی میدیدَم [1] |

(1) There is no word, in common use, in Persian, to correspond exactly with the English word "To dream"; but دَرخوابْ دیدَن or خوابْ دیدَن both mean, "To see while asleep," or "To see in sleep," *i.e.* "To dream."

**B.**

May it tend to good! What were you dreaming about?

( ب )

خَیْر باشَدْ² اَزْچه خوابْ میدیدید

**A.**

I dreamt that I was standing in a very spacious plain full of horses; and several persons on foot, each by turns having separated a single horse from the great herd, shewed it, first, to a personage, apparently their chief, who was standing close by; and afterwards, on a signal from him, having made the same horse pass in review before me, they allowed it to return into the herd: till, from amongst them, a vicious horse, becoming excited, kicked me in such a manner, that I started out of (my) sleep.

( ا )

خوابْ دیدَمْ کِه دَرْ مَیْدانی بِسْیار وَسیع
پُرْ اَزْ اَسْبْ ایْستادَهْ بُودَمْ وَچَنْدْ نَفَرْ
پِیادَهْ هَرْیَكْ بِنَوْبَتْ اَسْبی اَزْآن رَمَهٔ
بُزُرْگْ جِدا کَرْدَهْ اَوَّلاً بِشَخْصی ظاهِرًا
رئیسِشانْ که دَرْآن نَزْدیکی اَیْستادَهْ بُودْ
نِمُودَنْدی وَبَعْدْ باشارَتِ اُوْهَمانْ
اَسْبْ را بِنَظَرِ مَنْ گُذَرانیدَهْ بازْ بِرَمَهْ سَرْ
مِیدادَنْدْ تا آنکِه اَزْآنْ میانَهْ اَسْبی شَرِیرْ
چالاکی کَرْدَهْ چِنانْ لَگَدی بَرْمَنْ زَدْ کِه
اَزْ خوابْ بَرْجَسْتَمْ

**B.**

And found, that you had fallen on your back!

( ب )

وَدیدی کِه بَرْ پُشْتْ اُفْتادَهْ بُودی

**A.**

Friend!—*started up*, I say. How could I have fallen on my back?

( ا )

رَفیقْ بَرْجَسْتَمْ مِیگُویَمْ بَرْ پُشْتْ چِگُونَهْ
مِیتَوانِسْتَمْ اُفْتادَهْ باشَمْ

---

(²) A common Interjection, or ejaculatory expression, thrown out by the Persians on such occasions, or when one sneezes in company. It is also used frequently on occasions of surprise, or when any sudden or unexpected event, of a doubtful tendency or appearance, takes place;—pretty much the same as when one says in English, "What is the matter?" "I hope all is well!" &c. &c.

**B.** ( ب )

Then the danger was, that you might fall on your face?

پَسْ بِيمِ اِينْ بُودْ كِه بَرْرُوْ بِيُفْتِي

**A.** ( ا )

Joking apart;—come, and tell me, if you can, what is the interpretation of this dream!

مَزَاحْ بَرْكِنَارْ بِيَا وَاَگَرْ مِيتَوانِي بِگُوْ تَعْبِيرِ
اِينْ خَوابْ چِه چِيزْ اَسْتْ

**B.** ( ب )

You know that I, your humble servant, am not the Prophet Joseph.

شُمَا مِيدَانِيدْ كِهْ بَنْدَهْ يُوسُفِ پَيْغَمْبَرْ
نِيْسْتَمْ

**A.** ( ا )

Still you are jesting:—speak seriously; and let me know (*lit.* see) what can be the cause of this dream.

بَازْ شُوخِي مِيكُنِي رَاسْتِي بِگُوْ بِهْ بِينَمْ
سَبَبِ اِينْ خَوابْ چِه تَوانَدْ بُودْ

**B.** ( ب )

My dear fellow! the jest seems on your part: otherwise, I can hardly believe you to be really ignorant of the cause of your dream; for it appears very obvious.

عَزِيزِ مَنْ شُوخِي اَزْ طَرَفِ شُمَا مِي نِمَايَدْ
وَگَرْنَهْ مَنْ هَمْچُو نَمِيدَانَمْ كِهْ وَاقِعِي تُو
اَزْ سَبَبِ خَوابَتْ غَافِلْ بَاشِي چِرَا كِهْ
بِسْيَارْ بَدِيهِي مِينِمَايَدْ

**A.** ( ا )

With all this, I still wish to hear (*lit.* that I may hear) it from you.

بَا اِينْ هَمَهْ مَنْ مِيخَواهَمْ كِهْ اَزْ شُمَا بِشْنَوَمْ

**B.** ( ب )

Yesterday, for nearly four hours, we were on *horseback* together: just before riding,

مَا دِيرُوزْ قَرِيبِ چَهَارْ سَاعَتْ بَاهَمْ سَوَارِ
اَسْبْ بُودِيمْ پِيشْ اَزْ سَوَارِي دَرْمِيَانِ مَا

a discussion had arisen between us, the origin and the subject of which was "*Horse.*" Whilst riding, we returned to the same discussion, and (the mention of) *Horse,* and *Horses,* in various forms, passed between us, in our grammatical illustrations. Now, after all this, if the idea of *Horse,* even when you were asleep, again passed in your mind, ought we wonder at it?

گفتگوئي[3] برخاسته بود که اصل و
مبحثش اسب بود دربين سواري باز
بهمان مباحثه رجوع کرديم واسب
واسبها مکرر بانواع مختلف دراماثل
نحويه ما جاري بودند بعد ازاينها همه
اگر خيال اسب همين که درخواب
بوديد باز درخاطر شما گذشته باشد
ماباید ازآن تعجب بکنيم

## A. (١)

No; but my wonder is at the details, and other occurrences which could have had no connection at all with the subject of our discussion.

خير[4] ليکن تعجب من ازساير کيفيات و
وقايعيست که بمباحثه ما هيچ نسبتي
نتوانستند داشت

## B. (ب)

Our dreams are not always composed of elements which, in the same connected form,

رؤياي ما هميشه مرکب از اجزائي
نيستند که بهمان هيئات متصله گاهي

---

(3) See Note 8. Dialogue 1.

(4) The Persians, in polite conversations, seldom make use of the plain and decided Negative نَه "No." خَيْر "Good," is a common substitute for that expression. Several other ejaculatory expressions are likewise employed for the same purpose; such as, خُدا نَکُنَد "God forbid!" اَستَغفِرُالله "I pray God for mercy!" &c. &c. Many of the Adverbs also answer the same end; as, هَرگِز , مُطلَقاً , اَبَداً "Never," "Not at all," "For ever," &c. &c. But these last expressions are Emphatical Negatives: the former is only a Simple one.

may have at any time taken place in reality, or have passed in our imagination when awake. Coherence, consistency, exactitude, and order, do not necessarily enter the train of ideas which pass in our minds when dreaming. Nevertheless, this dream of yours is the most coherent of all the dreams of which I have ever heard; for there is not a single part in it, the connection of which, with a particular part in that discussion of ours, might not, after a little reflection, be traced. And I am rather pleased at this circumstance, because it shews that my explanations have made some impression on your mind.

دَرْ حَقِيقَتْ وَاقِعْ شُدَهْ يَا دَرْ بِيدَارِيْ
بِخَيَالِ مَا گُذَشْتَهْ بَاشَنْدْ رَبْطْ وَتَوَافُقْ وُ
تَسَاوِيْ وُتَرْتِيبْ حَتْمًا دَاخِلِ خَيَالَاتِيْ
نَمِيشَوَنْدْ كِهْ دَرْ خَوَابْ بِخَاطِرِ مَا مِيگُذَرَنْدْ
بَاوُجُودِ اِيْنْ اِيْنْ خَوَابِ شُمَا مَرْبُوطْتَرِينِ
خَوَابْهَا نِيسْتْ كِهْ مَنْ هَرْگِزْ شَنِيدَهْ اَمْ
چِرَا كِهْ دَرْ آنْ هِيچْ جُزْئِيْ نِيسْتْ كِهْ بَعْدْ
اَزْ اَنْدَكْ تَأَمُّلِي نِسْبَتَشْ رَا بِجُزْئِيْ
مَخْصُوصْ دَرْ آنْ مُبَاحِثَهٔ مَا نَتَوَانْ دِيدْ
وَمَنْ اَزْ اِينْ مَعْنِي خُوشْنُودَمْ چِرَا كِهْ هَمْچُو
مِينِمَايَدْ كِهْ تَقْرِيرَاتِ مَنْ دَرْ خَاطِرِ شُمَا
تَأْثِيرِيْ كَرْدَهْ اَنْدْ

A.

I know what you are about to say; the extent of which is this—that I may suppose *that spacious plain* to have been the long chapter which you repeated on grammar; and *the crowd of horses* in that plain to be, either the representation of a "Noun of Multitude," or of "*Horse, in the abstract.*" But what part of our discussion can point to *those perons* who, in that regular order, passed

(١)

مِيدَانَمْ كِهْ چِهْ مِيخَوَاهِيْ بِگُوئِيْ مُنْتَهَاشْ
اِينَسْتْ كِهْ فَرْضْ كُنَمْ كِهْ آنْ مَيْدَانِ
وَسِيعْ فَصْلِ طَوِيلِيْ بُوَدْ كِهْ شُمَا دَرْ
نَحْوْ تَقْرِيرْ فَرْمُودِيدْ وَاَنْبُوهِ اِسْبْهَا دَرْ آنْ
مَيْدَانْ مِثَالِ اِسْمِ جَمْعْ يَا اَسْبِ مُطْلَقْ
تَوَانَدْ بُوَدْ چِهْ جُزْءِ مُبَاحِثَهٔ مَا اِشَارَتْ
تَوَانَدْ كَرْدْ بِآنْ اَشْخَاصْ كِهْ بِدَانْ

the *horses* in review before me?

تَرْتِيبِ اَسْبهارا بِنَظَرِ مَنْ مِيگُذَرانِيدَنْد

**B.**

Perhaps the different *governing particles*, with which they transfer a Noun Substantive from one *grammatical case* into another.

( ب )

شايَدْ عَوامِلِ مُتَعَدِّدَه كِه بِدآنها اِسْمِي را اَزْ يَكْحالَتِ نَحْوِي بِدِيگَرِي نَقْلْ مِيكُنَنْد

**A.**

You do not jest badly; but can you give me any idea (*lit.* can you tell me at all) what relation that respectable personage, to whom they presented the horses first, and afterwards, by his direction, to me, can have to the subject of our discussion?

( ١ )

بَدْ مِزاحْ نَمِيكُنِي اَمّا هِيچْ مِيتَوانِي گُفْتْ كِه آنْ شَخْصِ مُشارٌ اِلَيْه كِه اَوَّلْ اَسْبهارا بِوَيْ مِينِمُودَنْد وَبَعْدْ بِاِشارَتِ اُوْ بِمَنْ چِه نِسْبَتْ بِمُباحِثَهٔ ما تَوانَنْد داشْت

**B.**

Since I see that you are enjoying my joke, there may be no harm in my saying (*lit.* if I were to say), that that *respectable personage* might represent your *humble servant;* who, having first examined, and properly weighed those *examples* in due order, presented them to the consideration of *your honour.*

( ب )

چُونْ مِي بِينَمْ كِه اَزْ مِزاحِ مَنْ حَظِّي مِيكُنِي پَرْوا نَباشَدْ اَگَرْ بِگُويَمْ كِه آنْ شَخْصِ مُشارٌ اِلَيْه مِيتَوانِسْتْ كِه بَنْدَهٔ مِسْكِينِ شُما باشَدْ كِه اَوَّلْ آنْ اَمْثِلَه را اِمْتِحانْ كَرْدَه وَسَنْجِيدَه بِتَرْتِيبْ مَعْرُوضِ رايِ مُبارَكْ مِيداشْت

**A.**

This, also, is not (*lit.* was not) very bad. But you can with difficulty get out of *this.*

( ١ )

اِيْنْ هَمْ بِسْيار بَدْ نَبُود اَمّا اَزْ اِيْنْ مُشْكِلْ بِيرُونْ بِرَوِي اَگَرْ مِيتَوانِي بِگُو كِه آنْ

Tell me, if you can, what might be *that vicious horse* which inflicted upon me so tremendous a kick?

اَسْبِ شَرِیر کِه چُنان لَگَدِی سَخْت
بَر مَن زَد چِه تَوانَد بُوَد

B.

( ب )

The *exasperated animal*, whom you originally goaded with the *three grammatical blunders*.

سِتُورِ بَرآشُفْتَه کِه بَاسِهٔ غَلَطِ نَحْوِیَّه
نُخُسْتِین بَر اُو مِهْمِیز هَمِی زَدِی

A.

( ا )

The truth of the matter is, that I wished to know to what extent you were a believer in dreams: but now I see that you, like myself, have no belief in dreams at all.

حَقِّ مَطْلَب اِینَسْت کِه مِیخْواسْتَم بِه
بِینَم کِه شُما تا چِه حَد بِخْواب مُعْتَقِد
بُودِید اَمّا حالا مِی بِینَم کِه شُما هَم مِثْلِ
خُودَم بِخْواب هِیچ اِعْتِقاد نَدارِید

B.

( ب )

I do not understand what you intend by the word "belief." I do certainly *believe* this — that several events, which I can now very well remember, have passed in my imagination when I was asleep.

مَن نَمِیفَهْمَم کِه اَز لَفْظِ اِعْتِقاد شُما چِه
قَصْد مِیکُنِید مَن اَلْبَتَّه مُعْتَقِدَم بَر اِینکِه
وَقایِعِی چَند کِه اَکْنُون اَز آنها خُوب یاد
مِیتَوانَم کَرد وَقْتِی کِه خوابِیدَه بُودَم
دَر خیالِ مَن گُذَشْتَه اَند

A.

( ا )

You again evade the question. I mean to say, that

باز اَز مَطْلَب تَجاهُل مِیکُنِی[5] مَن

---

(5) تَجاهُل (an Arabic Verbal Noun) means, "To feign ignorance," from جَهِلَ "He was ignorant." Whenever a Verb is expressed in this form in Arabic, it generally implies *fiction*; as, مَرَضَ "He was ill"; تَمارَضَ "*He feigned* illness"; &c. &c. The Persians have taken many Verbal Nouns of this sort from the Arabs, which they use for the same purpose; and, with the aid of the Persian Auxiliaries, Verbs are made of them.

it appears to me that you do not believe (*lit.* are not a believer in this), that the events which we see in our dreams can have any connection with the future; or, in other words (*lit.* other phrase), those events do not inform us beforehand of what may happen to us in time to come.

میخواهم بگویم که بمن چنین مینماید
که شما معتقد نیستید بر انیکه وقایعی
که ما در خواب می بینیم دخلی
بمستقبل داشته باشند یا بعبارة اخری
آن وقایع مارا پیش از وقت اخبار
نمیکنند از آنچه بعد برما واقع تواند شد

**B.**

Would that it were so, indeed! and that those events really gave intelligence of the future! Then I would never rise from bed, except to welcome a promised happiness, or to ward off a threatened evil. In this world, I would not wish for any other Paradise!

( ب )

کاش که حقیقت چنین بود و آن وقایع
راستی از آینده خبر میدادند من
آنوقت هرگز از رخت خواب[6] بر
نمیخاستم مگر باستقبال فرحی موعود
یا بدفع مصیبتی وعید در این
دنیا بهشتی دیگر نمیخواستم

**A.**

I, too, (would act and feel) in the same manner; but I fear that we might not find that Paradise in such a delightful state as we now fancy; and that, after two or three dreams, we would pray that our *visions* might all arise, either from fulness of stomach, or from lying (falling) upon our back, *i.e.* when asleep.

( ا )

من هم همچنین اما میترسم که آن
بهشت را بخرمی که حالا تصور میکنیم
نیابیم و بعد از دو سه خواب دعا کنیم
که خوابهامان همه یا از امتلاء معده
بر خیزند یا از بر پشت افتادن

---

(6) This elegant expression, رخت خواب, is not susceptible of a literal translation. The nearest, perhaps, is "Apparatus of sleep."

### B.

Why, and from what cause?

(ب)

چرا وَاَز چِه سَبَب

### A.

For this reason; that if there be really any good coming to you, it will doubtless come in due time: what more (would you) gain, if you were to know it beforehand? As for me, it is better that I should not know (any thing about it); for according to the degree of the pleasure which I may have anticipated while waiting for it (*lit.* from the expectation of it), in the same proportion my enjoyment, from the actual possession of it, will have been diminished. And if the interval between the dream and its realization may have been prolonged, then, perhaps, I shall derive no pleasure at all from it. On the other hand (side), if the dream foretells (gives intelligence) of a calamity or a misfortune, see what great misery it is to know it beforehand! And in the like manner, if the calamity be great, or the *interval* long, our reason in the meanwhile may give way, from the intensity of grief, or ourselves be altogether destroyed.

(۱)

اَز این سَبَب کِه اَگَر دَر حَقیقَت خَیری
بِشُما رَسیدَنی باشَد بی شَك کِه بِوَقت
خواهَد آمَد زیادَه چِه حاصِل اَگَر پیش
اَز پیش* آنرا بِدانید وَمَن بِهتَر اینکِه
نَدانَم چِرا کِه بِقَدریکِه اَز اِنتِظارَش
لَذَّت بُردَه باشَم بِهَمان قَدر حَظِّ مَن اَز
وُصولَش کَمتَر خواهَد بود وَاَگَر مُدَّت
مابَینِ خواب وَوُقوعِ طولی کَشیدَه باشَد
شایَد دَر آن وَقت مَن اَز آن هیچ لَذَّت
نَخواهَم داشت اَز آن طَرَف اَگَر خواب اَز
مُصیبَتی یا حادِثَهٔ خَبَر میدَهَد بِبین
کِه پیش اَز پیش دانِستَنَش چِه رَنج
گِرانیست وَبِهَمان طَور اَگَر مُصیبَت
عَظیم یا مُدَّت طَویل باشَد شایَد کِه
دَر این بَین اَز شِدَّتِ اَندوه عَقلِمان
زایِل گَردَد یا خود بِکُلّی هَلاك شَویم

* See Adverbs of Time, p. 120.

**B.** (ب)

Your statements are true; but more truths (other truths also) may be told on this subject. You only detailed the disadvantages of the proposition, and said nothing of its advantages.

تَقْرِيرَاتِ شُما حَقّ اَنْد اَمّا حَقايِقِ دِيْگَرْ
نِيْز دَرْ اِيْن بابْ مِيتَوانْ گُفْت شُما
هَمِيْن اَزْ مُضارِّ اِيْن مَعْنِي بَيان گَرْدِيد
وَاَزْ مَنافِعَش هِيْچ نَگُفْتِيد

But as the subject leads (us) into Metaphysics, we had better not plunge into it any deeper.

لِيْكِنْ چُون مَبْحَث بِاِلٰهِيّات مِيكَشَد
بِهْتَر كِهْ زِيادَهْ دَرْآنْ خَوْض نَكُنِيم

**A.** (ا)

Particularly as it now comes into my recollection, that I have an engagement somewhere, and must take my leave of you (*lit.* must be permitted to go). Will you honour my lodgings to-morrow? (*lit.* bring honour into your *servant's* lodging.)

خاصَهْ چُون حالا خاطِرَم مِي آيَد كِه
مَنْ جائِي وَعْدَهْ دارَم وَبايَد مُرَخَّص
شَوَم شُما فَرْدا بِبَنْدَهْ مَنْزِل تَشْرِيف
خواهِيد آوَرْد

**B.** (ب)

Please God! I will wait on you.

اِنْشاءَ اللّٰه* خِدْمَتِ شُما خواهَم رَسِيد

**A.** (ا)

At breakfast-time, at dinner-time, or both?

وَقْتِ نَهار[1] وَقْتِ شام ياهَرْدُو

---

* See the Interjections, pp. 81—84.

(¹) شام or نَهار, literally, mean "morning" and "evening" respectively; and the Persians apply them to the *two* meals which they take in the course of the day and night. The general mode of living in Persia is briefly thus:—The people get up in time to say their prayers before sun-rise. Soon after prayer, they partake of something very trifling, just to break their fast—part of a biscuit, with a small cup of coffee, or even hot water with a little ginger and sugar, &c. &c., and they call this ناشتا شكستن, literally, "*to break one's fast.*" But between eleven

| | |
|---|---|
| **B.** | ( ب ) |
| *To dinner,* I am engaged. | شام را که موعودم |
| **A.** | ( ا ) |
| Then, let it be at breakfast-time. | پس وقت نهار باشد |
| **B.** | ( ب ) |
| May your kindness never diminish! | محبت شما کم نشود |
| **A.** | ( ا ) |
| You will do me honour (*lit.* you will make me honoured). *Adieu!* | مشرف خواهید ساخت خداحافظ |
| **B.** | ( ب ) |
| God be with you! | خداهمراه شما |
| **A.** | ( ا ) |
| At breakfast-time, I shall expect you. | وقت نهار منتظر خواهم بود |

## DIALOGUE IV.

| | |
|---|---|
| A. (*calling his Servants.*) | ( ا ) |
| Boys!—Who is here? | بچها اینجا کیست |

---

eleven and twelve they make a substantial meal (hot and cold), which they term نهار, but not quite so substantial as the grand meal at night, called شام. The time for this meal varies according to the season, for it is never taken until an hour or two after sunset. This, however, is the habit of the better and more fashionable classes. Shop-keepers, and those people who are obliged to go early to their work, make a hearty meal at once, every one according to his means, before going to work, which they call ناشتا "fast," or "breakfast"; another at *noon*, which they call چاشت (meaning also the time of the day); and a third at *night*, *i.e.* the شام, which, however, they take generally earlier than the higher classes, who are not anxious to go to bed so early.

| | |
|---|---|
| A Servant. | ( خِدمَتکار ) |
| Yes, Sir! | بَلِي صاحِب[1] |
| A. | ( ا ) |
| I am to have (*lit.* I have) some guests at breakfast-time to-day. Be very attentive (*i.e.* have every thing properly arranged). | مَن اِمروز وَقتِ نَهار مِهمان دارَم خُوب مُتَوَجِّه باشید |
| Servant. | ( خِدمَتکار ) |
| Very well, Sir. What do you command us to prepare, besides the ordinary things? | بَلِي صاحِب چِه میفَرمائید دُرُست بکُنیم بِعَلاوَهٔ حاضِري[2] |
| A. | ( ا ) |
| Let there be both a pelaw and chilaw; several kabawbs of fowl and lamb; and whatever else you yourselves may think of (*lit.* may come into your minds). But tell the cook to be very careful about the cookery (*see Note* 2), and to make good dishes. | پِلاو وَچِلاو هَردُو باشَد چَند تا کَباب مُرغ وبَرّه وهَرچِه دیگَر که بِخاطِرتان بِرَسَد اَمّا باَش پَز بگُو که دَرپُختَني خَیلي دِقَّت بِکُنَد وخُورِشهاي خُوب بِسازَد[3] |

---

(¹) صاحِب (an Arabic word) literally means "*a companion*"; hence, the *master* or *owner* of any thing. The Indians apply this term to the English; and the Persians have borrowed it from them.

(²) حاضِري (of Arabic origin) means any thing *present*, or *always ready*. With regard to *eatables*, it is employed in contradistinction to پُختَني "things to be cooked," and implies all sorts of preserves, sweetmeats, cream, cheese, butter, fruits, &c. &c., as they are *always* ready, and may be had *presently*.

(³) There are several words in the above passage which require explanation, پُختَني ,کَباب ,خُورِش ,چِلاو , and پِلاو. *Pilaw*, I presume, is familiar to the English reader: it is made of rice dressed with meat, butter, spices, &c. &c: a dish

| | |
|---|---|
| **SERVANT.** | ( خِدمتگار ) |
| The tailor is here: he says you had ordered him to come (*lit.* that he should come). | خَیّاطْ اینجاسْت میگُویَد کِه شُما فَرمُودَه بُودید کِه بِیایَد |
| **A.** | ( ١ ) |
| Tell him to come (*lit.* say he may come) to-morrow afternoon: I have no leisure to-day. | بِگُو فَردا بَعدْ اَز ظُهر بِیایَد اِمرُوز فُرصَت نَدارَم |
| **SERVANT.** | ( خِدمتگار ) |
| The horse-dealer was again here to-day; and he was saying, "I know of several (*lit.* I have got a clue to) good horses." | دَلّالْ[4] هَم بازْ اِمرُوز اینجا بُود ومیگُفت کِه چَندتا اَسبهایِ خُوب سُراغ[5] دارَم |

---

a dish complete in itself, and eaten just as it is brought to table. *Chilaw* is also made of rice; but boiled plain, and eaten with خُورِش: this means any food made savoury and relishing, or pungent, by means of sauces. In conjunction with bread, it simply means condiment; as, نان خُورِش, which distinguishes it from the generic term خُورِش. Its foundation, however, is *meat* of any kind, dressed in a great variety of sauces, with dried fruits, spices, &c. &c. Each dish, so made, has its specific name: خُورِش may be said to take the place of curry on the table, in so far as it is eaten with plain boiled rice; but they are never made so hot as the Indian dish. کَباب, literally, means *meat roasted*, whether it be *fowl* or *flesh*, and it includes even *fish*. There is a great variety of this also made in Persia. پُختَنی, for the explanation of this word, see the preceding Note.

(4) This Arabic word, literally, means a "conductor"; hence, it is applied to all those persons who form a third party between the buyer and the seller, in order to *conduct* the bargain. It is, however, more commonly applied to dealers in cattle and other animals. دَلّالَه (in the feminine gender) is also a term applied to female hawkers, and the elderly women who negotiate to bring about a marriage.

(5) This word, literally, means "a trace," "a sign," or "indication"; and the

**A.** (۱)

Why did not you inform me, then? You knew that I had occasion for a good horse or two!

پس چرا مرا خبر نکردید شما
میدانستید که من یکدو تا اسب خوب
ضرور داشتم

**SERVANT.** (خدمتگار)

You had not yet risen from sleep, Sir. We told him, "Wait till the Sahib wakes" (*lit.* should wake); but he said, "I have business at another place, and must go; but if the Sahib wishes to see me, whenever he may think proper, if he sends a man [to say so], I will come directly."

شما هنوز از خواب برنخاسته بودید
صاحب ما گفتیمش صبر کن تا صاحب
بیدار شود اما او گفت که یکجای دیگر
کاردارم و باید بروم اما اگر صاحب
میخواهد که مرا ببیند هر وقت که صلاح
بداند آدم بفرستد من زود میآیم

**A.** (۱)

Does any one of you know his residence?

از شما کسی منزلش را میداند

---

the horse-dealer means to say, that he has got *scent of*, or *clue to*, some good horses. Here I take the opportunity of explaining, once for all, the difference between the idiom of the English and Persian, as to the manner of repeating the expressions of another person. In English, on such occasions, the speaker generally employs the third person or persons; as, "*He* said, *he* intended going to town", &c. &c.; or, "*They* told me, *they* had been up all night"; &c. &c. But in Persian, usually, the *exact* expressions of the parties are quoted by the present speaker, without any change in them whatsoever; as will be seen in the several instances (which I have purposely left undisturbed, in order to shew the idiom) in the statements of this Persian Servant. I may think it right, hereafter, to deviate from this *strictly literal* mode of translating, and follow the English idiom; if not always, at all events occasionally.

SERVANT. (خدمتکار)

Yes, Sir; I know his house (*lit.* I am a guide to it).

بلي صاحب من خانه اش را بلدم [6]

A. (۱)

Then go immediately, and say I wish to see him.—But what is the use of buying horses? So long as this groom remains in my stables, I shall never possess a horse fit for riding!

پس زود بروو بگو که من میخواهم به بینمش امّا چه حاصل از اسب خریدن تا این مهتر در طویلهٔ منست من هرگز اسب لایق سواری نخواهم داشت

---

(6) This is also an Arabic word, meaning, *strictly*, "a guide." It is, however, vulgar to use it in any other sense in Persian, as this Servant has done. Indeed, there are many other low phrases in the language assigned to this man in the Dialogue; such as, گجخلق بود , باش گفتم , خانه اش را بلدم , سراغ دارم , &c. &c., all of which should be avoided by persons wishing to speak the Persian language correctly or elegantly.

The generality of better servants, mechanics, and small tradesmen, throughout the greater part of Persia (owing perhaps to the circumstance of their not being kept at so great a distance, as they are in some other countries, by the more-educated classes of society), do not, in general, speak bad Persian. Their language, though necessarily devoid of classical taste and elegance, is, however, upon the whole, tolerably correct. But when we consider that *it* is the language of a very numerous class of men, the greatest number of whom, perhaps, can neither read nor write, we may wonder more at the general accuracy and tact with which they express themselves, than at their occasional mistakes or their uncouth phraseology. A beginner, however, had better avoid learning his Persian from them. On this account, in the course of these Dialogues, I shall introduce characters of this description very sparingly: and when I do introduce them, I shall make them speak, in point of grammar at all events, correctly.

The reader, if at all proficient in the Persian language, cannot have failed to observe already, in the few sentences which this man has uttered (independently of the low phrases above cited), the Syntactical looseness of his style; his ill-constructed sentences; the clumsy way in which he quotes, or rather puts, his own vulgar expressions into the mouth of another; and the difficulty which he seems to feel in delivering himself. There can be neither pleasure nor profit in the perusal of such language as this.

**Servant.**

Yesterday, I told him that the Sahib was very much vexed, because of the bay horse becoming lame: but he swore that he was not in fault (*lit.* had no fault), as the horse was quite lame when the Sahib bought it.

( خدمتگار )

من دیروز باش گفتم که صاحب خیلی کجخلق بود که اسب کهر میلنگید اما او قسم خورد که تقصیر من نیست این اسب وقتیکه صاحب خریدش شل بود

**A.**

Yes; but not so lame as his worse-than-the-offence excuse. I am greatly displeased with that man, for he does not appear honest. At all events, I can never confide in him any more; for he may kill me (for me) a horse daily. He must go away from my stables. Go, and tell him so (*lit.* say to him after this manner) ! !

( ا )

بلی امانه بلنگی عذر بدتر از گناه[7] او من ازان مردک[8] بسیار متنفرم چراکه صادق نمی نماید بهرحال من باو هرگز دیگر اعتماد نمیتوانم کرد که هر روز یک اسبی از برای من بکشد باید از طویله من برود بروو همین طور باو بگو

**B.** (*coming in.*)

Friend! O my dear friend! (*lit.* friend! friend!) May thy morn be good! for good comes of thy morning (*i.e.* morning's work). What unlucky being is the cause of this excitement? or perhaps you have had *another dream?*

( ب )

رفیق رفیق صبحت بخیر باد که خیر از صباح تست کدام بدبخت باعث این تغیر است یا مگر باز خوابی دیده

**A.**

Welcome, my friend! "*I had intended* (lit. *said*) *when*

( ا )

خوش آمدی ٭ رفیق گفته بودم چو بیائی

---

(7) See Note 5. Dialogue 1.

(8) See the Diminutive Nouns, p. 127.

غم دل با تو بگویم * چه بگویم که غم از دل برود چون تو بیائی[9] خواب تازهٔ ندیده‌ام اما تعبیر خواب کهنه ام بظهور آمده است چه حالا معلوم است که ستوریکه بالگد مرا از خواب بر خیزانید اسبی نبود که شما تعریف فرمودید بلکه این مهتر شریر من که اسبکهای[10] مرا چنان شل کرده است که بعد از این مگر در خواب دیگر سم از زمین بر توانند داشت

*you came, to tell you what had vexed me* (lit. *the grief of my heart*). *But what am I to say? since all the painful feeling is removed* (lit. *grief goes*) *from my heart, whenever you come.*" I have had (seen) no fresh dream; but the interpretation of my *old* dream has been realized (*lit.* into manifestation). For it is now certain, that *the animal which roused me out of my sleep with a kick,* was not the horse which you described, but [it was] this vicious groom of mine, who has lamed *my poor* horses so, that henceforth, perhaps, they may only be able to raise their hoofs (*lit.* raise the hoof) from the ground in a dream.

( ب )

سزای کفش تنگ پا از آن بیرون کردن ودوای درد دندان کشیدن نست چون مهتر بد باشد اخراجش باید کرد

B.

The remedy for a tight shoe is taking the foot out of it; and the cure for the toothache is extraction. When a groom is a bad one, he must be turned away.

( ا )

ببخشید که من لحق بسیار خجالت دارم که شما درچنین حالتی تشریف بیاورید باشما بودن واظهار نارضامندی

A.

Forgive me! for I really feel greatly ashamed that you should honour me (*lit.* bring honour) while in this state. To be in your com-

(9) This is a beautiful couplet, from Sādy.

(10) See the Diminutive Nouns, p. 127.

pany, and shew discontent, be the cause what it may, is, I confess, the extreme of ingratitude. But these servants are so very mischievous!

کردن سبب هرچه باشد من مقرم که
نهایت ناسپاسیست لیکن این خدام
بسیار اشرارند

B.

(ب)

There is no occasion to be ashamed at all! We are by ourselves: and if you wish me to prove still more that there is no stranger here, give me leave to correct a grammatical mistake in an expression of yours.

هیچ جای خجالت نیست ما خود مان
هستیم واگر میخواهید زیاده ثابت کنم
که غیری در اینجا نیست رخصت دهید
تا غلط نحویه در فرموده شما درست کنم

A.

(ا)

You will very much oblige me: may your favour be ever increasing! But to which of my mistakes are you alluding? for I fear that, in this state of vexation, I may have talked very much at random.

بنده را بسیار ممنون خواهید فرمود
لطف شما زیاد اما بکدام یک از غلطهای
من اشارت میفرمائید چه میترسم که
در بین این پریشانی نامربوط بسیار
گفته باشم

B.

(ب)

No; I was not aware of more than one very slight oversight.

نه من بیک جزئی سهوی بیشتر منتقل
نشدم

A.

(ا)

Which is it? Be so kind as to explain.

کدام است محبت فرموده بیان کنید

B.

(ب)

This only—when you said, "These servants are very mischievous." اشرار

همینکه فرمودید این خدام بسیار
اشرارند

A.

You say true: اَشْرار is an Adjective (Plural); and Adjectives in Persian, when used in the *Plural Number*, yield a *Substantive* signification; and the meaning of اَشْرار, by itself, is "*mischievous people*." Therefore, if I had said, "These servants are very شَرِير, the expression would have been correct; for in that form the Adjective would be in the Singular Number. But I have made a greater mistake than this; and you are not aware of it, because you had not then arrived (*lit.* you had not brought honour).

( ا )

راست میگوئید اشرار صفت است وصفات در فارسی چون بلفظ جمع استعمال شوند افادهٔ معنی ذات میکنند ومعنی اشرار خود مردمان شریر است پس اگر گفته بودم این خدام بسیار شریرند عبارت درست میبود چه در آن صورت صفت مفرد بودی لیکن من غلطی از این بزرگتر کرده ام وشما بدان منتقل نیستید چرا که آنوقت شما هنوز تشریف نیاورده بودید

B.

Do you remember (*lit.* is it in your recollection) what it was?

( ب )

در خاطرتان هست که آن چه بود

A.

Yes; I remember it very well. When I was talking to the other servant respecting that useless groom, I said, "I can never confide in him any more; for he may kill me *a horse daily*."

( ا )

بلی بسیار خوب یادم است وقتی که درباب آن مهتر بیکاره با آن نوکر دیگر گفتگو میکردم گفتم من باو هرگز دیگر اعتماد نمیتوانم کرد که هر روز یک اسبی از برای من بکشد

| | |
|---|---|
| **B.** Where is the mistake? For my part, (كه) I do not see any fault in this expression. | ( ب ) غَلَطْ دَرْ كُجَاسْتْ مَنْكِهْ دَرْاينْ عِبَارَتْ عَيْبِي نَمِي بِينَمْ |
| **A.** Do not you see يَكْ اَسْبِي can never be correct? | ( ا ) نَمِي بِينِيدْ يَكْ اَسْبِي هَرْگِزْ دُرُسْتْ نَتَوَانَدْ بُودْ |
| **B.** Why not? Would that your *horses* were always *as sound* as this! *i.e.* as this phrase is correct!—(a play upon the word دُرُسْتْ). | ( ب ) چِرا كَاشْ كِهْ اَسْبِهَايِ شُمَا هَمِيشَهْ بِايِنْ دُرُسْتِي بُودَنْدْ |
| **A.** A Cardinal Number, you observed, is not admissible before a Definite Noun; and اَسْبِي having already the ي of *unity* at the end of it, is, in itself, a Definite Noun. | ( ا ) لَفْظِ عَدَدْ شُمَا فَرْمُودِيدْ كِهْ بَرْسَرِ اِسْمِ مَعْرُوفْ دَاخِلْ نَمِيشَوَدْ وَاَسْبِي بَايَايِ وَحْدَتْ دَرْآخَرِشْ خُودْ اِسْمِيسْتْ مَعْرُوفْ |
| **B.** You are *now* making a mistake, undoubtedly; because the ي of unity conveys an indefinite sense, and an Indefinite Noun can never be definite (in its meaning). اَسْبِي indicates *a single* or *one* horse, certainly; but *it* may be *any one* horse: whereas يَكْ اَسْبِي implies some one *specific or parti-* | ( ب ) شُمَابِي شَكْ حَالا غَلَطْ مِيكُنِيدْ چِهْ يَايِ وَحْدَتْ اِفَادَهٔ تَنْكِير مِيكُنَدْ [11] وَاِسْمِ مُنَكَّرْ هَرْگِزْ مَعْرُوفْ نَتَوَانَدْ بُودْ اَسْبِي دِلالَتْ مِيكُنَدْ بَرْاَسْبِ وَاحِدْ يَامُفْرَدْ لاَمُحَالَهْ اَمَّا هَرْ اَسْبِي كِه بَاشَدْ لِيكِنْ يَكْ اَسْبِي دَلالَتْ مِيكُنَدْ بَرْيَكْ اَسْب |

(11) See Dialogue 2. Conversation on "Horseback," p. 147.

*cularized horse.* And you know, that if *any one* should kill *a horse, the horse,* in that state, would be definite and particularized.

معین ومحدود وشما میدانید که
اگر کسی اسبی را بکشد اسب درآن
حالت محدود ومعین خواهد بود

### A.

(١)

This is rather a nice point; but you have now made it quite clear to me: although I had much rather that my horses should always remain *unlimited,* and *uncircumscribed* in number, than that this *hack* of a groom should *define* and *particularize* them.

این نکته اندك دقیق است لیکن شما
حالا خوب برمن واضحش کرده اید
اگرچه من خیلی ترجیح میدهم که
اسبهای من همیشه منکرو نامحدود
بمانند تا این الاغ مهتران آنهارا
معروف ومحدود گرداند [12]

### B.

(ب)

Whoever wants his horse for the purpose of riding, would be your partner in this sentiment.—But, since we are now upon the subject, I wish very much to explain to you two or three more points concerning *Adjective, and Substantive Nouns qualified by Adjec-*

هرکه اسبش را برای سواری میخواهد
درآین عقیدت شریك شما خواهد بود
لیکن چون حالا برسر مطلبیم من خیلی
میخواهم که دو سه نکتهٔ دیگر درباب
صفت وموصوف که درآن روز تنگی

---

([12]) This play, or pun, upon grammatical terms cannot be exactly translated into English without the risk of rendering the passage unmeaning: suffice it to state, that these technical phrases (viz. منکر، نامحدود، معروف، محدود—) apply both to Grammar and to Horses, in the Persian Language; and consequently make good puns.

| | |
|---|---|
| *tives,* which, on that day, the lateness of time prevented me from explaining. | وَقتْ اَزْبَيانْ مانِع شُدْ اَكْنُونْ اَزْ بَرايِ شُما بَيانْ كُنَمْ |
| A. | (١) |
| You are doing me a great kindness; but if it be no trouble, and in the like manner as before you will again explain yourself in English, it will add to the obligation. | بِسْيارْ لُطْف ميفَرْمائيدْ اَمّا اَگَرْ زَحْمَتْ نَباشَدْ وبِهَمانْ طَورْ بازْدَرْ اِنْگِليسي بَيانْ فَرْمائيدْ مَزيدِ مِنَّتْ خواهَدْ بُودْ |
| B. | (ب) |
| The (letter) *zau* of زَحْمَتْ, among sincere friends, is always without a dot. | زايِ زَحْمَتْ دَرْمِيانِ دُوسْتانِ خالِص هَمِيشَهْ بي نُقْطَهْ اَسْتْ[13] |

An Adjective, whether Simple or Compound, must always be in the Singular Number, whether its Substantive be so or not. As to its proper situation with regard to the Substantive which it qualifies;—when the Noun is Indefinite or Definite, but not in *apposition,* the Adjective must invariably follow it, and the final or connecting زيرْ (ِ) be added to the Substantive; as, مَرْدِ خُوبْ اَزْ خُدا ميتَرْسَدْ "A good man fears God"; اَسْبِ عَرَبي هَمِيشَهْ لاغَر ميانَسْتْ "An Arabian horse is always *thin-waisted*"; اَسْبِ سِياهِ مَنْ دَرْطَويلَهْ بُودْ "My *black* horse was in the stable"; مَرْدانِ دِلاوَرْ اَزْ جَنْگْ باكْ نَدارَنْدْ "*Brave men* have no dread of battle"; دُوسْتانِ مِهْرْبانِ تُوحاضِرَاَنْدْ "Thy *affectionate* friends are present"; &c. &c. But when the Noun is in apposition, the Adjective may either precede or follow the

---

(13) If the first letter (ز) of the word زَحْمَتْ "trouble," is not *dotted*, the word will be read رَحْمَتْ, which signifies *blessing*, or *mercy*.

Substantive; and in either case, instead of the زِیر (ِ), the descriptive ي must be added to the Substantive or to the Adjective, but generally to that which immediately precedes the Verb; as, پدرِ تو خوب مردیست or پدرِ تو مردِ خوبیست "Thy father is a good *man*." But when the sentence becomes more complicated, the good taste and the judgment of the writer or speaker must, in a great measure, guide him in the manner of arranging his words; for then the Adjective may even be expressed after the Verb itself; as, لَنْدَن شَهریست بِسیار بزرگ, or لَنْدَن بِسیار شَهرِ بزرگیست, or لَنْدَن بِسیار بزرگ شَهریست, or لَنْدَن شَهرِ بسیار بزرگیست, all of which expressions equally mean, "London is a very large city," and are all idiomatic. One rule, however, is generally to be observed; viz. that if the Adjective expresses more than a *simple abstract* quality, such as *good* or *bad*, or if it is of Arabic extraction, or a compound, it is to be placed after the Substantive, whether expressed before or after the Verb: for instance, you may say in Persian, نوکرِ تو بد مرد یست, or نوکرِ تو مردِ بدیست, or نوکرِ تو مرد یست بد, all meaning, "Thy servant is a bad *man*"; but if an Arabic Adjective, say شَرِیر "wicked," be substituted for the Persian بَد, you may say نوکرِ تو مردِ شَرِیریست, or نوکرِ تو مرد یست شَرِیر; but it would not be quite idiomatic, except in poetry, to say نوکرِ تو شریر مرد یست. Adjective Adverbs, or Adverbs of Quantity, such as, بِسیار, خَیلي, "much," "very," &c. &c., brought to increase the force of an Adjective, may be placed immediately before (never after) the Adjective, and the second Noun of the apposition may also intervene between them; as, اِنگلند مَملکتِ بسیار,

اِنْگْلَنْد خَيْلِي خُوبْ, or اَنْگْلَنْد بِسيار مَمْلَكَتِ خُوبِيسْت, or خُوبِيسْت, or اَنْگْلَنْد مَمْلَكَتِيسْت خَيْلِي خُوبْ, or مَمْلَكَتِيسْت: all of these expressions equally mean, "England is a very good kingdom," or, "a very fine country."

With regard to the Cardinal Numbers, the Nouns to which they are joined (whether they be with, or without an Adjective) must always be in the Singular Number; as, هَزار مَرْد "a thousand *men* (literally, *man*)," or يَكْهَزار مَرْد "one thousand *man*"; صَدْ گُوسْفَنْد, or يَكْصَدْ گُوسْفَنْد, "one hundred *sheep*," &c. &c.; but *not* مَرْدان, or گوسْفَنْدان. The same also when the Noun is with an Adjective; as, بِيسْتْ مَرْدِ دِلاوَر "twenty brave *man*"; پانْصَدْ ودُو اَسْبِ بِسيار خُوبْ "five hundred and two very good *horse*"; &c. &c. Respecting the order in which the numbers should be arranged, the greatest number is expressed first, and the rest following in the same order; as, دَوِيسْت وپَنْجاه وچِهار هَزار و هَفْتصَد و هَشْتا دُو سِه گُوسْفَنْد "two hundred and fifty-four thousand seven hundred and eighty-three *sheep*." There is one exception to this rule however; namely, that from eleven to nineteen the smaller number is always expressed first: and from twenty to forty-nine, the smaller number *may be* expressed first; but only in counting or telling, and *never* in conversation or writing. For instance, you *may tell* دُوبِيسْت, چِهارسِي, پَنْج چِهِل, &c. &c., instead of counting بِيسْت ودُو, سِي وچِهار, چِهِل وپَنْج, *i.e.* twenty-two, thirty-four, and forty-five; though the latter is the best mode of expressing these numbers. But there is no *choice* from eleven to nineteen*.

---

* See the Numerals, pp. 10, 11.

*A Definite Noun* may be used in the Plural, to answer to the Cardinal Number; but it must be in a complete sentence, when the Plural Noun is expressed first, then the Cardinal Number, and lastly the Verb; as, مردان دو هزار بودند "*the men* were two thousand"; اسبهای سیاه چهار بودند "The black *horses* were four"; &c. &c.

In concluding this subject, however, let me assure you, that if you will only be a little careful in the course of your reading, you will discover more rules with regard to the Persian Syntax, and understand them even much better, than any Grammarian could explain them to you by his isolated examples or quotations. Besides having access to books, you now possess another advantage over those foreigners who study a language by themselves, or far from where it is spoken. You are now at present in Persia, and in constant intercourse with the natives: the best Grammar for you, therefore, is to attend to the conversations and idioms of the educated classes of the people, with whom you are so frequently in communication, and may ask them any questions you may think proper.

## DIALOGUE V.

| | |
|---|---|
| A. | (ا) |
| To-day, the air is very warm. | امروز هوا بسیار گرمست |
| B. | (ب) |
| I wonder that you should complain of the heat! | من تعجب میکنم که شما از گرما شکایت کنید |
| A. | (ا) |
| Why? Perhaps you supposed that I had no bodily feeling? | چرا مگر شما همچو میدانستید که بنده حس بدنی نداشتم |

B.

Not so: but you having said that you had resided ten years in India, and had been staying chiefly in Bengal—and the climate of India, especially Bengal, being much warmer than Persia, and to-day also not being a particularly hot day—I was surprised when you complained of the heat!

( ب )

نَه هَمچنین لیکِن چون شُما فَرموده
بودید کِه دَه سال دَر هِندوستان
تَشریف میداشتید واَغلَب دَر بَنگالَه
مُتَوَقِّف میبودید وَهوایِ هِندوستان
خُصوصًا بَنگالَه اَز ایران بِسیار
گَرمتَر است وامروز هَم بِخُصوصِه روزِ گَرمی
نَمیبود مَن مُتَحَیِّر شُدَم کِه شُما اَز گَرما
شِکایَت کَردید

A.

Notwithstanding these good reasons why such should not be the case, I feel a strange heat all over my body; and, moreover, I have a great thirst upon me, and my head also aches.

( ا )

باوُجودِ این وُجوهِ مَعقولَه کِه حال
چِنین نَباشَد بَندَه حَرارَتِ غَریبی دَر
بَدَن اِحساس میکُنَم وَبِعَلاوَه عَطَش
هَم بِسیار دارَم وَسَرَم هَم دَرد میکُنَد

B.

God grant that you may have no fever! Let me feel (*lit.* see) your pulse. Do not be alarmed: you have a slight fever; take care (of yourself): please God, it will soon be removed.

( ب )

خُدا نَکُنَد کِه تَب نَداشتَه باشی نَبضَترا
بِبینَم تَشویش مَکُن تَبَک* خَفیفی
داری اِحتیاط بِکُن اِنشاءَ اللّٰه زود رَفع
میشَوَد

* See the Diminutive Particles, pp. 127—129.

(۱)

**A.**

I fear I may have caught cold: there is a bad taste in my mouth; and I feel a shivering in my back and side.

مَن مِیتَرسَم چاهِیدَه باشَم دَهَنَم
بَدمَزَه اَست وَرَعشَه دَرپُشت وپَهلُو
اِحساس مِیکُنَم

(ب)

**B.**

There is no doubt you have caught cold: you must abstain from fruit altogether. At this season, fever and ague are very prevalent (*lit.* has a great prevalence) in Persia. People, in these warm nights, sleep mostly on the tops of their houses; and it sometimes happens, that in the course of the night a slight cold may have settled on a person, and he may not be aware of it: and, in the earlier part of the day, people incautiously eat fruit: and most of the agues and fevers, and other maladies which prevail at this season, arise from these sources.

شَك نِیست کِه چاهِیدَه اِید اَزمِیوَه
مُطلَقاً بایَد پَرهِیز کُنِید دَراِین مَوسِم
تَب ولَرز دَرایران عُمُومِي دارَد مَردُم
دَراِین شَبهايِ گَرم اَغلَب بَرپُشتِ
بامها مِیخوابَند وگاه باشَد کِه دَربَینِ
شَب اَندَك چاهِشِي عارِض شُدَه باشَد
وشَخص اَزآن مُخبِر نِیست وَدَراَوایِلِ
روزبِي اِحتِیاط مِیوَه مِیخورَند واَکثَرتَب
ولَرزها وسایِرِ اَمراضِي کِه دَراِین فَصل
مُتَداوَلَند اَزاِین جِهات بَرمِیخِیزَند

(۱)

**A.**

You say true: last night, about two or three hours past midnight, I woke, and felt very much chilled. I found (saw) the night-cap

راست مِیگُوئِید مَن دِیشَب دُوسِه
ساعَت اَزنِصف شَب گُذَشتَه بِیدار
شُدَم وخَیلِي سَردَم بود دِیدَم کِه شَب

had fallen off my head, and the quilt even was not over me; and I sneezed also twice or thrice: perhaps that may have been the commencement of my cold.

کلاه از سرم افتاده بود ولحاف هم رویم نبود دوسه بارهم عطسه کردم شاید که ابتدای زکام من ازآن باشد

B.

( ب )

Notwithstanding these several warnings, I still fear you may not have abstained from your usual custom of eating fruit before breakfast.

باوجود این تنبیهات متعدده هنوز میترسم که از عادت مستمری پیش از نهار میوه خوردن پرهیز نکرده باشید

A.

( ا )

Why conceal it from you? The truth of the matter is, that this morning the gardener of the English Envoy brought me several baskets of fresh ripe fruits. Without exaggeration, I had never seen grapes, figs, and melons, in such a state of perfection and delicacy.—Moreover, with what neatness and elegance had that tasteful gardener arranged them, mixed with roses and jessamines, in those baskets of green myrtle! At all events, I enjoyed the pleasure of partaking of those forbidden fruits: now I must pay the penalty of my indiscretion.

ازشما چه پنهان حق مطلب اینست که امروز صبح باغبان ایلچی انگلیس چند سبد میوهای تازه ورسیده از برای من آوردبی اغراق من هرگز انگور و انجیر و خربزه بآن خوبی ولطافت ندیده بودم بعلاوت بچه تنقیه ونزاقت آن باغبان باسلیقت آنها را باگل ویاسمن درآن سبد های مورد سبز درهم چیده بود بهرحال من ازآن میوهای ممنوعه لذتی بردم واکنون باید جریمت ناپرهیزی خود را بدهم

**B.**

You must not alone pay the whole of the penalty: since the Envoy's gardener has tempted you to eat the fruit, justice requires that the Envoy's doctor should pay a part of the penalty, in the shape of medicine and attendance. I have some business in the neighbourhood of the Ambassador's house; and, as I am passing that way, I will see the English doctor myself, and send him to see you directly.

( ب )

شما تنها تمام جریمت را نباید بدهید
چون باغبان ایلچی شما را بخوردن میوه
ترغیب کرده است انصاف مقتضیست
که حکیم ایلچی یکحصهٔ جریمت را
بصورت دوا و پرستاری بدهد من
نزدیکی خانهٔ ایلچی کاری دارم چون
از آن راه میگذرم من خودم حکیم
صاحب را می بینم و اورا زود بدیدن
شما میفرستم

**A.**

May your affection never diminish! But there is no necessity for you to take the trouble (*lit.* that you should take the trouble): I can write to the doctor myself, and beg him to come.

( ا )

محبت شما کم نشود اما ضرور نیست
که شما زحمت بکشید من خودم میتوانم
بحکیم بنویسم والتماس کنم که بیاید

**B.**

It is no trouble at all! I must pass that way: what difference will it make, if I were to see the doctor for two or three minutes?—Moreover, when I see him, I can explain your case to him; and he perhaps, forming some judgment of it by

( ب )

هیچ زحمت نیست من باید از آن راه
بگذرم چه تفاوت میکند اگر دو سه
دقیقه حکیم را ببینم بعلاوت من چون
اورا ببینم میتوانم احوال شما را بیان
کنم و او شاید از گفتهٔ من استنباطی

my statement, should any medicine be necessary, he can at once bring it with him; and in this manner the matter may be expedited.

کَرْدَهْ اَگَرْ دَوائِي ضَرُورْ باشَدْ يَكْدَفْعَهْ هَمْراهِ خُودْ بِياوَرَدْ وَبِاينْ طَوْرْ اَنْدَكِي كارْ پِيشْ اُفْتَدْ

A.

I am much obliged to you! Although we say, in English, "I would do as much for you;" yet I hope to requite you, for these affectionate offices, at your wedding, and not in your illness!

( ا )

مَنْ اَزْ شُما بِسْيارْ مَمْنُونَمْ اَگَرْچِهْ ما دَرْ اِنْگِلِيسِي مِيگُوئِيمْ مَنْ هَمِينْ قَدْرْ را زْبَراي شُما خواهَمْ كَرْدْ اَمّا مَنْ اُمِيدْ وارَمْ كِهْ تَلافِيِ اينْ مِهْرْبانِيها را دَرْ عَرُوسِيِ شُما بِكُنَمْ نَهْ دَرْ بِيمارِيتانْ

B.

May it please God to restore you to health first!—Now I will leave you quiet: and do you repose a little, until the doctor comes.

( ب )

خُدا اِنْشاءَ اللّهْ اَوَّلْ بِشُما شَفا بِدِهَدْ مَنْ حالا شُمارا آرامْ مِيگُذارَمْ وَتا آمَدَنِ حَكِيمْ اَنْدَكِي اِسْتِراحَتْ بِكُنِيدْ

A.

I have a great thirst upon me; and am afraid of drinking cold water, lest it should do me harm.

( ا )

عَطَشْ بِسْيارْ دارَمْ وَآبِ سَرْدْ مِيتَرْسَمْ بِخُورَمْ[1] مَبادا ضَرَرْ بِكُنَدْ

---

(1) The Verb خُورْدَنْ does not always signify "To eat" in Persian. It signifies also "To drink"; as, آبْ خُورْدَنْ "To drink water"; مَيْ خُورْدَنْ "To drink wine"; &c. &c. It means also "To suffer," and "To feel"; as, غَمْ خُورْدَنْ "To suffer grief"; تَأَسُّفْ خُورْدَنْ "To feel regret." In fact, خُورْدَنْ, in Persian, corresponds more with the English Verb "To take," than any other Verb; for they say in English, "To take pains," "To take trouble," "To take dinner," "To take wine," &c. &c.; for all of which خُورْدَنْ may be used in Persian.

**B.** (ب)

I will tell the cook to make some barley-water for you: that will quench (your) thirst.

مَنْ بآشْ پَزْ میگُویَمْ تا اَنْدَکِي ماءِ شَعِیرْ
اَزْ بَرایِ شُما دُرُسْتْ بِکُنَدْ آنْ تَسْکِینِ
عَطَشْ مِیکُنَدْ

**A.** (ا)

May your kindness and affection increase!

لُطْفْ و شَفْقَتِ شُما زِیادْ

**B.** (ب)

Boys! Boys!!—No one answers! (*lit.* gives an answer.) They are all dead! —Boys!!!

بَچّها بَچّها هِیچْکَسْ جَوابْ نَمِیدِهَدْ
اِیْنْها هَمَهْ مُرْدَهْ اَنْدْ بَچّها

**Servant.** (خِدْمَتْکارْ)

Sir! yes Sir!!

صاحِبْ بَلِي صاحِبْ

**A.** (ا)

You see, at last, that I am ill! why do you, all of you, vanish together?—For God's sake, let one of you, at least, be always near at hand, to answer when I call! It is *your special duty* always to be in the coffee-room: where had you gone?

آخِرْ شُمامِي بِبِیْنِیْدْ کِهْ مَنْ بیمارَمْ چِرا
هَمَتانْ باهَمْ گُمْ مِیشَوِیْدْ اَزْ بَرایِ خُدا
بِگُذارِیْدْ اَقَلّا یِکِیْتانْ هَمِیشَهْ اِیْنْ
نَزْدِیکیها باشَدْ تاوَقْتِیکِهْ آوازْ مِیکُنَمْ
جَوابْ بِدِهَدْ کارِ مُعَیَّنِ تُو اِیْنَسْتْ کِهْ
هَمِیشَهْ دَرْ قَهْوَهْ خانَهْ [2] باشِي کُجا رَفْتَهْ
بُودِي

---

(2) An ante-room leading into the audience-chamber, where the *coffee*, &c. غَلْیانْ "ghalyaun," are prepared, and handed in to the guests.

SERVANT. (خِدمَتکار)

I was gone to the kitchen, to fetch the barley-water, which the cook had prepared for you.

مَنْ تُويِ آشپزخانَهْ رَفتَهْ بُودَمْ كِهْ ماشَعْير كِهْ آشپز بَرايِ شُما ساخْتَهْ بُودْ بِيارَم

A. (ا)

Mind you well, that to-day, excepting the doctor, and the gentleman who just went out, whoever else may call (come), you must say that I am not well, and cannot see any body!—Dost thou understand, or not?

خُوبْ خاطِرتانْ باشَدْ كِهْ اِمْرُوزْ بِغَيْر اَزْ حَكِيمْ واينْ صاحِبْ كِهْ حالا بيرُونْ رَفْتْ هَرْكَسي دِيگَرْ كِهْ بِيايَدْ بِگُوئيدْ كِهْ اَحْوالَمْ خُوشْ نيستْ وكَسيرا نَميتَوانَمْ بِهْ بِينَمْ ميفَهْمي يانَهْ

SERVANT. (خِدمَتکار)

Yes, Sir; very well.

بَليْ صاحِبْ بِسْيارْ خُوبْ

A. (ا)

Now, bring (me) some barley-water.—Ah! this is too hot; I cannot drink it.

حالا قَدْري ماشَعْير بِيارْ آه اينْ خَيْلي گَرْمَسْتْ مَنْ نَميتَوانَمْ اينْرا بُخورَمْ[3]

SERVANT. (خِدمَتکار)

It is not (a) long (time) since it has been taken off the fire; and it is not yet cooled.

خَيْلي وَقْتْ نيستْ كِهْ اَزْ رُويِ آتَش بَرْداشْتَهْ شُدَسْتْ وَهَنُوزْ سَرْدْ نَشُدَه اَسْتْ

(³) See Note 1. Dialogue 5.

(۱)

A.

Go, and pour it all into a glass (bottle); and put the bottle into ice, that it may cool the sooner. I am very thirsty! But do not bring it till I ask for it: I may be asleep, and will not have any one disturb me.

بِرُو وَهَمَه را دَرْيَكْ شِيشَهٔ بِرِيزْ وَشِيشَه را
مِيانِ يَخْ بِگُذارْ تا زُودْتَرْ سَرْدْ بِشَوَدْ مَنْ
بِسْيارْ تِشْنَه اَمْ اَمّا تا نَخْواهَمْ[4] مَيارْ
شايَدْ خْوابْ باشَمْ وَنَمِيخْواهَمْ كَسِي
بِيدارَمْ كُنَدْ

*(Two Servants talk.)*

( دُو خِدْمَتْكار بايَكْدِيگَر )

1st Servant.

(۱)

What is the matter with master to-day?

صاحِبْ[5] اِمْرُوزْ چِه خَيرِشْ اَسْتْ[6]

2d Servant.

(۲)

What do I know?—He says *he is ill.*

مَنْ چِه مِيدانَمْ مِيگُويَدْ كِه بِيمارَمْ[7]

1st Servant.

(۱)

If he is ill, he *is* ill: if he is not ill, he *is not* ill: but you, who go in and come out so often, if you be not an ass, must, at all events, know one thing or the other.

اَگَرْ بِيمارَسْتْ كِه بِيمارَسْتْ اَگَرْ
بِيمارْ نِيسْتْ كِه بِيمارْ نِيسْتْ اَمّا تُو كِه
اِنْقَدَرْ تُو مِيرَوِي وَبِيرُونْ مِي آيِي اَگَرْ
خَرْ نَباشِي آخِرْ بايَدْ كِه يَكْ چِيزِي بِدانِي

---

([4]) The reader will here again observe the difference of idiom between the Persian and English. In the former, the Negative form تا نَخْواهَمْ مَيارْ "So long as I shall *not* ask for it, do not bring it," is strictly idiomatic. In English, it is the reverse: "Until I *do* ask for it, do not bring it."

([5]) See Note 1. Dialogue 4.

([6]) See Notes 2 and 4. Dialogue 3.

([7]) See Note 5. Dialogue 4.

2d Servant.

If you ask me, I tell you, that these Englishmen, so long as they possess a *pulse* and a *watch*, they are never in health. With one hand, He holds his watch; and with the other, feeling his pulse—thus. He looks at *this* a little, and counts something to himself; and all at once exclaims, "Alas! it is ninety!—it is ninety-five!—O dear, it is a hundred!!!—Woe is me! I am ill!—Bring the doctor!—Prepare some medicine!—Make some barley-water!—Let no one speak!—Let no one knock at the door!—I cannot see any one!"—and I know not what! But, thank God! he is now asleep. Would that, before his waking, his *watch* may stop!—then all would be right.

(٢)

اگر ازمن میپرسي من بات میگویم که
این انگلیسها تاوقتیکه یك نبضي
ویکساعتي دارند هرگز چاق نیستند
یکدست ساعتش را میگیرد ویکدست
نبضشرا همچو یکخوردهٔ باین نگاه
میکند و یکچیزي پیش خودش
میشمارد و یکمرتبه فریاد میکند که
امان [8] نود تاست نود و پنجتاست واویلا
که صد تاست اَي واي که من بیمارم
حکیم بیارید دوابسازید ما شعیر
درست بکنید کسي حرف نزند کسي
در نزند من هیچکس را نمیتوانم ببینم
وچه میدانم که چه امّا شکر خدا که
حالا خوابست کاشکه پیش از بیدار
شدنش ساعتش وامي ایستاد آنوقت
همه درست میشد

1st Servant.

You talk a great deal of nonsense! Methinks

(١)

تو خیلي چرند میگوئي گویا عقلترا گم

(8) For this and the following exclamations, see the Interjections, pp 117—19.

you have lost your wits. If the *man* were not really ill, do you think the doctor was a fool, like yourself, to take so much blood from him for no purpose?

کَرْدَهْ باشِي اَگَرْ مَرْدِ کَه راسْتِي بِیمارْ نَبُودْ
آنْ حَکِیمْ تُوْ هَمْچُومِیدانِي مِثْلِ خُوْدَتْ
یَكْ اَحْمَقِي بُودْ کِهْ اینْ هَمَهْ خُونَشْ
بِگِیرَدْ بَرایِ هِیچْ چِیزْ

(۲)

2d Servant.

After all, he (the doctor) is an Englishman too, and has a watch also. What did *he* do, when he came? First of all, he pulled out his watch, and, like Master himself, held it in one hand, and with the other hand he felt the Master's pulse, and in the same manner he began counting: then he said something to Master, and Master put out his tongue. As soon as he looked at Master's tongue, he fumbled with his hand in his pocket and pulled out his lancet; and cried out, "Boys! bring the jug and basin!" You know the rest (*lit.* the rest of it is known), *i.e.* he bled him.

آخِرْ اُوْهَمْ اِنْگْلِیسْ اَسْتُ وِیَکْساعَتِي هَمْ
دارَدْ مَگَرْ چِهْ کارْ کَرْدْ وَقْتِي کِهْ آمَدْ اَوَّلْ
هَمَهْ ساعَتَشْ را بیرُونْ آوَرْدُ و مِثْلِ
صاحِبْ خُوْدَشْ بِیَکْدَسْتَشْ گِرِفْتُ
وِبِیَکْدَسْتِ دِیگَرَشْ نَبْضِ صاحِبْ را
گِرِفْتْ وَبِهَمانْ طَوْرْ بِنا کَرْدْ بِشُمُرْدَنْ
آنْوَقْتْ یَكْ چِیزِي بِصاحِبْ گُفْتُ
وصاحِبْ زَبانَشْ را بیرُونْ آوَرْدْ هَمِینْکِهْ
بِزَبانِ صاحِبْ نِگاهْ کَرْدْ دَسْتَشْ را تُوْيِ
جِیبَشْ اَنْداخْتُ ونِیشْتَرَشْ را بیرُونْ
آوَرْدُ وبانْگْ زَدْ کِهْ بَچِّها آفْتابَهْ لَگَنْ
بِیارِیدْ باقِیشْ مَعْلُومَسْتْ

(۱)

1st Servant.

Do you mean to say that

تُوْ مِیخْواهِي بِگُوئِي کِهْ حَکِیمْ خُوْدَشْ

the doctor *himself* bled Master, and did not send for a barber?!

صاحِبرا خُونْ گِرِفْتْ وَپِيْ دَلّاكْ نَفِرِسْتادْ

2d Servant.

( ۲ )

Barber! They are their own barbers. Have you ever seen an Englishman who could not shave himself?—Their doctors, also, both bleed and extract teeth. —Listen! somebody knocks at the door.— —Yes, yes! Coming!

دَلّاكْ اِينْها دَلّاكِ خُودِ شانَنْدْ هَرگِزْ يَكْ اِنْگِلِيسِي دِيدَهٔ كِهْ رِيشِ خُودَشْرا نَتَوانَدْ بِتَراشَدْ حَكِيما نِشانْ هَمْ هَمْ خُونْ مِيگِيرَنْدْ وَهَمْ دَنْدانْ مِيكَشَنْدْ بِشْنَوِيدْ كَسِي دَرْ مِيزَنَدْ بَلِي بَلِي آمَدْ

A Messenger.

( آدَمِي بارُقْعَهٔ )

I have brought a note for the Gentleman; and want an answer to it.

بَراي صاحِبْ يَكْ رُقْعَهٔ آوَرْدَهْ اَمْ وجَوابَشْرا مِيخواهَمْ

Servant.

( خِدْمَتْكار )

Master is not well, and is asleep: I cannot just now give him the note. But, hark! I hear him cough. I think he is awake (or has awoke). Give me the note!

صاحِبْ اَحْوالَشْ خُوشْ نِيسْتْ و خوابِيدَهْ اَسْتْ مَنْ نَمِيتَوانَمْ كِهْ حالا رُقْعَهْرا بِاِشْ بِدِهَمْ اَمّا يَواشْ مِيشْنَوَمْ كِهْ سُرْفَهْ مِيكُنَدْ مَظَنَّهْ كِهْ بِيدارْ شُدَهْ اَسْتْ رُقْعَهْرا بِدِهْ بِمَنْ

A.

( ۱ )

Boys! Bring me some water to drink!—What is the time? Bring candles, that I may see!

بَچِّها قَدْرِي آبِ خُورْدَنْ بِيارِيدْ چِهْ وَقْتَسْتْ شَمْعْ بِيارِيدْ بِبِينَمْ

**Servant.**

Yes, Sir. We are coming. Make haste [*to a fellow-servant*], and light these candles! or he will be angry again.

(خِدمتکار)

بَلي صاحِب آمَديم زود باش اين شمعهارا روشن کُن که باز کَج خُلق ميشَوَد

*Another Servant.*

Your prayer has been granted! Master's watch *is stopped.* Do you not see, he asks, "What is the time?"

(خادِمي ديگر)

دُعات مُستَجاب شُد ساعَت صاحِب ايستاده اَست نَمي بيني که ميپُرسَد چه وَقتست

**Servant.**

Do not talk nonsense! Give me the candles!

Sir! a person has brought this note for you, and wishes for an answer to it.

(خِدمتکار)

چَرَند مَگو شمعهارا بِدِه بِمَن

صاحِب يَك کَسي اين رُقعه را براي شُما آوَرده اَست وجَوابشرا ميخواهَد

**A.** (*reads.*)

My Dear Friend!

Although it is unkind to leave a valued friend alone when he is ill; and justice itself, under such circum-

(۱)

دُوستِ عَزيزِ مَن[9]

اَگَرچه يارانِ گِراميرا دَرحالَتِ بيماري تَنها گُذاشتَن طَريقِ مِهرباني

(9) I have not been strictly literal in translating some parts of this epistle; because, in the vain attempt to *Anglify* the *untranslatable* phrases of Persian courtesy, the English becomes so bad, I may even say so ridiculous, as to degrade, rather than elucidate, the peculiar phraseology of the original. The learner, if he has been a learner at all, by the time he comes to this part of the Grammar, must see, and be able to understand, the difference of the idiom and grammatical construction of the two languages, in this, as well as in many other similar instances, in these Dialogues.

stances, does not reckon any excuse sufficient for absence. Nevertheless, on account of an important and necessary business, the transaction of which is indispensable, I fear I may not be able to have the honour of waiting on you until to-morrow morning; unless (which God forbid!) your indisposition should be so great as to make you think my presence necessary: in that case, to attend upon you will, of course, become the most urgent of all important affairs. I pray that the Almighty Giver of all gifts, in His infinite mercy, may grant you a speedy cure! Your very sincere friend, B.

نیست وانصاف خود درچنین احوال
غیبت را هیچ عذری موجه نمیشمارد
لیکن بسبب مهمی ضروری که
انصرامش لا بدست میترسم که تا فردا
صبح شرف خدمت حاصل نتوانم کرد
مگر آنکه خدا نکرده تکسر مزاج مبارک
بحدی باشد که حضور مخلص را درکار
دانند درآنصورت پرستاری آنجناب
البته اهم مهمات خواهد بود امید که
حضرت واهب العطایا از رحمت بی
نهایت خود شفای عاجل بذات
مبارک عطا فرماید دوست بی ریا (ب)

A.

There is no necessity to write an answer. Send my compliments, and say, "Thank God! I feel much better to night. The doctor has visited me twice; and, after bleeding me, he sent me some medicine: his remedies have proved of great benefit; and I am in hopes that by to-morrow,

(ا)

احتیاج بنوشتن جواب نیست ازمن
دعا وسلام بفرست وبگو که الحمد لله
امشب احوالم بسیار بهترست حکیم
دوبار عیادت کردند وبعد از فصد دوا
فرستادند ومعالجاتشان بسیار مفید
افتاده اند وانشاء الله امیدوارم که تا فردا

God willing! no illness will remain."—As soon as you have sent this message, bring me some tea.

دیگر هیچ ناخوشی نمانده باشد
همینکه این پیغام را فرستادی قدری
چای بیار

**Servant.** (خدمتگار)

Very well, Sir. Do not you wish for something to eat with (your) tea?

بلی صاحب همراه چای چیزی
نمیخواهید بخورید

**A.** (ا)

No; I want nothing (more). But mind, and remember, before going to rest to-night, to bring me some warm water, that I may bathe my feet; and, that an hour after tea is *the time.*

نه هیچ نمیخواهم امّا خاطرت باشد که
پیش از خوابیدن امشب قدری آب
گرم بیاوری تا پاهایم را بشویم و یکساعت
بعد از چای وقتست

## DIALOGUE VI.

**B.** (ب)

O, my thornless rose! O, my "Companion of the cave!" peace be upon you! "May thy person never be a supplicant before the self-sufficiency of the doctors! May thy delicate frame never be afflicted with sickness!"

ای گل بیخار و ای یار غار[1] من سلام علیکم
تنت بناز طبیبان نیازمند مباد ٭
وجود نازکت آزرده گزند مباد ٭ *

---

(1) Mohammed, during his flight, when closely pursued by his enemies, was obliged for a time to conceal himself in a cave, wherein none of his followers was with him, excepting أبابکر "Ababakr" (afterwards the first Khalif); and hence he obtained the appellation of یارِغار "The Companion of the cave." It is now used occasionally, in Persian, to signify a very sincere and intimate friend. The couplet is by Hāfiz.

* See Optative Mood, p. 67.

I trust that the disinterested prayers of your sincere friends have been heard in your behalf, and that you are now completely free from indisposition!

اُمِيدْ كِهْ دَعَواتِ بِي غَرَضِ دُوسْتانِ خالِصْ دَرْ بارَهٔ اَتْ مُسْتَجابْ اُفْتادَه اَكْنُونْ بِالْمَرَّه اَزْ مَرَضْ آزادِي

### A.

Thanks be to God! I have no illness to-day. My fever has left me (*lit.* is broken off); my headache is completely gone; and my appetite is also very good: what more dost thou want? But the truth is, that so long as a person does not suffer illness, he does not know the value of health. How much it behoves me now to praise God, who has bestowed on me the blessing of health! but when I compare my state of yesterday with that of to-day, I acknowledge that it is impossible for me to thank God as I ought.

(ا)

اَلْحَمْدُ لِلّٰهْ اِمْرُوزْ هِيچْ ناخُوشِي نَدارَمْ تَبَمْ شِكَسْتَه اَسْت دَرْدِ سَرَمْ بِكُلِّي رَفْع شُدَه اَسْت وَاِشْتِهامْ هَمْ بِسْيارْ خُوبَسْت دِيگَرْ چِه مِيخْواهِي اَمّا حَقّ اَسْت كِه تا كَسِي بِيمارِي نَكَشَدْ قَدْرِ صِحَّت نَمِيدانَدْ وَمَنْ حالا چِه قَدْرْ خُدارا شُكْر بايَدْ بِكُنَمْ كِه نِعْمَتِ صِحَّت بِمَنْ عَطا فَرْمُودَه اَسْت لِيكَنْ چُونْ حالَتِ دِيرُوزْرا با اِمْرُوزَمْ بَرْآوَرْدْ مِيكُنَمْ مِي بِينَمْ كِه مُحالَسْت كِه خُدارا چِنانْكِه بايَدْ وَشايَدْ شُكْر تَوانَمْ كَرْد

### B.

It is incumbent upon us every moment to thank God; for there is no instant that we are free from the exercise of His goodness. The divine bounty is like water, and we like fish; we cannot exist a moment without it.

(ب)

شُكْرِ خُدا دَرْ هَرْ آنْ بَرْ ما واجِبْ اَسْت چِه ما گاهِي نِيسْت كِه اَزْ فَيْضِ اُو خالِي باشِيمْ نِعْمَتِ اِلٰهِي مانَنْدِ آبَسْت و ما چُونْ ماهِي دَمِي بِي آنْ زِنْدَه نَتَوانِيمْ

It is from our ingratitude and neglect that we thank God only from time to time for some particular bounty of His; otherwise, His universal grace every moment demands renewed thanks. Dost thou not recollect the passage in Sādy?

بُوَدْ این اَزْکُفْرانُ وغَفْلَتِماسْتْ کِهْ هَمِینْ
گاهْگاهِي خُدارا بِجِهَتْ نَعْمَتِي مَخْصُوصْ
سِتایِشْ میکُنِیمْ وَالّا اَلْطافِ عَمِیمِ اُوْهَرْآنِي
اِقْتِضايِ شُکْرِي تازَهْ میکُنَدْ عِبارَتِ
سَعْدِي خاطِرَتْ نیسْتْ

**A.**

No: to what passage do you allude?

(ا)

خَیْرْ بِکُدامْ عِبارَتْ اَشارَتْ میکُنِیدْ

**B.**

In the preface of his incomparable (work) "Gulistān," On the praise of the Almighty Creator, he says, "Every breath, when inhaled, is a prolonger of life; and when exhaled, a reviver of nature: so that in every single respiration there exists two bounties of God; and for every bounty, a separate thanksgiving becomes due. Whose power and whose language is sufficient to fulfil the duty of gratitude to Him?!"

(ب)

دَرْ دِیباچَهٔ گُلِسْتانِ بِي نَظِیرَشْ دَرْ
سِتایِشِ بارِي تَعالِي میگُویَدْ
هَرْ نَفَسِي کِهْ فُرُو میرَوَدْ مُمِدِّ حَیاتَسْتْ
وَچُونْ بَرْمِي آیَدْ مُفَرِّحِ ذاتَسْتْ
پَسْ دَرْ هَرْ نَفَسِي دُو نَعْمَتْ مَوْجُودْ
وَبَرْ هَرْ نَعْمَتِي شُکْرِي واجِبْ
اَزْ دَسْتْ[2] وَزَبانِ کِهْ بَرْآیَدْ ⁂
کَزْ عُهْدَهٔ شُکْرَشْ بِدَرْ آیَدْ ⁂

(2) دَسْتْ in Persian, means "*hand,*" as well as "*power.*" The English reader need not be reminded of the same in his own language. But the passage may also be translated thus: "What can the hand or tongue express sufficiently, to perform the requisite duty of gratitude?"

A.

The chief beauty of these passages is in the truths which they express, although the expressions [themselves] are also quite perfect in point of eloquence.

( ۱ )

حُسْنِ کُلِّيِ اینْ فقراتْ دَرْ تحقیقاتیستْ
کهْ بیانْ میکُنَنْدْ اَگَرچهْ عِباراتْ خُودْ
دَرْ فصاحَتْ هَمْ تامَّنْدْ

B.

What can be more beautiful than *truth?* My belief is, that man ought not to be called "the lord of the creation" merely because of the power of speech; but rather on this account, that he can speak *truth.*

( ب )

اَزْ راسْتْ چهْ نیکوتَرْ تَوانَدْ بُودْ اِعْتقادِ
مَنْ اینَسْتْ کهْ اِنْسانْ را بحَسَبِ نُطْقِ
محْضْ اَشْرَفِ مخلُوقاتْ نَبایَدْ گُفْتْ
بَلْکهْ بحَسَبِ اینکهْ راسْتْ تَنَطُّقْ
میتَوانَدْ کَرْدْ

A.

You speak *truth;* therefore you are *the lord of the creation.* But, My Lord of the Creation, this is a very antiquated truth. Should there be any new truths in your noble thoughts, I shall be much delighted to hear it.

( ۱ )

شُما راسْتْ میگُوئیدْ پَسْ شُما اَشْرَفِ
مَخْلُوقاتیدْ لیکِنْ اَيْ اَشْرَفِ مَخْلُوقاتْ
اینْ راسْتیستْ بِسیارْ قَدیمْ اَگَرْ تَحْقیقِ
تازَهٔ دَرْ خاطِرِ شَریفْ باشَدْ مَنْ اَزْ
شَنیدَنَشْ خَیْلي مَحْظُوظْ خواهَمْ شُدْ

B.

Do you believe, then, that *truth* also, like the customs and fashions of nations, has its novelty and antiquity?—that to-day, *this colour* is *liked;* and to-morrow, *that?*

( ب )

شُما هَمْچُو میدانید کهْ راسْتْ هَمْ مِثْلِ
رُسُومْ وعاداتِ طَوایِفْ تازَگيْ وکُهْنَگي
دارَدْ کهْ اِمْروزْ اینْ رَنْگْ مَرْغُوبَسْتْ و
فَرْدا آنْ اِمْسالْ اینْ بُرِشْ مُتَعارَفْ بَرايِ

—this year, *this is the fashionable* cut of a coat; and *this was* last year's, and is unfashionable;—and so on? However, if such really be your notion, I hope that you will stop at *this limit*, and will not carry the analogy to its full extent! For as, in the one case, you may say, for instance, "This is an old coat, or its colour is unfashionable;" or, "The cut of these breeches is vulgar, and I am ashamed to wear them;" in the other case you will be obliged also to say, "This *truth* is very antiquated, and every body knows it; and is now become very vulgar, and I am ashamed to discuss it;"—and so forth.

لباس است واین برش سال گذشته
است ونامرغوب وهمچنین بهرحال
اگر واقعي اعتقاد شما چنین باشد امید
که دراین حد توقف فرمائید وقیاس را
بنهایت نرسانید چه چون دریك
صورت میتوانید گفت مثلاً این قبا
کهنه است یارنگش نامرغوبست
یابرش این شلوار مبتذلست ومرا از
پوشیدنش عار مي آید درصورت
دیگرهم میباید بگوئید که این راست
خیلي قدیمست وهمه کس آنرا میداند
واکنون بسیار مبتذلست ومرا از
گفتگویش شرم مي آید وعلي هذا

(۱)

A.

I like your diction better than your logic; for in *that*, there is much eloquence; but in *this*, a great deal of fallacy. Who in this world, excepting yourself, could pervert my simple remark in so hideous a manner?

من نطق شمارا از منطقتان بهتر مي
پسندم چه در آن فصاحت بسیار اما
دراین فلسفت بیشمار ست کي دراین
عالم بغیر از خودت میتوانست که
گفت سادهٔ مرا باین صورت زشت
معوج گرداند

B.

Where is the fallacy? Be so kind as to point it out.

( ب )

فلسفت در کجاست لطف فرموده بیان کنید

A.

I said, "This truth is antiquated," meaning, *long established;*" but you interpreted it in the sense of "*old, and worn out,*" which was not my meaning. By قديم, I meant "*ancient,*" as opposed to حادث "*casual.*" The word, as it is employed in logic, signifies "*eternal,*" and *not* "worn out." Moreover, قديم is one of the attributes of the Deity, meaning "without beginning, and without end."

( ١ )

من گفتم که این راست قدیمست یعني دیرپا و شما آنرا بکهنه ومندرس تعبیر کردید وآن مقصود من نبود قصد من از قدیم نقیض حادث بود چنانکه در منطق مستعملست یعني ازلي نه مندرس بعلاوت قدیم یکي از صفات الهیست یعني بي ابتدا وبي انتها

B.

There is no doubt that you have proved (the existence of) a *fallacy;* but, I fear, *more* in your own statement than in my saying. You must surely know, that it often happens that a word has been employed in a science, or idiomatically, to express a particular meaning; but, in common conversation, it has a more extensive signification, which, for the most part, is restricted by the context. You did not *merely* say, "This is

( ب )

شك نیست که شما فلسفتي ثابت کردید امّا میترسم که بیشتر در فرمودهٔ خودتان تا در گفتهٔ من شما باید بدانید که بساست که لفظي در علمي یا اصطلاحي از براي معني مخصوص موضوعست امّا در محاورات معنیش عمومیّت دارد که اغلب از قراین محدود میگردد شما نه همین گفتید که این

an *antiquated* truth;" but you added, "Should there be any *new* truth," &c. &c. It is therefore quite clear, from these contexts, that you used the word قديم (*old*), as opposed to نو (*fresh*), and not as opposed to حادث (*casual*); and your meaning, in using the word "*antiquated*," could only have been "*old and common*," and not "*eternal*." Moreover, you expressed yourself ironically at my defective explanation, and shewed some signs of weariness; and *these*, too, are additional proofs that you used the word "antiquated" in its *worst sense*.

راست قديم است بلكه علاوت كرديد
كه اگر تحقيقِ تازه در خاطرِ شريف
باشد وغيره پس از اين قراين
معلومست كه شما لفظ قديم را در مقابلِ
نو استعمال كرديد نه در مقابلِ حادث
ومقصودِ شما از قديم كهنه ومبتذل
ميتوانست بود نه ازلي بعلاوت شما
ببيانِ ناقصِ من استهزائي فرموديد
واظهارِ ملالتي نموديد وانيها نيز دلايل
ديگرند كه شما لفظ قديم را باقبحِ
معانيش استعمال فرموديد

A.

Do you not know, that I am an Englishman, and that Persian is not my native tongue? What wonder is it, if I should have employed a word rather out of its proper place?

( ا )

مگر شما نميدانيد كه من انگليسم
وفارسي زبانِ اصليِ من نيست چه
عجب اگر لفظي را اندك بيجا استعمال
كرده باشم.

B.

Although your excuse is *very lame*; yet, as you have *so recently* (lit. *newly*) risen from sickness, I will not, for *old* friendship's sake, be too hard upon you.

( ب )

اگرچه عذرت بسيار لنگست ليكن
چون تازه از بيماري برخاسته بخاطرِ
دوستيِ قديمِ من برتو سخت نميگيرم

A.

May your affection ever increase! But, with all this kindness and consideration, I still see that you do not quite forget the "*new*" and the "*old*."

(١)

محبت شما زیاد لیکن با اینهمه موالات
ومهربانی هنوز می بینم که از تازه
وقدیم فراموش نمیفرمائید

B.

This is only to shew you, how words, according to idioms and contexts, give various significations.

But now let us change the subject: for, as you say in English, "This is rather too much of a good thing," we say in Persian, "Eating too much of sweetmeats produces heartburn."

(ب)

این همین است که بشما بنمایم که الفاظ
چگونه بحسب محاورات وقراین معانی
عدیده می بخشند لیکن حالا بگذار
مطلب را تغییر دهیم چه چنانکه شما
در انگلیسی میگوئید این اندکی افراط
است در چیز خوب ما در فارسی میگوئیم
حلوا بسیار خوردن دلسوزش می آرد

A.

Now, I well remember, that, two or three days ago, I settled with a dealer that he should bring several good horses, in order that I might see them, and, if I approved of any, might make a purchase. He came yesterday; but I was not very well, and told him to come another time. If you have a mind,

(١)

حالا خوب یاد میکنم دوسه روز پیش
از این بایك دلالی[3] قرار داده بودم که
چند تا اسب خوب بیارد تا من ببینم
واگر از آنها چیزی به پسندم بخرم او
دیروز آمد اما من حالم خوش نبودو
گفتم وقت دیگر بیاید اگر شما میل

(3) See Note 4. Dialogue IV.

I will send a man, to desire him to come to-morrow morning; and, if you happen not to have any other engagement, have the kindness to come here, that we may see the horses together.

داريد من آدم ميفرستم كه فردا صبح بيايد واسبهارا هم بياورد واگر شما شغلي ديگر نداشته باشيد محبت فرموده اينجا تشريف بياوريد تا اسبهارا باهم به بينيم

**B.**

(ب)

Very well!—I have an engagement now, and shall take my leave (*lit.* become permitted); but to-morrow morning, I will be here again.

بسيار خوب من هم حالا شغلي دارم ومرخص ميشوم وفردا صبح باز اينجا خواهم بود

**A.**

(ا)

God be with you! To-morrow morning, I shall expect you.

خدا همراه شما فردا صبح منتظر شما خواهم بود

## DIALOGUE VII.

**A.**

(ا)

I am very much pleased with that bay horse. What say you?

من ازآن اسب كهر خيلي خوشم مي آيد شما چه ميگوئيد

**B.**

(ب)

It is a fine horse: but I like that chesnut better: it possesses several very good marks.

خوب اسبيست اما من آن كرن را بهتر مي پسندم چند تا نشان بسيار خوب دارد

**A.**

(ا)

It is true; but, to my taste, it is rather too small.

راستست اما بسليقهٔ من اندكي

If that horse had been half a hand taller, he would have been worth any sum you might mention.

کوچکست اگر آن اسب نیم وجب بلند
تر بود هرچه میگفتی می ارزید

**Dealer.**

(دلّال)

Sir, a thorough-bred Arab horse seldom happens to be taller than this. By your own head[1]! in the stable of the prince even, a better horse than this cannot be found! But what need is there for me to describe it? You (as heaven has willed) yourself understand horses very well; and your friend himself also is a perfect judge of a horse.

صاحب اسب عربی خالص کمتر از این
بلند تر اتّفاق می افتد بسر[1] خودت که
در طویلهٔ شاهزاده هم از این بهتر اسب
بهم نمیرسد اما چه ضرور که من
تعریفش بکنم شما خودتان ماشاء الله که
خوب اسب می شناسید ورفیقتان هم
که خودش اسب شناس تمامیست

**A.**

(ا)

You say that "an Arab horse seldom happens to be taller than this." Is not that bay an Arab?

تو میگوئیکه اسب عربی کمتر از این
بلند تر اتّفاق می افتد مگر آن کهر
عربی نیست

**Dealer.**

(دلّال)

That bay horse, also, is worthy of being mounted by the king. It is of mixed blood (*lit.* is of two veins)—the Arab and the Turkoman; but it has more of the Arab blood.

آن اسب کهر هم قابلیّت سواری شاه را
دارد آن دورگه است عربی وترکمانی
اما رگ عربیش بیشتر است

---

(1) A form of adjuration common among the Persians.

**B.**

What do you think (say) of that piebald? See what a beautiful head and neck he has!

( ب )

اَزْآنْ اَبْلَقْ چِهْ مِيگُوئِي بِهْ بِبِيْنْ چِهْ سَرُوگَرْدَنِ مَقْبُولِي دَارَدْ

**A.**

In respect of *shape*, he does not appear to be a bad horse, though his chest is rather narrow: but, I do not know why, I never fancy a piebald horse, however good his blood may be (*lit.* good-veined).

( ا )

اَزْ حَيْثِيَّتِ تَرْكِيبْ بَدْ اَسْبِي نَمِي نَمَايَدْ اَگَرْچِهْ سِينَهْ اَشْ اَنْدَكِي تَنْگَسْتْ اَمَّا نَمِيدَانَمْ چِرا مَنْ اَزْ اَسْبِ اَبْلَقْ هَرْگِزْ خُوشَمْ نَمِي آيَدْ هَرْچَنْدْ خُوشْ رَگْ بَاشَدْ

**B.**

That is another thing. But if a horse be of good blood, and [possess] good marks, I seldom look at his colour.

( ب )

آنْ اَمْرِيسْتْ عَلَيحِدَّهْ اَمَّا اَگَرْ اَسْبْ خُوشْرَگْ وخُوشْنِشَانْ بَاشَدْ مَنْ بِرَنْگَشْ كَمْتَرْ نِگَاهْ مِيكُنَمْ

**A.**

At all events, out of these six horses, I approve only of that bay and that chesnut.

( ا )

بِهَرْحَالْ مَنْ اَزْ اِينْ شِشْ تا اَسْبْ هَمَانْ كَهَرْ وكَرَنْرا مِي پَسَنْدَمْ وبَسْ

**B.**

Do you not admire that dun-coloured horse? I very much wonder! See how handsome he is! In point of beauty and *marks*, that horse, in my opinion, is quite perfect. Short back — broad shoulders —

( ب )

آنْ اَسْبِ سَمَنْدْرا نَمِي پَسَنْدِي مَنْ خَيْلِي تَعَجُّبْ مِيكُنَمْ بِبِيْنْ چِهْ قَدْرْ شَكِيلَ اَسْتْ دَرْحُسْنْ ونِشَانْ آنْ اَسْبْ بِاعْتِقَادِ مَنْ تَمَامَسْتْ پُشْتِ كُوتَاهْ شَانَهْ

open chest; slender waist; wide between the thighs; clean and straight legs; expansive forehead; dark-grey eyes; taper ears; handsome head and neck; white teeth; elegant form; graceful actions; altogether (*literally*, all having grown upon each other), there is not a single good mark which this horse does not possess.

عَرِيضْ سِينَهْ وَسِيعْ مِيانِ بارِيكْ شَلْوارِ
گُشادَهْ ساقْهايْ پاكْ وراسْتْ پيشانِيْ
پَهْنْ چَشْمْهايْ سِياهِ شَهْلا گُوشْهايْ
قَلَمِيْ سَرْوگَرْدَنِ شَكِيلْ دَنْدانْهايْ
سَفِيدْ خُوشْ اَنْدامْ خُوشْ حَرَكَتْ هَمَهْ
رُويِهَمْ رَفْتَهْ هِيچْ نِشانِ خُوبِيْ نِيسْتْ كِهْ
اِينْ اَسْبْ نَمِيدارَدْ

**A.** (١)

I am, however, much more pleased with the other two; and, if their owner is inclined to treat with me (*lit.* have an intention to do business), I have no objection to purchase both.

مَگَرْ اِينْكِهْ مَنْ اَزْآنْ دُوتا خَيْلِيْ خُوشْتَرَمْ
مِيْ آيَدْ وَاَگَرْ صاحِبِشانْ [2] سَرِ مُعامِلَتْ
داشْتَهْ باشَدْ مَنْ مُضايِقَتْ نَدارَمْ كِهْ
هَرْدُورا بِخَرَمْ

**Dealer.** ( دَلّالْ )

Let your mind be easy on that account, Sir: my business is, to sell *horses*; and I have no doubt that a better purchaser than yourself cannot be found.—Why, then, should not our business be done?

خاطِرِ شُما اَزْآنْ بابَتْ جَمْعْ باشَدْ صاحِبْ
شُغْلِ مَنْ اَسْبْ فُرُوخْتَنْ اَسْتْ وشَكْ
نَدارَمْ كِهْ مُشْتَرِيْ اَزْ شُما بِهْتَرْهَمْ يافْتْ
نَمِيشَوَدْ پَسْ چِرا مُعامِلَمانْ نَشَوَدْ

**A.** (١)

For one important reason;

بَرايْ يَكْسَبَبِ كُلِّيْ وَآنْ اِينَسْتْ كِهْ اَگَرْ

---

(2) See Note 1. Dialogue IV.

and that is, *if you should ask too much* for them: then it may become difficult for us to proceed.

قیمتشانرا خیلی بخواهی آنوقت مشکل
باشد که معاملمان بشود

**Dealer.**

(دلال)

God grant you happiness, Sir! What words are these which you are pleased to utter? I would never ask too high a price from you. Every body knows me; and all know, that no merchant can sell horses cheaper than myself.

خدا خیرت بدهد صاحب این چه
حرفهاست که میفرمائید من از شما
هرگز قیمت زیاد نخواهم خواست همه کس
مرا میشناسد و همه میدانند که هیچ
تاجری از من ارزان تر اسب نمیتواند
بفروشد

**A.**

(ا)

That must be tried.—Well! say now, How much do you want for that bay horse? Tell me the lowest (*lit.* the final) price of it, that the business may be shortened.

آن را امتحان باید کرد خوب حالا بگو
از برای آن اسب کهر چند میخواهی
قیمت آخرش را بگو تا کار کوتاه شود

**Dealer.**

(دلال)

The very lowest price of that bay horse is two hundred and thirty tumāns; and the price of the chesnut horse, two hundred and twenty tumāns; or, the two together, four hundred and fifty tumāns.

قیمت آخر آخر[3] آن اسب کهر دویست و
سی تومانست[4] و قیمت اسب کرن
دویست و بیست تومان یا هر دو باهم
چهار صد و پنجاه تومان

---

(3) Adjectives and Adverbs are often thus repeated in Persian, for the sake of emphasis.

(4) A gold coin, the highest in circulation in Persia, worth about ten shillings English money. It is a Turkish word.

**A.**

Did I not say, that "if you should ask too much, our bargain would not proceed?" Four hundred and fifty tumāns is a great deal too much!

(١)

مَنْ نَگُفْتَمْ کِهْ اَگَرْ زِیادْ بِپُرْسِي مُعامِلَمان نَمیشَوَدْ چِهارْصَدْ وپَنْجاهْ تُومانْ خَیْلِي زِیادَسْت

**Dealer.**

By your own head, they are very cheap! If I were to send those two horses to Bushire, your own merchants would give them no respite[5], and, at the lowest, they would give six hundred tumāns for them. From here to Bushire, the expenses of two horses and a groom would not even be ten tumāns. But at present I have occasion for money, and cannot wait. You yourself are a very good judge of horses, and your friend is also perfect in this respect: reflect, both of you, and say whether these horses are cheap, at the price I asked, or not?!

(دَلّالْ)

بِسَرِ خُودَتْ کِهْ بِسْیارْ اَرْزانَنْدْ اَگَرْ مَنْ آنْ دُوْتا اَسْبْرا بِهْ بُوشِهْرْ بِفِرِسْتَمْ تاجِرْهايِ خُودِ تانْ اَمانِشانْ نَمیدِهَنْدْ وَاَقَلّا شِشْصَدْ تُومانْ بَرآیِشانْ مِیدِهَنْدْ اَزایْنجا تا بُوشِهْرْ اِخْراجاتِ دُوْتا اَسْبْ و یَكْ مِهْتَرْ دَهْ تُومانْ هَمْ نَمیشَوَدْ اَمّا مَنْ حالا وَجْهْ ضَرُورْ دارَمْ وصَبْرْ نَمیتَوانَمْ بِکُنَمْ شُما خُودِ تانْ اَسْبْ شِناسِیدْ ورَفیقِتانْ هَمْ کِهْ دَرایْنْ بابْ تَمامَسْتْ خُودِ تانْ فِکْرْ بِکُنِیدْ وبِگُوئِیدْ ایْنْ اَسْبْها بِقِیمَتِیکِهْ مَنْ پُرسِیدَمْ اَرْزانَنْدْ یانَهْ

**A.**

Will you consent to whatever this gentleman may say?—I will be satisfied

(١)

هَرْچِهْ ایْنْ صاحِبْ بِگُویَدْ قَبُولْ مِیکُنِي مَنْ بِهَرْقِیمَتِي کِهْ اُوقَرارْ بِدِهَدْ راضِي

---

(5) The meaning of this passage is, that "your English merchants would eagerly purchase the horses," *i.e.* suffer *no time* to be lost in securing them.

with whatever price he shall fix.—Let him be the arbiter between us.

خواهم شد بگذار او در میانِ ما حکم باشد

**Dealer.**

( دلّال )

Though I do not believe that he would, out of friendship for you, propose what is unfair (*lit.* transgress justice); yet, since this is not the proper way of selling and purchasing, I cannot positively engage to take whatever he may mention: but still, there is no objection to his stating what he thinks fair.—Perhaps I shall be satisfied.

اگرچه من همچو نمیدانم که ایشان بسببِ رفاقتِ شما از انصاف بگذرند اما چون این قاعدهٔ خرید وفروش نیست من نمیتوانم شرط بکنم که هرچه ایشان بفرمایند بگیرم اما هنوز مضایقه نیست که هرچه صلاح بدانند بفرمایند شاید من راضی خواهم شد

**B.**

( ب )

If you ask me, I say at once, that four hundred tumāns is a fair price for the two horses. Let one give, and the other take; and so let the bargain be closed. I have not a single word more to say.

اگر از من میپرسید من یکدفعه میگویم که چهارصد تومان برای هردو اسب خوب قیمتیست یکی بدهد و دیگری بگیرد تا معامله ختم شود من یك کلمهٔ دیگر ندارم که بگویم

**A.**

( ا )

I, likewise, since I referred [the matter] to you, have no more to say; and am willing to pay the four

من هم چون بشما حوالت کردم دیگر هیچ ندارم بگویم و راضیم که چهارصد

hundred tumāns. Let him take it, if he chooses: otherwise, he knows best.

تومان را بدهم اگر میخواهد بگیرد والا
خودش بهتر میداند

DEALER.

(دلّال)

Four hundred tumāns are too little, Sir; but, as I represented to you, that having great occasion for money, I must sell the horses;—there is no help.

چهارصد تومان خیلي کمست صاحب
امّا همچو که عرض کردم چون پول
بسیار ضرور دارم باید اسبها را بفروشم
چاره نیست

A.

(ا)

Very good! now all is right. Tell me, What do you wish—money, or a bill of exchange?—To me it makes no difference.

بسیار خوب حالا همه درستست
بگو که چه میخواهي وجه نقد یا برات
براي من هیچ تفاوت نمیکند

DEALER.

(دلّال)

If you will have the kindness to give me a bill of exchange, payable to my partner at Bombay, I shall be very thankful to you.

اگر شفقت بفرمائید ویك براتي بدهید
که درمنبئي بشریك من داده شود من
از شما بسیار شاکر خواهم شد

A.

(ا)

Certainly; there is no objection. If it would not be too much trouble, come to-morrow morning, or send some person: the bill shall be ready.

البتّه هیچ مضایقه نیست اگر شما را
زیاده زحمت نباشد فرداصبح بیائید
یا کسي را بفرستید برات آماده
خواهد بود

**Dealer.**

May your kindness never be less! I will wait on you myself.

( دلّال )

لطف شما کم نشود بنده خودم خدمت شما میرسم

**A.**

See, in order to buy a couple of horses, what waste of breath is necessary. As for me, I am really fatigued; and if I, who have purchased two such good horses, and anticipate so much pleasure in riding them, say so, what must you say, who have had nothing else, excepting the trouble of talking?

( ا )

به بین که برای دو تا اسب خریدن چه قدر نفس ضرورست من که للحق خسته شده ام واگر منکه دو تا اسب باین خوبی خریده واز سواریشان امید لذتها دارم همچو بگویم شما چه باید بگوئید که بغیر از زحمت گفتگو چیز دیگر نداشتید

**B.**

You make a mistake! My pleasure, in having done you a service, is greater by many degress than the pleasure which you may have from riding those horses. Moreover, my pleasure is more permanent; because it will, at all events, be with me as long as my life lasts: but your pleasure depends upon the lives of the horses, which I trust may be, by many years, shorter than your own life.

( ب )

شما سهو میفرمائید لذت من در اینکه بشما خدمتی کرده ام بمراتب بیشتر است از لذتیکه شما از سواری آن اسبها خواهید داشت بعلاوه لذت من دوامش بیشتر است چرا که آن بهرحال تا عمر من باشد با من خواهد بود لیکن لذت شما متعلق بعمر اسبهاست که امید وارم که بسالهای بسیار از عمر شما کوتاه تر باشد

A.

What you express, proceeds, doubtless, from your extreme kindness towards me: nevertheless, it so appears, that the pleasures of this world—which, after all, must sooner or later entirely perish—stimulate our inclination towards them according to their *nature* and *quality*, and *not* in proportion to the extent of duration which each may have, in comparison with others. And very often we prefer a pleasure which we know to be of short duration, to that which we are certain is by many degrees more lasting; because there is more probability of *excitement* in *that*, than in the *other*. Therefore the value of our pleasures must not be estimated by the time of their continuance; but rather, they ought to be appreciated according to the sensations they create, and the interest we feel in them.

( ۱ )

آنچه شما میفرمائید بی شبهت ناشی
است از کمالِ محبّتِ شما نسبت
ببنده لیکن چنین مینماید که لذّات
این جهانی که بالآخره زودتر یا دیرتر
بالمرّه فانیند بحسبِ طبایع وکیفیاتِ
خود مارا بخودِ شان استمالت میکنند نه
موافقِ دوامیکه هریك نسبت بدیگران
میدارد وبساست که مالذّتی را که
میدانیم اندك دوامست ترجیح
میدهیم برآنکه یقین میداریم که
دوامش بمرّات بیشتر است چراکه
احتمالِ شعف درآن زیاده است از
دیگری پس قدرِ لذّات را از امتدادِ
اوقاتِ دوامشان نباید سنجید بلکه
برآوردِ آنها را بحسبِ نشئات واغراضی
که از آنها احساس میکنیم باید کرد

B.

No doubt! But the tastes and the dispositions of men are of different kinds; and

( ب )

بلاشك امّا مذاق وطباعِ ناس متفاوتند
واین بخودِ شخص بسته است مطلقا که

it entirely depends upon the individual himself which pleasure he would prefer, and in *which* he would take most interest, or imagine there is most excitement: for there is no species of pleasure in this world of which it can be said, "*This*, of itself, contains *such and such* a degree of excitement," or "*that much* gratification," and "*every body* would feel the same amount of satisfaction from the acquisition of it." And hence it is, that we frequently see that a person takes pleasure in a thing in which others have no interest, or to which they even have a dislike: therefore, if I, in serving you, in fact, receive only the same amount of pleasure that you receive from riding those horses, still, the strong probability that "the duration of my pleasure will be greater than that of yours" gives, *to that extent*, a superiority to my pleasure over yours. But if, in reality, my pleasure of itself *be superior* — that is, in a given space of time — I become more gratified from serving you, than you

کدام لذّت را ترجیح دهد ودر کدام
غرض بیشتر داشته باشد یا شعف
زیادت تصوّر کند والّا در دنیا هیچ لذّتی
نیست که از آن توان گفت این بنفسه
متضمّن این مقدار شعف یا آن قدر
تفریحست وهرکس از حصولش همان
مبلغ خوشنودی احساس میکند
واز اینجاست که مکرّر می بینیم که
شخصی از چیزی لذّت میبرد که
دیگران را بدان اعتنائی نیست یا خود از
آن تنفّر دارند پس اگر من در واقع از
خدمت شما همان قدر لذّت یابم وبس
که شما از سواری آن اسبها هنوز ظنّ
غالب براینکه دوام لذّت من بیشتر از
آن شما خواهد بود لذّت مرا بهمان قدر
بر لذّت شما باز مزیّت میدهد امّا اگر
حقیقتاً خود لذّت من زاید باشد
یعنی در آنی محدود من از خدمت شما
زیادت محظوظ گردم که شما از سواری

from riding; then, my pleasure, in point of quantity also, will be more than yours.

آنوقت لذّت من بحسب کمّیّت نیز از
لذّت شما بیشتر خواهد بود

A.

Your arguments all turn upon this, that my horses may die before me; for in that case alone, a portion only of your dogmas can become verified. But, what if the horses should survive me?

(ا)

دلایل شما همه براین برمیگردند که
اسبهای من پیش از من بمیرند چه
تنها درآنصورت بعضی از بیانهای شما
محقّق تواند شد وبس امّا چه اگر
اسبها بعد از من بمانند

B.

You admit, by this statement, that in your life-time there may be a period when the enjoyment of riding those horses may not be attainable by you; as they may perhaps be dead, or some other person may have become their owner. But, as it is not *quite* possible that I should die before *myself*, therefore, whilst I am living, my pleasure can always be attained.

(ب)

شما ازاین گفته مسلّم میدارید که در
حیات شما زمانی تواند بود که شمارا
لذّت سواری آن اسبها ممکن نباشد
چه آنها شاید مرده باشند یا دیگری
مالکشان شده باشد امّا چون ممکن
نیست که بنده پیش از خودم بمیرم
پس تا زنده ام لذّت من همیشه
حاصل تواند بود

A.

This, likewise, depends upon my remaining alive as long as you live: but it

(ا)

این هم منوطست برآنکه بنده تا شما
زنده اید زنده باشم لیکن محتملست

is probable that I may die before you: in that case—as it pleased you to say that your pleasure consisted in serving me—there may be a period also, in your time, when the pleasure of serving me may not be attainable by you.

کِهْ مَنْ پیشْ اَزْ شُما بِمیرَمْ دَرْ آنحالْ
چُونْ شُمارا چِنینْ خُوشْ آمَدْ کِهْ فَرمُودیدْ
کِهْ لَذَّتِ شُما بِخِدْمَتِ بَنْدَهْ بَسْتَهْ بُودْ
دَرْ حَیاتِ شُما نیزْ زَمانی تَوانَدْ شُدْ کِه
لَذَّتِ خِدْمَتِ مَنْ شُمارا مُمْکِنْ نَباشَدْ

B.

( ب )

I was speaking of the pleasure which I had already acquired from serving you; and not of that which, in time to come, I might acquire. And (if it has not escaped your memory) in the beginning of these discussions, when you asked me to excuse you—fearing I might have been vexed at the altercation between you and the horse-dealer—my answer was this:—"You make a mistake! My pleasure, in *having done you a service*, is greater, by many degrees, than the pleasure which you may have in riding those horses!" Therefore it makes no difference to me, whether you die before me, or

مَنْ اَزْ لَذَّتی گُفْتگُو میکَرْدَمْ کِهْ بِنَقْدْ اَزْ
خِدْمَتِ شُما حاصِلْ کَرْدَهْ بُودَمْ نَهْ اَزْ
آنْچِهْ سِپَسْ اَزْ خِدْمَتِ شُما تَحْصیلْ
میتَوانِسْتَمْ کَرْدْ وَاَگَرْ اَزْ خاطِرِ شَریفِ
شُما نَرَفْتَهْ باشَدْ دَرْ اِبْتِدایِ اینْ مُکالَماتْ
چُونْ شُما اَزْ مَنْ عُذْرْ خواسْتیدْ کِهْ مَبادا
اَزْ مُقالاتِ میانِ شُما وُ دَلّالْ مَلُولْ شُدَهْ
بُودَمْ جَوابِ مَنْ اینْ بُودْ کِهْ شُما سَهْو
میفَرْمائیدْ لَذَّتِ مَنْ دَرْ انیکِهْ بِشُما
خِدْمَتی کَرْدَهْ اَمْ بِمَراتِبْ بیشْتَرْ اَسْتْ
اَزْ لَذَّتیکِهْ شُما اَزْ سَوارِیِ آنْ اَسْبْها
خواهیدْ داشْتْ پَسْ هیچْ تَفاوُتْ
نَمیکُنَدْ مَرا کِهْ شُما پیشْ اَزْ مَنْ بِمیریدْ

survive me. The source of my pleasure is attained, and it already exists within me; and I shall take pleasure in the contemplation of it, whilst I live.

یا بعد از من زنده مانید منشاء لذت
من حاصل است و بالفعل در من موجود
و تا زنده ام از خیالش لذت میبرم

A.

( ا )

Suppose that I and my horses should all survive you. In that case, I shall take pleasure in riding them at a time when you are not alive to take any pleasure from your contemplation: the duration of my pleasure, therefore, would then be greater than that of yours.

فرض کن که من و اسبهایم همه بعد از
شما بمانیم در آن حال من از سواري آنها
لذت میبرم در حالتي که شما زنده
نیستید که از خیال خود لذت برید
پس دوام لذت من از آن شما زیادت
خواهد بود

B.

( ب )

Our conversation was on the subject of the enjoyments of *this life:* but when a person is not in *this world,* of what enjoyment can he be deprived?

گفتگوي ما بر سر لذات این عمر بود اما
چون کسي در این دنیا نباشد از چه
لذت محروم تواند بود

A.

( ا )

Of the enjoyment of *salvation,* which is the greatest of all enjoyments! When a person, in this world, is deprived of any pleasure, he may perhaps, at some other time, recover the same, or may find an equivalent which may afford him consolation for the loss of it. But the pleasures of futurity

از لذت رستگاري که معظم لذاتست
چون کسي در این عالم از لذتي محروم
گردد شاید وقتي دیگر همانرا باز یابد لي
که اورا از فوت آن تسلي دهد دریابد
اما لذات اخروي نه همین بي بدل نند

are not only without equivalent, but the loss of them is, to us, a sure sign of *eternal condemnation and misery!*

بَلْکه فَوْتِ آنْها مارا عَلامَتِ فَلاکَتْ
وَعِقابِ اَبَدِیْسْتْ

**B.**

( ب )

I see, again, you are mixing the subjects of the debate; and, with *all this piety*, you are about to confound both worlds together. It is, therefore, better we should here conclude the discussion, *and suffer the heavens and the earth to remain in their respective places.*

بازْمي بْينَمْ کِه خَلْطِ مَبْحَثْ ميکُنيْ وَبا
اينْهَمَه تَقْوىِ ميخواهيْ کِه هَرْدُو عالَمْرا
بَرْهَمْ زَنيْ پَسْ بِهْتَرَسْتْ کِه دَرْ اينْجا خَتْمِ
سُخَنْ کُنيمْ وآسْمانْ وزَميْنْرا بِجايْ خُودْ
بِگُذاريمْ

---

## DIALOGUE VIII.

**A.**

( ا )

Heigh-ho! — The world cannot go round without madmen! Come, take *this*, and read it! and see *what is* written in it. — If this man be not mad, then, no madman can be found on the whole earth!—Read aloud; —read aloud!

هَيْ هَيْ عالَمْ بِيْ ديْوانَگانْ نَميگَرْدَدْ بِيا
اينْرا بِگيرُو بِخوانْ وَبِه بيْنْ کِه دَرْ اينْ
چِهْ نِوِشْتَه اَسْتْ اَگَرْ اينْ مَرْدَکَه[1] ديوانَه
نَباشَدْ پَسْ دَرْ تَمامِ دُنْيا ديْوانَه يافْتْ
نَميْتَوانَدْ شُدْ بُلَنْدْ بِخوانْ بُلَنْدْ بِخوانْ

**B.** (*reads a Letter.*)

( ب رُقْعَه ميْخوانَدْ )

" Sir,

صاحِبْ

" The religious controversies, which passed yesterday between us, have made

مُباحِثاتِ دينِيَّه کِه ديرُوزْ دَرْ ميانِ

---

(1) See the Diminutive Particles, pp. 128, 129, &c. &c.

me very anxious on the subject (*lit.* concerning the affairs) of your future existence.

ماگُذَشْت مَرا دَرْ بابِ اُمُورِ آخِرَتِ شُما
بِسْيار مُشَوَّش گَرْدانِيدَه اَنْد

"It is one of the blessed maxims of our holy religion (and, indeed, philanthropy and humanity also require it), that we should not, by our piety and devotion, seek to obtain the glories and salvation of futurity for ourselves alone; but we ought to endeavour at the same time, by our admonitions and exhortations, to the utmost of our power, to guide likewise unto the abode of salvation those [of our fellow-creatures] who, by the temptations of Satan, having wandered from the right path, are, in the fearful desert of perdition, bewildered in the labyrinth of misery.

يَكِي اَزْ قَوانِينِ مَرْضِيَّهٔ مِلَّتِ شَرِيفِ
ماسْت وَمَرْدُم دُوسْتِي وَآدَمِي مَنِشِي نِيز
اِقْتِضا مِيكُنَنْد كِه ما دَرَجاتْ وَنَجاتِ
عُقْبِيٰ را نَه هَمِين بِتَقْوِي وَرِياضاتْ اَزْ
بَراي خُود تَحْصِيل كُنِيم وَبَس بَلْكِه
بِمَواعِظ وَنَصائِحِ حَتَّيْ الْوُسْع نِيز ساعِي
گَرْدِيم تا آنانِيرا هَم كِه بِوَساوِسِ شَيْطانِي
اَزْ راهِ راسْت بِيرُون رَفْتَه دَرْ بادِيَهٔ
هَوْلْناكِ ضَلالَتْ سَرْگَشْتَه طَرِيقِ شَقاوَتَنْد
بِسَرْمَنْزِلِ نَجاتْ دَلالَتْ كُنِيم

"And it is come down to us, in the authentic Traditions of the Prophet—(but as I suppose you do not understand Arabic, I send you a translation of the prophetic saying in Persian)—it is in the Traditions, that '*all children* are born to be of the

وَدَرْ حَدِيثِ [2] صَحِيحْ وارِدْ شُدَه اَسْت اَمّا
چُون مَظَنَّه شُما عَرَبِي نَمِيدانِيد مَن
تَرْجَمَهٔ حَدِيثِ نَبَوِي را دَرْ فارْسِي اَزْ بَراي
شُما مِيفِرِسْتَم دَرْ حَدِيث اَسْت كِه
اَطْفالْ هَمَه اَزْ پِي مِلَّتِ اِسْلام مُتَوَلَّد

(²) The حَدِيث is a body or code of recognised Traditions of the Prophet Mohammad, considered to have equal validity, in point of authenticity, with the Korân itself. This passage, therefore, cannot be *literally* translated into English; there being, as I presume, no such Traditions among Christians.

religion of Islam; but *their parents* make them 'Jews, Christians, and *Majūs* [Magi or Fire-worshippers]'. I therefore hope, that since the Divine favour has now guided you into the country of the Faithful, the exhortations of *pious people* may conduct you also to the abode of salvation! One of the disinterested counsels of *your well-wisher* is this, *that*, while you are in Persia, you *do not* associate with those cursed Soofies; for they not only go to hell themselves, but, without a doubt, they take their associates (be they willing or not) with them likewise, into the infernal regions!—Oh! how do I tremble for your soul—like the willow-tree before a mighty wind! Free yourself from the chains of the *wicked*; and enter the circle of the *pious* people of Islam, in order that, in company with *them*, you may enter Paradise!—And peace be upon him who follows the true guide!' "

میگردند لیکن پدر و مادر شان ایشانرا
یهود و نصاری و مجوس میگردانند لهذا
امید وار چنانم که چون اکنون توفیق
الهی شمارا ببلاد اسلام هدایت کرده
است مواعظ اهل تقوی نیز شمارا
بسر منزل نجات دلالت کند یکی از
نصایح بی غرض این خیرخواه شمارا
اینست که مادا میکه در ایرانید با این
صوفیهای ملعون معاشرت نکنید که
ایشان نه همین خود تنها بجهنم میرو
ند و پس بلکه مصاحبان خودرا نیز بی
شك خواهی نخواهی با خود باسفل
السافلین خواهند برد آه که چگونه از
برای جانت میلرزم مانند درخت بید
در مقابل بادصرصر از سلسلهٔ اشرار
خودرا آزاد گردان و در حلقهٔ صلحای
اسلام داخل شو تا بمصاحبت ایشان
داخل بهشت گردی والسلام علی من
تبع الهدی

What is this? And who is it from? and what is the meaning of it? It has neither a seal nor signature, whereby one may know who has written it!

اين چه چيز است و از كيست و چه معني دارد نه مهري دارد و نه نشاني كه كسي بداند كي نوشته است

A. (۱)

I will now tell you all about it. I know who has written it.

من حالا همه اش را از برات ميگويم من ميدانم كي نوشته استش

Yesterday, after you went away from this place, I went also, to return a visit of the Minister for Foreign Affairs. While I was sitting in the Minister's apartment (where a number of people were also present), there entered a Mulla (Doctor), apparently about sixty-one or two years of age; but, up to that time, I had never seen so strange a figure! — white turband, white garments, white mantle! — in short, from head to foot, excepting his beard, which by dint of dyeing looked blacker than jet, he resembled snow newly fallen on the mountain-top; — having just come out of the bath, with his head and neck shaven as clean and as smooth as the interior of the pearl-oyster, and with

ديروز چون شما از اينجا رفتيد منهم بباز ديد وزير امور خارجه رفتم چون در مجلس وزير نشسته بودم و جمعي هم حاضر بودند يك ملائي داخل شد ظاهراً بسن شصت و يك و سال اما من تا آنوقت هرگز همچو هيئات غريبي نديده بودم منديل سفيد لباس سفيد رداي سفيد خلاصه از سر تا پا بغير از ريشش كه بضرب رنگ* از شبه سياه تر مي نمود مثل برفي مي مانست كه تازه بر سر كوه افتاده باشد از حمام تازه بيرون آمده با سر و گردني مثل اندرون صدف صاف و پاك تراشيده باريشي

* رنگ literally means "colour"—any colour; but in abstract, it is applied to the leaves of the indigo-plant, which are pounded and made into a paste with which they dye the beard.

a beard most diligently trimmed, and rounded like a half-moon in a state of total eclipse, mocking, as it were, the ordinary course of nature!—his mustaches cut close to his upper lip, and his lips busily employed in muttering ejaculations as he approached;—a very neat staff in one hand, and a rosary of large beads in the other;—and, putting all together, he appeared the very personification of austerity and devotion! As he was entering, the assembly all reverentially stood up; and the apartment itself became filled, at his entry, with the scent of ottar of roses. The Minister ran out, barefooted, as far as the door of the coffee-room, to meet him, and, with the utmost reverence and respect, brought and seated him in the highest place; and himself—respectfully leaving a space between them wide enough for two or three persons—took his seat lower down.

دَرْ كَمالِ دِقَّتْ تيمارْ كَرْدَهْ وَمُدَوَّرْ شَبيهِ
نيمهٔ ماهي مُخالِفِ عادَتِ طَبيعَتْ گوئي
دَرْ خُسوفِ تامْ شارِبَشْ تا مُحاذيِ لَبِ
بالا بمِقْراضْ كَرْدَهْ وَلَبْهاشْ مَشْغولِ
هَمْهَمَهٔ ذِكْر چون نَزْديكْ مِيآمَدْ عَصايِ
بِسْيارْ مُنَقَّحي بِيِكْ دَسْتْ وَتَسْبيحي
بادانَهايِ بُزُرْگْ بِدَسْتِ ديگَرْ وَهَمَه
رُويِهَمْ رَفْتَهْ خُودْ شَخْصِ تَقْويٰ وَرِياضَتْ
مي نِمودْ چون داخِلْ ميشُدْ اَهْلِ مَجْلِسْ
هَمَهْ بِتَواضُعْ بَرْخاسْتَنْدْ وَمَجْلِسِ خُودْ
اَزْ دُخولَشْ اَزْ بويِ عِطْرِ گُلْ پُرْشُدْ وَزير
تا دَرِ قَهْوَهْ خانَهْ[3] بِاسْتِقْبالَشْ پابِرَهْنَهْ
بيرونْ دَويدْ وبِاعْزازْ وَاِحْتِرامِ تَمامْ اُورا
آوَرْدْ و بَرْصَدْرْ نِشانيدْ وَخُودْ بِفاصِلَهٔ
دُوسِهْ كَسْ حَريمي[4] فيمابَيْنْ واگُذاشْتَهْ
پائينْ تَرْ اَزْ اُو نِشَسْتْ

(3) See Note 2. Dialogue V.

(4) حَرِيم, an Arabic word, literally signifies "a sacred place" or "sanctum." It has, besides this, a technical or conventional meaning, in which sense the word has here been employed; namely, "the vacant place" left by a person between himself and another, out of respect to the latter.

**B.**

Ah! how much prolixity you are giving to your story! Say, at once, what was his name. Although, I have an idea that I already know of whom you are speaking.

( ب )

آه شما چه قدر تفصیلش میدهید
یکمرتبه بگو که اسمش چه بود اگرچه
حدس من اینست که میدانم از کي
میگوئي

**A.**

They were addressing him, "The Rev. Hajee Mūlla-Zayn-ūll-Aubedeen."

( ا )

اورا جناب حاجي ملا زین العابدین
خطاب میکردند

**B.**

Now, *you have* relieved me! — It is the same! — Everybody knows him! — He is among the most celebrated of the "Khūshks."

( ب )

حالا فارغم کردي همانست همه کس
اورا میشناسد او از مشاهیر خشکهاست

**A.**

What is "Khūshk"? and what does it mean?

( ا )

خشك چه چیز است وچه معني دارد

**B.**

"Khūshk" means *dry* and *inflexible,* like a *hard stick,* which does not bend in any direction: but in Persian, it is also a metaphor for those *superstitious people* who, in regard to matters of religion, are *injudiciously scrupulous.*—They call *them,* also "Khar-sauleh."

( ب )

خشك یعني یابس وسخت مثل چوب
خشکي که بهیچ طرف خم نمیشود
ودر فارسي کنایت است از مردمان
وسواسي که درباب دین بي بصیرت
محتاط اند وایشا نرا خرصالح نیز
میگویند

**A.**

Be so kind as to explain the meaning of "Khar-

( ا )

معني خرصالح راهم نیز محبت فرموده

sauleh" as well; for *this* word also, like "Khūshk," is new to me (*lit.* has a novelty for me).

بیان نمائید که این لفظ هم مثل خشک از برای من تازگی دارد

**B.**

(ب)

"Khar-sauleh" means a *pious donkey.*—This is also *another* metaphor, in Persian, for a blockhead, in whom real stupidity is combined with the external forms of devotion. That is, his folly is natural and real; but his piety is merely imitation and blind zeal, without discrimination or judgment in those actions which render a man truly pious and acceptable to God. And such persons as these are to be found in every nation, and in all religions: thus, in English, you call them "Bigots."

خرصالح یعنی حمار پرهیزگار واین نیز در فارسی کنایتیست دیگر مرکودنیرا که دروی معنی حماقت باصورت عبادت مجتمع باشد یعنی حمقش ذاتی وواقعی باشد ولیکن صلاحش محض تقلید وتعصب بی امتیاز وبصیرت در افعالی که آدمی را حقیقتاً مورع ومقبول خدا میگرداند وچنین اشخاص در هر قوم وهرملت یافت میشوند چنانچه در انگلیسی شما ایشانرا بیگت میگوئید

**A.**

(ا)

Be he a "Khar-Sauleh," or "Khūshk," or both, whatever you please; nevertheless, he did not appear to me deficient in sense; for many of his proofs and arguments were well weighed, and appeared very plausible.

خرصالح یا خشک یا هردو هرچه بخواهی امّا او بنظر من کم عقل نمی نمود چه دلایل وبراهینش بسیاری سنجیده ومستحسن می نمودند

**B.**

(ب)

Are any of them still remaining in your recollection? What was he saying; and what was he arguing about?

هیچ از آنها در خاطرتان مانده اند چه میگفت واز چه بحث میکرد

A.

The controversy was on the topic of Faith and Religion—whether the Mohammadan or the Christian Religion was the true faith.—I said thus:—"As the followers of Islam already believe that Christ was sent by God, and his religion was true, *this* alone is quite sufficient to enable us Christians to establish the truth of our religion; as there can be no proof better than the voluntary admission of the opponent himself. Therefore it is now for the Mūslems to prove the truth of their religion, and shew that Mohammad was the Apostle of God, and, by His command, the abrogator of the religion of Jesus."

He answered: "The same evidences and proofs which teach us to believe the truth of the Christian faith—that is, the Kūrān and the Tra-

( ۱ )

مُباحثهٔ بَرسرِ دینْ و مَذهَبْ بودْ کِه
آیا مِلّتِ مُحَمّدیْ بَرحَقْ اسْتْ یا دینِ
عیسَوِیْ[5] مَنْ گُفتَمْ کِه چونْ اَهلِ اسْلامْ
مُعْتَقِدَنْدْ بَراینکِه عیسیِ فِرِسْتادهٔ خُدا
بودْ ودینَشْ بَرحَقْ ما عیسَوِیانْ راهَمینْ
بَرِاثْباتِ حَقیقَتِ دینِ مانْ کافیسْتْ
چِهْ هیچْ دَلیلْ اَزاِذْعانِ خودِ خَصْمْ بِهتَرْ
نَمیتَوانَدْ بودْ پَسْ اَکْنونْ اَهْلِ اسْلامْ
راسْتْ کِه راسْتیِ دینِ خودْرا ثابِتْ
کُنَنْدْ وبِنَمایَنْدْ کِه مُحَمّدْ رَسولِ خُدا
وَبِاَمرِ اُوْ ناسِخِ دینِ عیسیِ آمَدْ
جوابْ دادْ کِه هَمانْ دَلایِلْ وبَراهینیْ
کِه حَقیقَتِ دینِ عیسَوِیْ را بِما تَعلیمْ
میکُنَنْدْ یَعْنیْ قُرآنْ واَحادیثْ هَمانْها

---

(5) In these colloquies, the Persian idiom, or manner of quoting, has been preserved; that is, to make a person repeat his own expressions, as well as to repeat one's own expressions, in the very words in which they were uttered when spoken. This peculiarity of Oriental phraseology has been already remarked upon (Note 5. Dialogue 4.); and it has been adhered to in the translation, in many places, even when not consistent with English phraseology. But, as it happens that, in this instance, the personification is quite admissible according to English, it has with propriety been preserved.

ditions—the same also instruct us in the truth of the Mohammadan religion."

نیز مارا از راستیِ دینِ محمّدی
می آگاهانند

I said: "Since we Christians do not consider Mohammad a true prophet (*lit.* true), we cannot believe in the Kūrān and the Traditions; for Mohammad himself is the author of them. Therefore, to prove the truth of the religion of Islam to us, other proofs and testimonies are necessary."

مَن گفتم که چون ما عیسویان محمّد را
صادق نمیدانیم بقرآن واحادیث
معتقد نمیتوانیم بود چه محمّد خود
منشاء آنهاست پس در اثباتِ حقیقت
دینِ اسلام مارا احتیاج ببراهین وادلّهٔ
دیگر است

He answered: "The case is confined to one or the other (*lit.* is not out) of these two positions.—Mohammad was either true or false. If we believe him to have been true, we must believe the whole of his statements; and if otherwise, we must look upon the entire of his sayings and doings with doubt, or even reject them altogether. For it cannot be, that we should consider only a portion to be true, and the other portion false; so as to believe implicitly in some (points), and to reject others as absolute falsehoods. For instance; you cannot expect that the Mūslems should believe Mohammad, when he

جواب گفت که حال ازاین دو بیرون
نیست محمّد یا صادق بود یا کاذب اگر ما
اورا صادق دانیم باید بتمام گفتهای وی
معتقد باشیم واگرنه باید که در تمامی
اقوال وافعالِ او بتشکیک بنگریم یا خود
همه را بکلّی رد کنیم ونمیشود که پارهٔ را
راست دانیم وپارهٔ را دروغ چنانچه در
بعضی یقینِ کامل کنیم وبعضی را چون
کذبِ محض رد نمائیم مثلاً شما متوقّع
نمیتوانید بود که اهلِ اسلام از محمّد
باور کنند وقتی که میگوید عیسی از

says 'Jesus was sent by God,' and to reckon him a liar when he again says that he himself was also sent by God!"

I said, in reply, "The belief of a person, or even a nation, in an event, does not make it *necessary* for others also to believe in it; and this *fact* alone — that the Mūslems believe Mohammad to be true in his testimony with regard to the mission of Jesus—is sufficient to warrant Christians in saying to you (Mohammadans), 'We have no need of any other evidence to prove the mission of the Messiah; for if the use of proofs be to establish *a truth*, you already *believe* and *confess* it.' And since *you* consider Mohammad to be true in this part of his statement, you may also suppose him so in what he may have stated with regard to his own mission: but it is by no means incumbent upon us Christians to agree with you in this belief, as we do not avail ourselves of what your Prophet has stated concerning the mission of the Messiah; and our faith

جانبِ خدا مبعوث بود و اورا کاذب
شمرند چون میگوید که خودش هم نیز
از جانبِ خدا مبعوث بود

من جواب گفتم که اعتقادِ شخصی
یا قومی در امری مستلزمِ اعتقادِ دیگران
نیست و همینکه اهلِ اسلام محمد را در
شهادتش برسالتِ عیسی صادق
میدانند عیسویان را کافیست که
بگویند که مارا احتیاج نیست که
رسالتِ مسیح را بادلّهٔ دیگر از برای شما
ثابت کنیم چه اگر مقصود از حجّت
ثبوتِ حقی باشد شما خود بالفعل بآن
معتقد و مقرّید و چون شما محمد را
در این گفتهٔ او صادق میدانید میتوانید
که او را نیز در آنچه نسبت برسالتِ خود
هم گفته باشد صادق پندارید لیکن
هرگز بر ما مسیحیان لازم نیست که در
این اعتقاد با شما موافقت کنیم چه ما از
آنچه پیغمبرِ شما در بابِ رسالتِ مسیح

in our own religion does not depend upon the testimony *he* bears to the mission of the Messiah."

گفته است بهره نميگيريم واعتقاد مادر
دين خود منوط بگواهي وي در باب
رسالت مسيحا نيست

He said: "It is quite incumbent upon Christians, in their controversies with the Mūslems (especially when they invite the latter to embrace the religion of Jesus), to prove the mission of the Messiah, and the truth and perpetuity of his religion, by arguments and testimonies distinct from what Mohammad has stated in that respect. For, suppose that I have abandoned the faith of Islam, and become a Christian, *because* I consider Mohammad sincere in his testimony respecting the mission of the Messiah; yet, immediately that I become a Christian, it becomes a vital principle of my faith to turn round and consider Mohammad a liar. Hence, I am bound to consider Mohammad *sincere*, in order *to prove him* to be a liar; and to become a Christian through the testimony of a man in whom Christianity itself teaches me to disbelieve!"

او گفت كه بر عيسويان لازمست كه در
مباحثات خود با مسلمانان خاصه
چون ايشانرا بملت عيسوي دعوت
ميكنند رسالت مسيح وحقيقت ودوام
مذهب اورا بدلايل وبراهين ديگر غير
آنچه محمد در آن باب گفته است ثابت
كنند چه فرض كن كه من ترك دين
اسلام كرده عيسوي شدم بسبب اينكه
محمد را در گواهيش نسبت برسالت
مسيحا صادق ميدانم اما بمجرد اينكه
من عيسوي شدم يكي از اصول دين
من ميگردد كه برگردم ومحمد را كاذب
دانم لهذا مرا بايد كه محمد را صادق
دانم تا اورا كاذب ثابت كنم وعيسوي
گردم بگواهي شخصي كه خود عيسويت
مرا تعليم ميكند كه ويرا باور نكنم

**B.**

Aha! I see that the "Akhfash's goat" shakes his head at logic too!

(ب)

هامي بينم كه بزِ اخفش بمنطق هم سري مي جنباند

**A.**

Akhfash's goat?! What does this mean? This expression is also new to me!

(ا)

بزِ اخفش اين چه معني دارد اين عبارت هم از براي من تازه است

**B.**

Akhfash is one of the celebrated grammarians of Arabia. They say, that at the beginning of his studies, whether because he had a bad delivery, or had not as yet acquired any knowledge worthy of being delivered, or both—God knows best!—but, certain it is, that at that time he could not find a pupil to whom he might repeat what he was in the habit of acquiring at public lectures or by private studies, and by this means sharpen his own wits. Now, you must know, that in Eastern Countries, amongst

(ب)

اخفش يكي از مشاهير نحويّهٔ عربست گويند كه در مبادي تحصيلش بسبب آنكه تقريري بد داشت يا آنكه هنوز علمي كه لايق تقرير باشد نميداشت ياهردو خدا بهتر ميداند امّا اين معيّن است كه درآنوقت تلميذي نميتوانست يافت كه آنچه باستفاده[6] يا مطالعه حاصل هميكردي بوي تكرار نمودي وبدين وسيلت فهم خودرا تيز گردانيدي وشما اين را بايد بدانيد كه در

---

(6) استفاده (an Arabic word) is *deriving*, or *seeking*, *benefit*. It may be from any thing. But its conventional meaning (which, in this place, the context of the story also indicates) is, *attending public lectures*. In like manner مطالعه (also an Arabic word) of itself signifies, *looking into*, or *perusal*; but, contrasted with *public lectures*, its conventional meaning is, *private study by oneself*.

the students, the repeating of what they have learned from Public Lecturers, either to each other or to other pupils, is of much greater importance than the listening to the Professor alone. And this Arabic maxim is well known amongst them, viz. "The lecture is equal only to *one word*, but the *repetition* is a thousand." However, the poor Akhfash was for a long time quite unhappy and distressed, and at a loss how to supply the want of a pupil. At length, he (*literally*, his thoughts) hit upon this expedient. He bought a little kid, and taught it while yet young; until, by degrees, it became quite perfect in the part Akhfash expected it to perform, which was this:—As soon as Akhfash opened any book, and placed it before himself, the little goat also instantly bounded on the other side of the book, opposite to Akhfash, and, bending both its fore-legs, rested on its knees, and, fixing both its eyes on the face of the *teacher*, waited with profound attention. Akhfash would begin lecturing; and whenever he came to the end of a preposition,

بِلادِ مَشرِقِیَّه دَرْمِیانِ طُلّابْ تِکْرارِ آنچِهْ
اَزْ مُدَرِّسْ اِقْتِباسْ کَرْدَه اَنْد بایَکْدِیگَرْ
یابِتَلامِیذِ دِیگَرْ اَهَمّ اَسْتْ اَزْ اِصْغا نِمُودَنِ
بِمُدَرِّسْ وَایْن مَثَلِ عَرَبِی دَرْمِیانِشانْ
مَشْهُور اَسْتْ کِهْ اَلدَّرْسُ حَرْفٌ وَالتَّکْرارُ
اَلْفٌ بِهَرْحالْ اَخْفَشِ مِسْکِینْ مُدَّتِی
مَدِیدْ اَفْسُرْدَه وَمَهْمُوم مِیبُودْ وَمُتَحَیِّر
کِهْ تَلافِیِ عَدَمِ تِلْمِیذْرا چِگُونَهْ نِمایَدْ
بِالْآخِرَهْ خَیالَشْ بِایْن تَمْهِیدْ بَرْخُورْدْ
یَکْ بُزْغالَهٔ کُوچِکِی خَرِیدْ وَدَرْکُوچِکِی
آنْرا آمُوخْتْ تا آنْکِهْ بِتَدْرِیجْ دَرْآنچِهْ
اَخْفَشْ اَزْآنْ مَنْظُورْ داشْتْ کِهْ بِعَمَلْ
آوَرَدْ کامِلْ گَرْدِیدْ وَآنْ اِیْنْ بُودْ کِهْ تا
اَخْفَشْ کِتابِیْرا بازْکَرْدِی وَپِیشِ خُودْ
نِهادِی بُزَکْ نِیزْ بِالْفَوْرْ دَرْ آنْطَرَفِ کِتابْ
بَرْجَسْتِی وَدَرْمُقابِلِ اَخْفَشْ هَرْدُو
دَسْتْ خَمْ کَرْدَه بَرْزانُو مِی اِیسْتادْ وَهَرْدُو
چَشْمْ بَرْرُوی مُعَلِّمْ نَصْبْ کَرْدَه دَرْ
کَمالِ تَوَجُّهْ مِیماندْ اَخْفَشْ بِنایِ اِفادَهْ

or to a pause, he would look the goat in the face, and, in a louder tone of voice, ask, "*Didst thou understand?*" when the goat, in reply as it were, nodded its head thrice, as much as to say, "Yes!"

میکرد وهرگاه بآخر مسئله یا بوقفی
رسیدی روببز کردی وبآوازی بلندتر
پرسیدی که فهمیدی وبزگوئی در
جواب سه بار سرخودرا جنبانیدی
وگویا گفتی بلی

Since that time, "Būzé Akhfash" has become a nick-name for those *simpletons* who have no more active brains in their heads than [had] Akhfash's goat, and, like the same animal too, when a conversation is going on upon some intellectual subject, of which they have not the least notion, *shake their heads and beards*, as much as to say, "*We understand also.*"

وبز اخفش ازآن وقت کنایت شده
است مراشخاص ساده لوحی راکه در
سرخود مغزی گرم تراز بز اخفش ندارند
ومانند همان جانور نیز چون در
مناظرات عقلیه که ازآن مطلقا خبری
ندارند بحثی میرود سرو ریشی
میجنبانند یعنی که ماهم می فهمیم

A.

(۱)

You bear too hard upon the Rev. Hajee Mūlla-Zayn-ūll-Aubedeen! —— I fear there is *another* cause, which prompts you to disparage him. *I know* he has not much *friendship for the Soofies.*

شما برجناب حاجی ملازین العابدین
زیادت سخت میگیرید میترسم که
سبب دیگر باعث است شمارا
برتعییب او ومن میدانم که او باصوفیان
دوستی چندان ندارد

**B.**

There *may be something in this, too.* But look, my friend, at my watch! By the Persian way of reckoning, it is now an hour after midnight; and, according to the English, one o'clock in the morning!—Sleep is necessary: so, Good night! and God bless you!

( ب )

شايَدْ كِهْ دَرْاينْ هَمْ چيزْكيْ باشَدْ ليْكِنْ
رَفيقْ بِساعَتِ مَنْ نِگاهْ كُنْ بِحَسابِ
ايْرانِيانْ اَكْنُونْ يكْساعَتْ بَعْدَ اَزْنِصْفِ
شَبَسْتُ وبِقاعِدَهٔ اِنْگِلِيْسانْ ساعَتِ
يَكْ اَزْصُبْحْ خوابْ لازِمَسْتْ شَبِ شُما
خُوشْ بادُ وخُدا حافِظِ شُما

# ALPHABETICAL LIST

OF THE

## ENGLISH AND PERSIAN TERMS OF GRAMMAR.

---

THESE Terms are in common between the Arabian and the Persian Grammarians, and owe their origin entirely to the former language.

---

Ablative. If "*by*" is prefixed to a Noun in English, the corresponding term in Persian is مَفْعُولٌ بِهِ; and if "*from*," or "*with*," مَفْعُولٌ عَنْهُ, or مَفْعُولٌ مَعَهُ, respectively.

Abridgment, مُخْتَصَر.

Abstract Noun, حاصِلِ مَصْدَر.

Accent, تَلَفُّظ. To accent, تَلَفُّظ كَرْدَن.

Accentuation, لَهْجَت, or تَلَفُّظ.

Accusative, مَفْعُول, or مَفْعُولٌ مُطْلَق.

Accusative Case, حالَتِ مَفْعُولِيَّت; *i.e.* a Noun in the Accusative Case.

Action, عَمَل.

Active Participle, اِسْمِ فاعِل; *i.e.* Noun, or name of agent.

Active Verb, فِعْلِ مُتَعَدِّي

Active Voice, فِعْلِ مَعْرُوف

Addition, اِلْحاق

(Active Verb / Active Voice / Addition:) A Verb in the Active Voice, if it be a Transitive Verb, is termed فِعْلِ مُتَعَدِّي; but if only *Active*, in contradistinction to Verb Neuter, it is termed فِعْلِ لازِم.

Additional Letters, or Particles, حُرُوفِ زَوایِدْ, or مُلْحَقَاتْ; also زَوایِدْ.

Adjective, صِفَتْ, or وَصْف.

Adjunct, مُلْحَقْ, or اِلْحَاقْ.

Adverb, حالْ, or ظَرْف.

Adverb of Time, ظَرْفِ زَمانْ.

Adverb of Place, ظَرْفِ مَكانْ.

Affirmative Particle, حَرْفِ اِثْباتْ, حَرْفِ اِيجابْ, حَرْفِ تَأْكِيدْ, or (if to swear "*by*") حَرْفِ قَسَمْ. Plural, حُرُوفْ for all.

Affirmative Form, حالَتِ اِثْباتْ, حالَتِ اِيجابْ, حالَتِ تأكِيدْ.

Affirmative Verb, فِعْلِ مُثْبِتْ.

Affix. The corresponding term to this is never used in the Singular Number; لَواحِقْ, or مُلْحَقاتْ, both being Plural. But they are rendered Singular, by placing يكي اَزْ ("one of") before them; thus, يكي اَزْ لَواحِقْ.

Agent (of a Verb), فاعِلْ.

Agent (of a Participle, &c. &c.) اِسْمْ.

Agreement, مُوافِقَتْ, or تَوافُقْ.

Allegorical } كِنايَتْ, or اِيْهامْ.
Allegory

Alphabet (letters of), حُرُوفِ تَهَجّي.

Ambiguous, اِيْهامْ, or مُوهِمِ اِيْهامْ.

Annotations, حاشِيَهْ. Plural, حَواشي.

Antecedent, مُبْتَدا.

Antithesis, ضِدّ.

Aorist, مُضارِع.

Apposition, بَدَلْ.

Article, حَرْفِ تَعْرِيف, or عَلامَتِ تَعْرِيف.

Auxiliary, رابِطَهْ. Auxiliary Verbs, اَفْعالِ رَوابِطْ.

Copulative (Conjunction), حَرْفِ عَطْف.

Case, حالَتْ, or اِعْرابْ.

Causal Verb, فِعْلِ مَجْبُور.

Clause, فَقَرَهْ, or جُمْلَهْ.

Commentary, تَفْسِير, or شَرْح.

Comparative Particle, حَرْفِ تَشْبِيهْ, or حَرْفِ تَفْضِيلْ.

Comparative Degree, حالَتِ تَفْضِيلْ.

Comparison (Degrees of) مَراتِبِ تَفْضِيلْ.

Composition, تَأْلِيف. Plural, تَأْلِيفاتْ, or عِبارَتْ. Plural, عِباراتْ.

Compound, مُرَكَّبْ.

Concrete (as opposed to "Abstract"); مُقَيَّدْ.

Conditional, شَرْطِيّ.

Conditional Participle, حَرْفِ شَرْطْ.

Conditional Clause, جُمْلَهٔ شَرْطِيَّهْ.

Conjugation, بابْ, or تَصْرِيفْ. To conjugate (a Verb), صَرْفْ كَرْدَنْ.

Conjunction, عَطْفْ.

Connective Particle, حَرْفِ رَبْطْ, or رابِطَهْ. Plural, حُرُوفِ رَوابِطْ or رَوابِطْ.

Consonant (as opposed to Vowel), حَرْفِ مُعَرَبْ. Plural حُرُوفِ مُعَربَهْ.

Consequence, نَتِيجَهْ.

Context, قَرِينَهْ, or فَحْوايِ كَلامْ.

Dative Case, مَفْعُولٌ فِيهْ.

Dedective, اِشْتِقاقْ. Dedected, مُشْتَقْ, or مَأْخُوذْ.

Declension, تَحْوِيلْ, or صَرْفْ.

Declinable (Noun), اِسْمِ مُنْصَرِفْ.

Defective, ناقِصْ.

Defective Verb, فِعْلِ ناقِصْ.

Definite, مَعْرُوفْ, or مَعْرِفَهْ.

Definitive Particle, حَرْفِ تَعْرِيفْ.

Definition, تَعْرِيفْ, or حَدّ.

Demonstrative Pronoun, اِسْمِ اِشارَهْ.

Derivative, مُشْتَقْ, or مَأْخُوذْ.

Descriptive Particle, حَرْفِ تَوْصِيفْ.

Diminutive, تَصْغِيرْ.

Discriminative, تَمْيِيزْ.
Disjunctive Particle, حَرْفِ تَرْدِيدْ, or حَرْفِ اِسْتِثْنا.
Dual, تَثْنِيَه.

Ellipsis, مَفْهُومْ, or مُقَدَّرْ; *i.e.* any thing understood or supposed.
Elocution, مُعانِيْ بَيانْ.
Emphasis, تَأْكِيدْ.
Epithet, لَقَبْ.
Etymology, اَصْلِ لُغَتْ; *i. e.* the original meaning of a word.
Example, مِثالْ. Plural, اَمْثِلَه.
Explanatory Particle, حَرْفِ تَفْسِيرْ.
Expression, كَلامْ.

Feet (in Prosody), تَقْطِيعْ.
Feminine, مُؤَنَّثْ.
First Person, مُتَكَلِّمْ. *Literally,* Speaker.
Future, مُسْتَقْبَلْ.
Form ; Formation ; بِنا, or مَبْنِيْ.

Gender, جِنْسْ (or, Genus).
Generic Noun, اِسْمِ جِنْسْ.
Genitive, اِضافَه. The Noun which is in the Genitive Case is termed مُضافِ اِلَيْه; and that which governs it, مُضافْ.

Gerund, اِسْمِ حالیّه. A kind of Verbal Noun; which governs Cases, like a Verb.

Grammar, نَحْو, or صَرْف ونَحْو.

Idiom, مُحاوَرَت.

| | | |
|---|---|---|
| Idiomatic, | مُوافِقِ مُحاوَرَت | بَروَفْقِ مُحاوَرَت |
| Idiomatically, | مُطابِقِ مُحاوَرَت | اَزقرارِ مُحاوَرَت |

all equally meaning *idiomatically*, or according to *idiom*.

Imperative Mood, اَمْر, or فِعْلِ اَمْر, or صیغَهٔ اَمْر.

Imperfect Tense, ماضِیِ اِسْتِمْراري (for, "*I was* doing"); or, ماضِیِ قَریب (for, "I *have* done").

Imperfect Verb. *See* Defective Verb.

Infinitive Mood, مَصْدَر.

Index, فِهْرِسْت.

Indeclinable, غَیرِمُنْصَرِف.

Indefinite, نَکِرَه.

Indicative Mood, فِعْلِ مُطْلَق, or, simply, فِعْل.

Intransitive Verb, فِعْلِ لازِم.

Interjunction, صَوْت. Plural, اَصْوات, or نِدآء.

Introduction, مُقَدَّمَه.

Irregular, سَماعي. When a Noun, or a Verb, deviates from the ordinary Rules of Grammar, it is termed سَماعِي, i.e. *heard* from the *natives* who have so used it. But if such instances of deviation are few, or uncommon, the *Irregular* is then termed شاذّ, i.e. *rare*.

Masculine Gender, مُذَكَّر.

Metaphor, Metaphorical, Metaphorically, اِسْتِعارَت, اِسْتِعارَتًا; Plural اِسْتِعارات.

Measure, وَزن, Plural اَوزان; or (in Poetry) بَحر, Plural بُحُور.

Multitude, Noun of, اِسمِ جَمْع.

Name, Proper, عَلَم. (Also Appellation.)

Negation, نَفْي. Negatived, مَنْفِيّ.

Negative Particle, حَرفِ نَفْي.

Negative Form, مَنْفِيّ, or حالَتِ نَفْي.

Nominative, فاعِلْ.

Nominative Case, حالَتِ فاعِلِيَّتْ.

Neuter Gender. The Arabs have but two Genders, Masculine and Feminine; to either of which only a Noun may belong, according to its *sex*, or other grammatical circumstances.

Neuter Verb, فِعْلِ لازِمْ.

Noun, اِسم.

Noun Adjective, صِفَتْ.

Noun Derivative, اِسمِ مُشْتَق, or مَأخُوذ.

Noun Primitive, اِسْمِ جامِد, or اَصْلِيّ.

Noun Substantive (as distinguished from Adjective), اِسْمِ ذاتْ.

Noun of Time, اِسْمِ زَمانْ.

Noun of Place, اسمِ مَكانْ.

Noun of Instrument, اِسْمِ آلَتْ.

Object (as governed), مَعْمُولْ.

Object (as intended), مَطْلَبْ.

Objective Case, حالَتِ مَعْمُولِيَّت. A Noun governed by another, or by a Verb. It may be in the Accusative, Dative, Ablative, or Vocative Case, &c. &c.; for any of which, see under their respective heads.

Oblique Cases. *See* Objective Case.

Original (meaning of a word), دَرْاَصْل, or اَصْلِيّ.

Optative Mood, فِعْلِ تَمَنّي, or فِعْلِ دُعائي.

Optional, اِخْتِياري.

Ordinal Number, اِسمِ عَدَدْ.

Paragraph, فَقَرَتْ.

Paraphrase, حاصِلِ مَعْنِي.

Parenthesis, مُعْتَرَضَهْ, or (for a whole sentence) جُمْلَهٔ مُعْتَرَضَهْ.

Particle, حَرْفْ. Plural, حُرُوفْ.

Participle. See *Active*, and *Passive*.

Passive Voice, فِعْلِ مَجْهُولْ.

Passive Participle, اِسْمِ مَفْعُولْ.

Past Tense, ماضِيْ, or فِعْلِ ماضِيْ.

Perfect Tense, ماضِيِ مُطْلَقْ.

Perfect Verb, فِعْلِ تامّ; *i.e.* a Verb having all the Regular Tenses and Moods. It is used in contradistinction to an Imperfect or Defective Verb.— فِعْلِ ناقِصْ.

Pluperfect Tense, ماضيِ بَعيْدْ.

Plural, جَمْعْ.

Potential, مُمْكِنْ. Potential Mood, فِعْلِ مُمْكِنْ.

Predicate (in Logic), تالِيْ; (in Grammar), خَبَرْ.

Poetry, نَظْمْ, or شِعْرْ.

Preface, دِيْباچِه. (This *term* is purely Persian.)

Prefix, حَرْفِ وَصْلِ. Plural, حُرُوفْ.

Preposition, حَرْفِ جَرّ, or اَداتْ. Plural, حُرُوفِ جارَّهْ.

Pronoun, ضَمِيرْ. Plural, ضَمايِرْ.

Pronoun, Separate or Personal, ضَمِيرِ مُنْفَصِلْ. Plural, ضَمايِرِ مُنْفَصَلَهْ.

Pronoun, Adjunct or Affix, ضَمِيرِ مُتَّصِلْ. Plural, ضَمايِرِ مُتَّصَلَهْ.

Pronoun, Relative, مَوْصُولْ. Plural, مَوْصُولاتْ.

Pronoun, Demonstrative, اِسْمِ اِشارَهْ. Plural, اَسْماءِ اِشاراتْ.

Pronoun, Reciprocal, ضَمِيرِ مُشْتَرَكْ. Plural, ضَمايِرِ مُشْتَرَكَهْ.

Pronoun, Interrogative, اِسْمِ اِسْتِفْهامْ. Plural, اَسْماءِ اِسْتِفْهامْ.

Pronoun, Possessive, ضَمِيرِ مُضافٌ اِلَيْهْ.

Pronunciation, تَلَفُّظْ, or تَكَلُّمْ.

Prose (as distinguished from Poetry), نَثْر.

Proposition (in Grammar) جُمْلَه: (in Logic or Mathematics) شَكْل.

Prosody, عَرُوض.

Qualified Noun, اِسْمِ مَوْصُوف, or مَوْصُوف.

Quality (or the power of any one Part of Speech grammatically), عَمَل, or خاصِيَّت.

Quantity, وَزْن, or مِيزان. Plural, اَوْزان, or مَوازِين.

Quiescent, ساكِن, خَفِيفَه, or مُخَفَّف.

Quadriliteral, رُباعِي.

Quadriliteral Noun, اِسْمِ رُباعِي.

Quadriliteral Verb, فِعْلِ رُباعِي مُجَرَّد.

Reflective Verb, فِعْلِ مُتَعَدِّي بِنَفْس.

Regular, قِياسِي.

Relation (as between Parts of Speech), نِسْبَت, or تَعَلُّق.

Relative (as subjoined to Antecedent), خَبَر.

Rhyme or Rhythm, قافِيَه, or سَجْع.

Root, اَصْل, مَنْشَأ, or مَصْدَر.

Sentence, كَلام, جُمْلَه, or فَقَرَه.

Sequel, نَتِيجَه, حاصِلِ كَلام, or فائِدَهٔ بَيان.

Simple, مُطْلَق, مُفْرَد, سادَه, or بَسِيط.

Simple Noun, اِسْمِ مُفْرَدْ, or بَسْيطْ.

Simple Adjective, صِفَتِ مُفْرَدْ, or وَصْفِ مُفْرَدْ, &c. &c.

Plural, صِفات مُفْرَدَهْ, اَوْصافِ مُفْرَدَهْ, or اَوْصافِ بَسْيطَهْ.

Simple Verb, فِعْلِ مُطْلَق, or فِعْلِ بِلاتَقْيِيدْ, (as opposed to Subjunctive).

Simple Peterite, ماضِيِ مُطْلَق.

Singular (Number), واحِدْ, or مُفْرَدْ, or صِيْغَهٔ واحِدْ, &c. &c.

Speech (the Parts of), جُزْءِ كَلامْ. Plural, اَجْزآءِ كَلامْ.

Speech (the Faculty or Power of), نُطْق, or قُوَّهٔ ناطِقَهْ.

Speech (an Oration), خُطْبَهْ, or خِطابْ.

Style (of Writing), عِبارَتْ. Title (Appellation), لَقَبْ.

Subject (of a Predicate), مُقَدَّم.

Subject (of a Discourse), مَضْمُونْ, or مَطْلَبْ.

Subjunctive Verb, or Mood, فِعْلِ مَشْرُوطْ, or فِعْلِ مُقَيَّدْ, if the Verb be Conditional; فِعْلِ مَظْنُونْ, if Suppositive; and فِعْلِ مَشْكُوكْ, if Doubtful.

Superlative Degree, تَفْضِيلْ, مَرْتَبَهٔ تَفْضِيلْ, or رُتْبَهٔ تَفْضِيلْ. Plural, مَراتِبْ, &c. &c.

Supplement, لاحِق. Plural, لَواحِق, or مُلْحَقاتْ; also خاتِمَهْ.

Suppositive, مَظْنُونْ.

Syntax, نَحْو, or اِعْرابُ وبِنا.

Term, اِصْطِلاحْ. Plural, اِصْطِلاحاتْ.

Terms of Grammar, اِصْطِلاحاتِ نَحْوِيَّهٔ وَصَرْفِيَّهٔ.

Terms of Logic, اِصْطِلاحاتِ مَنْطِقِيَّه.

Terms of Mathematics, اِصْطِلاحاتِ رِياضِيَّهْ.

Terms of Philosophy, اِصْطِلاحاتِ فَلْسَفَهْ, or حِكْمَتْ. Of Philosophers, اِصْطِلاحاتِ حُكَماء, or فَلاسِفَهْ.

Terms Technical (in general), اِصْطِلاحاتِ مَخْصُوصَهْ.

Text (as opposed to Commentary), مَتْن.

Title (of a book), اِسْمِ كِتابْ. Proper Name, عَلَمْ. Appellation, لَقَبْ. Plural, اَلْقابْ.

Title-page, سَرْلَوحْ, or سَرْصَفْحَهْ.

Triliteral, ثُلاثِيْ, or ثُلاثِيْ مُجَرَّدْ.

Triliteral Verb, فِعْلِ ثُلاثِيْ مُجَرَّدْ. Noun, اِسْمِ ثُلاثِيْ مُجَرَّدْ. Root, مَصْدَرِ ثُلاثِيْ مُجَرَّدْ.

Typical (Emblematical), دالّ, نِشانَهْ, عَلامَتْ.

Typography (Printing), طَبْع, چاپْ, باسْمَهْ.

Vacation (Holidays), تَعْطِيلْ, or اَيّامِ تَعْطِيلْ.

Vague, مُبْهَمْ.

Variable (Declinable), مُنْصَرِفْ.

Variation (of Cases), تَغْيِيراتِ اِعْرابِيْ.

Verb, فِعْلْ.

Verbal Noun (the Infinitive), مَصْدَرْ.

**Verbatim**, لَفْظاً بِلَفْظ.

**Verse**, شِعْر, or نَظْم.

**Version** (Translation), تَرْجَمَة.

**Vocabulary** (Dictionary), لُغَت, or كِتابِ لُغَت.

**Vocative** (a Noun in Vocative Case), مُنادآء.

**Vocative Particle**, حَرْفِ نِدآء.

**Voice.** *See* Active and Passive.

**Volume** (a Book), جِلْد, or كِتابْ.

**Vowel** (Points), اِعْراب, or اِعْرابات.

**Vulgar** (People), عَوامْ, or عَوامُ النّاس.

**Vulgar** (Diction), گُفتارِ عَوامْ, or مُحاوِراتِ عَوامْ.

**Unambiguous**, نامُبْهَم, or واضِح.

**Unaspirated** (*h*, or *ه*), هآءِ خَفِيفَه, or هآءِ ساكِنَه; *i.e.* the quiescent *ه*.

**Unchangeable.** *See* Indeclinable.

**Uncommon** (rarely used), نادِر, or شاذّ.

**Unconnected** (not coherent), as applied to Composition, نامَرْبُوط, (which also means, "Nonsense.")

**Unity** (between the Parts of Speech, or in composition), تَوافُق, or رَبْط.

**United** (Grammatically), مُتَّصِل, or مُنْظَم. (*See* Pronoun.)

**Utterance**, تَلَفُّظ.

**Word**, لَفْظ, or كَلَمَة.

# APPENDIX.

## ON THE USE OF THE ARABIC WORDS.

The Persian of the present day being so much mixed with Arabic words, I think it almost indispensable for a student of the former language to acquire some slight knowledge of the rudiments of the latter.

Independently of quotations, and whole Arabic phrases, with which the Persian writings abound, there is scarcely a Persian line, or sentence, which does not contain some words, either purely Arabic, or of Arabian origin. Notwithstanding this great influx of foreign words, the genius of the Persian language remains unchanged. The *aliens*, however, are all subjected to the same laws, and are governed by the same rules of Grammar, as if they were purely native words. They may be considered as so many abstract words, denoting certain, but *indefinite*, meanings: if they are used as Nouns, *they are declined, in all respects*, the same as the Persian Nouns; and if as Verbs, they must be conjugated in the same manner. In the instances of the former kind, the Arabic words admit of the same grammatical Particles being *affixed* or *prefixed* to them, with which the Persian Nouns are uniformly declined; and in those of the latter, they are simply prefixed (without any alteration) to all the Persons, in both Numbers, throughout the Tenses and Moods of one of the Auxiliary Persian Verbs, both in the Active and the Passive Voices.*

* See the Persian Compound Verbs, p. 85.

The Arabic words, thus used by the Persians, do chiefly belong to some one or other of the following original classes.

## THE MOST COMMON FORMS OF THE MASDAR مَصْدَرْ, OR VERBAL NOUNS OF TRILITERAL RADICAL VERBS,

## مَصَادِرِ اَفْعَالِ ثُلَاثِي مُجَرَّدْ.

| SIGNIFICATION. | EXAMPLES. | MEASURES. | |
|---|---|---|---|
| Slaughter, | قَتْلْ | فَعْلْ | 1. |
| Vice, | فِسْقْ | فِعْلْ | 2. |
| Employment, | شُغْلْ | فُعْلْ | 3. |
| Mercy, | رَحْمَةْ | فَعْلَةْ | 4. |
| Science, | حِكْمَةْ | فِعْلَةْ | 5. |
| Power, | قُدْرَةْ | فُعْلَةْ | 6. |
| Search, | طَلَبْ | فَعَلْ | 7. |
| Falsehood, | كَذِبْ | فَعِلْ | 8. |
| Conquest, | غَلَبَةْ | فَعَلَةْ | 9. |
| Theft, | سَرِقَةْ | فَعِلَةْ | 10. |
| Childhood, | صِغَرْ | فِعَلْ | 11. |
| Guidance, | هُدَيٰ | فُعَلْ | 12. |
| Going, | ذَهَابْ | فَعَالْ | 13. |
| Standing, | قِيَامْ | فِعَالْ | 14. |

| SIGNIFICATION. | EXAMPLES. | MEASURES. | |
|---|---|---|---|
| Asking, | سُؤَالْ | فُعَالْ | 15. |
| Hating, | عَدَاوَةْ | فَعَالَةْ | 16. |
| Worshipping, | عِبَادَةْ | فِعَالَةْ | 17. |
| Bravery, | شُجَاعَةْ | فُعَالَةْ | 18. |
| Directing, | دَلِيلْ | فَعِيلْ | 19. |
| Entering, | دُخُولْ | فُعُولْ | 20. |
| Accepting, | قَبُولْ | فَعُولْ | 21. |
| Plundering, | غَنِيمَةْ | فَعِيلَةْ | 22. |
| Cold, | بُرُودَةْ | فُعُولَةْ | 23. |
| Necessity, | ضَرُورَةْ | فَعُولَةْ | 24. |
| Intention, | مَقْصَدْ | مَفْعَلْ | 25. |
| Gaming, | مَيْسِرْ | مَفْعِلْ | 26. |
| Station, | مَرْتَبَةْ | مَفْعَلَةْ | 27. |
| Praising, | مَحْمِدَةْ | مَفْعِلَةْ | 28. |
| Claiming, | دَعْوَي | فَعْلَي | 29. |
| Mentioning, | ذِكْرَي | فِعْلَي | 30. |
| Congratulation, | بُشْرَي | فُعْلَي | 31. |
| Concealing, | كِتْمَانْ | فَعْلَانْ | 32. |
| Disappointment, | حِرْمَانْ | فِعْلَانْ | 33. |

| SIGNIFICATION. | EXAMPLES. | MEASURES. | |
|---|---|---|---|
| Pardoning, | غُفْرَانْ | فُعْلَانْ | 34. |
| Palpitation, | خَفَقَانْ | فَعَلَانْ | 35. |
| Disliking, | كَرَاهِيَةْ | فَعَالِيَةْ | 36. |
| Measurement, | مِقْدَارْ | مِفْعَالْ | 37. |
| Distraction of mind, | مَفْتُونْ | مَفْعُولْ | 38. |
| Usage, | مَرْسُومَةْ | مَفْعُولَةْ | 39. |
| Safety, | عَافِيَةْ | فَاعِلَةْ | 40. |
| Dominion, | مَمْلَكَةْ | مَفْعَلَةْ | 41. |
| Sleeping at mid-day, | قَيْلُولَةْ | فَعْلُولَةْ | 42. |
| Peril, | تَهْلُكَةْ | تَفْعُلَةْ | 43. |
| Travelling, | تِمْشَاءْ | تِفْعَالْ | 44. |
| Extreme playfulness, | تَلْعَابْ | تَفْعَالْ | 45. |
| Excessive cutting, | تِقِطَّاعْ | تِفِعَّالْ | 46. |
| Enormous falsehood, | كِذَّابْ | فِعَّالْ | 47. |
| Great enmity, | بَغْضَاءْ | فَعْلَاءْ | 48. |

INCREASED TRILITERALS, ثُلَاثِيِّ مَزِيدْ.

| | | | |
|---|---|---|---|
| Expulsion, | اِخْرَاجْ | اِفْعَالْ | 1. |
| Arrangement, | تَرْتِيبْ | تَفْعِيلْ | 2. |

| SIGNIFICATION. | EXAMPLES. | MEASURES. | |
|---|---|---|---|
| Learning by degrees, | تَعَلُّمْ | تَفَعُّلْ | 3. |
| Pretending ignorance, | تَجَاهُلْ | تَفَاعُلْ | 4. |
| War, or Reciprocal slaughter, | مُقَاتَلَةْ | مُفَاعَلَةْ | 5. |
| Avoiding, | اِجْتِنَابْ | اِفْتِعَالْ | 6. |
| Asking assistance, | اِسْتِنْصَارْ | اِسْتِفْعَالْ | 7. |
| Being broken, or fatigued, | اِنْكِسَارْ | اِنْفِعَالْ | 8. |
| Travelling with haste, | اِجْلِوَّاذْ | اِفْعِوَّالْ | 9. |
| Wearing a rough garment, | اِخْشِيْشَانْ | اِفْعِيْعَالْ | 10. |
| Excessive redness, | اِحْمِرَارْ | اِفْعِلَالْ | 11. |
| Excessive blackness, | اِدْهِيْمَامْ | اِفْعِيْلَالْ | 12. |
| Causing to put on a sheet, | جَلْبَبَهْ | فَعْلَلَهْ | 13. |
| Deputing, | صَيْطَرَةْ | فَيْعَلَهْ | 14. |
| Causing to put on foot-socks, | جَوْرَبَةْ | فَوْعَلَةْ | 15. |
| Causing to put on a hat, | قَلْنَسَهْ | فَعْنَلَةْ | 16. |
| Pruning, | شَرْيَفَةْ | فَعْيَلَةْ | 17. |
| Causing to put on drawers, | سَرْوَلَةْ | فَعْوَلَةْ | 18. |
| Causing to put on a cap, | قَلْسَاةْ | فَعْلَاةْ | 19. |
| Putting on a sheet, | تَجَلْبُبْ | تَفَعْلُلْ | 20. |
| Putting on a garment without sleeves, | تَخَيْعُلْ | تَفَيْعُلْ | 21. |

| SIGNIFICATION. | EXAMPLES. | MEASURES. | |
|---|---|---|---|
| Putting on stockings, | تَجَوْرُب | تَفَوْعُل | 22. |
| Putting on a hat, | تَقَلْنُس | تَفَعْنُل | 23. |
| Being pruned, | تَشَرْيُف | تَفَيْعُل | 24. |
| Putting on drawers, | تَسَرْوُل | تَفَعْوُل | 25. |
| Going backwards, | اِقْعِنْسَاسْ | اِفْعِنْلَالْ | 26. |
| Reposing on the back, | اِسْلِنْقَاءْ | اِفْعِنْلَاءْ | 27. |

## VERBAL NOUNS OF RADICAL AND INCREASED QUADRILITERAL VERBS, مَصَادِرِ اَفْعَالِ رُبَاعِيْ مُجَرَّدْ وَمَزِيْدْ.

| | | | |
|---|---|---|---|
| Exciting, | بَعْثَرَةْ | فَعْلَلَةْ | 1. |
| Putting on a vest, | تَسَرْبُلْ | تَفَعْلُلْ | 2. |
| Assembly, | اِحْرِنْجَامْ | اِفْعِنْلَالْ | 3. |
| Shrinking from fear, | اِقْشِعْرَارْ | اِفْعِلَّالْ | 4. |

Forms and Examples of Attributives, or Participle Actives, as derived from the Infinitives of Triliteral Radical Verbs, in order to denote Excess; and are termed اَسْمَاءْ مُبَالِغَهْ, *i. e.* Nouns of *Excess*. (The Singular اِسْمِ مُبَالِغَهْ, Noun of Excess.)

| | | | |
|---|---|---|---|
| Extremely cautious, | حَذِرْ | فَعِلْ | 1. |
| Extremely knowing or learned, | عَلِيْم | فَعِيْل | 2. |
| A great striker, | ضَرُوْب | فَعُوْل | 3. |

| SIGNIFICATION. | EXAMPLES. | MEASURES. | |
|---|---|---|---|
| A great discriminator, | فاروق | فاعول | 4. |
| A great cutter, | قُطّاعْ | فُعّالْ | 5. |
| A great speaker, | مِنْطَق | مِفْعَل | 6. |
| A great warrior, | مِحْرابْ | مِفْعالْ | 7. |
| A great deceiver, | مِخْدِيع | مِفْعِيلْ | 8. |
| A great drinker, | شِرِّيْب | فِعِّيلْ | 9. |
| A great changer, | صَرّافْ | فَعّالْ | 10. |
| A great laugher, | ضُحَكَة | فُعَلَة | 11. |
| A great alterer, or changer, | قُلَّبْ | فُعَّلْ | 12. |
| Extremely fearful, | هَيِّبْ | فَعِّلْ | 13. |
| Extremely silent, | سُكَّيْت | فُعَّيلْ | 14. |
| A great fomenter of disturbance, | شِغَبّ | فِعَلّ | 15. |
| Extremely impatient, | جُزاعْ | فُعالْ | 16. |
| A great eater, | سِرْواطْ | فِعْوالْ | 17. |
| Extremely timorous, | هَيْبانْ | فَعْلانْ | 18. |
| A great talker, | تِقْوَلَة | تِفْعَلَة | 19. |
| A great sleeper, | يَرْقُود | يَفْعُول | 20. |

It is proper to remark, that of the Twenty Measures which have been noticed and exemplified here, there are only three or four which can be considered as of frequent occurrence, either in the Persian or Arabic language: and of these, in a peculiar degree, the measures فَعّال, فَعُول, and فَعِيل are worthy to be impressed upon the memory with care.

In addition to the examples offered in the Table, the following may also be remembered, as mostly occurring in the Persian language:—

عَلّام Very wise, or *omniscient* (an attribute of the Deity).

خَلّاق A great *Creator* (also an attribute of the Deity).

رَزّاق An *universal provider*.

غَفُور *Very forgiving*.

بَصِير *Very discerning*.

رَحِيم *Most merciful*;

رَحمان (or, as it is generally written, رَحْمٰن) *Most compassionate*:

سَمِيع *All-hearing*:

خَبِير *Universally-informed*: (all attributes of the Deity.)

صَبُور Very patient.

ظَلُوم Very unjust.

شَكُور Very grateful.

جَهُول Very ignorant.

نَمّام A great calumniator, or tale-bearer.

Forms and Examples of Irregular Participle Passives, as derived from the Infinitives of Triliteral Radical Verbs, and employed as Attributives, having a Transitive مُتَعَدّي signification:—

| SIGNIFICATION. | EXAMPLES. | MEASURES. | |
|---|---|---|---|
| Wounded, | جَرِيح | فَعِيل | 1. |
| Accepted, | قَبُول | فَعُول | 2. |

| SIGNIFICATION. | EXAMPLES. | MEASURES. | |
|---|---|---|---|
| Sacrificed, or having the throat cut, | ذِبْح | فِعْل | 3. |
| Seized, or possessed, | قَبْض | فَعْل | 4. |
| Concealed, | كاتِم | فاعِل | 5. |
| Broken, | حُطام | فُعال | 6. |
| Cut, or filed, | قُراضَه | فُعالَه | 7. |
| Drunk at a single draught, | جُرْعَه | فُعْلَه | 8. |

In addition to the above forms, it may be observed, also, that the following Participle Passives are of most frequent occurrence, as Attributives, in the Persian language.

شَهير, synonymous to مَشْهور, *celebrated.*

حَبيب, for مَحْبوب, *beloved.*

ذَميم, for مَذْموم, *blamed,* or *reproached.*

طَريد, for مَطْرود, *banished,* or *expelled.*

رَجيم, for مَرْجوم, *stoned to death,* or *detested* (an appellation of the devil).

قَتيل, for مَقْتول, *slain.*

ذَبيح, for مَذْبوح, *sacrificed.*

قَبول, for مَقْبول, *accepted.*

رَسول, a *messenger,* or *prophet,* but literally *sent,* which invariably supplies the place of the Regular Participle, مَرْسول.

Forms and Examples of ATTRIBUTIVES, or DERIVATIVE NOUNS, as flowing from the Infinitives of Triliteral Radical Verbs, which are in themselves uniformly Neuter and Intransitive, or occasionally admit of a Neuter and Intransitive Acceptation; and are termed, صِفاتِ مُشَبَّهَه *Collectively*, or صِفَتِ مُشَبَّهَه *Singly*; *i.e.* Adjectives resembling, or having the same import as Participles.

| SIGNIFICATION. | EXAMPLES. | MEASURES. | |
|---|---|---|---|
| Generous, or noble, | كَرِيْم | فَعِيْل | 1. |
| Jealous, or high-minded, | غَيُوْر | فَعُوْل | 2. |
| Of deep-red colour, | اَحْمَر | اَفْعَل | 3. |
| Resplendent, or shining, | بَرّاق | فَعّال | 4. |
| Chief (a term applied to the descendants of the Prophet Mohammad), | سَيِّد | فَيْعِل | 5. |
| Virtuous, good, or beautiful, | حَسَن | فَعَل | 6. |
| Joyful, or glad, | فَرِح | فَعِل | 7. |
| Thirsty, or dry, | عَطْشان | فَعْلان | 8. |
| Polluted, or impure, | جُنُب | فُعُل | 9. |
| Yellow, or bile, | صَفْرآء | فَعْلآء | 10. |
| Thirsty (*feminine*), | عَطْشَي | فَعْلَي | 11. |
| A shepherd cruel to his flock, | حُطَم | فُعَل | 12. |
| Aged, or great, | كابِر | فاعِل | 13. |
| Brave, or enterprising, | شُجاع | فُعال | 14. |

| SIGNIFICATION. | EXAMPLES. | MEASURES. | |
|---|---|---|---|
| Difficult, or arduous, | صَعْبٌ | فَعْلٌ | 15. |
| Empty, or cipher, | صِفْرٌ | فِعْلٌ | 16. |
| Hard, or solid, | صُلْبٌ | فُعْلٌ | 17. |
| Intelligent, or sagacious, | نَدُسٌ | فَعُلٌ | 18. |
| Cowardly, or timorous, | جَبانٌ | فَعالٌ | 19. |
| Noble, chief, or aged, | كُبّارٌ | فُعّالٌ | 20. |
| Pregnant (applied to rational beings only), | حُبْلَي | فُعْلَي | 21. |
| Naked, or stripped, | عُرْيانٌ | فُعْلانٌ | 22. |
| Starting (generally, an ass) at one's own shadow, | حَيَدَي | فَعَلَي | 23. |
| A white-haired camel, | هِجانٌ | فِعالٌ | 24. |
| Living (an animal), | حَيَوانٌ | فَعَلانٌ | 25. |
| Mean or contemptible, | حَيْقَرٌ | فَيْعَلٌ | 26. |
| Ingenious, or clever, | لَوْذَعٌ | فَوْعَلٌ | 27. |
| Eloquent, | بِلَغٌ | فِعَلٌ | 28. |
| A pregnant camel, in the tenth month of gestation, | عُشَرآءُ | فُعَلآءُ | 29. |
| Fat, stout, or bulky, | بِلِزٌ | فِعِلٌ | 30. |

The Student will observe, that although the above thirty measures are of frequent and promiscuous occurrence in Arabic, yet all of them are not commonly met with in the

Persian language. Those صِفاتِ مُشَبَّهَة which are of *most* frequent occurrence in the Arabic language, and are *chiefly* used by the Persians, are the following measures; viz. فَعَل , فَعِيل , فَعْل , فَعُول , فُعال , فَعال , فِعْل , فُعُول , and أَفْعَل ; as,

| | | | |
|---|---|---|---|
| حَسَن | Good, or beautiful. | جَبان | Fearful, or cowardly. |
| شَرِيف | Noble, or honourable. | خَشِن | Rough, coarse, or harsh. |
| صَعْب | Hard, or difficult. | جُنُب | Impure, or polluted |
| ظَلُوم | Unjust, or tyrannical. | غَيُور | Jealous, or high-minded. |
| شُجاع | Heroic, or brave. | أَبْلَه, أَحْمَق | Foolish, idiotic, or simpleton. |

## NOUN OF SUPERIORITY, اِسْمِ تَفْضِيل.

The measures of this Noun, in Arabic, is, for the masculine, أَفْعَل; and for the feminine, فُعْلَي ; as, أَكْبَر , or أَعْظَم , both meaning "greater," or "greatest"; and كُبْرَي , or عُظْمَي , the same.

In Arabic, this Noun supplies the place of the Comparative, and Superlative, in other languages. Although the Persians have a proper Comparative and Superlative in their own language, yet they not unfrequently employ the Arabic forms also.

## NOUNS OF INSTRUMENT, اِسْم, or اَسْمآءِ آلَتْ.

These Nouns have three Measures, مِفْعَلْ, مِفْعَلَةْ, and مِفْعالْ; as,

مِحْلَبْ A milk-pail, or the *instrument* of milking.

مِكْنَسَةْ A broom, or the *instrument* of sweeping.

But the measure مِفْعالْ is of the most frequent occurrence, and is very extensively used in Persian; as,

مِفْتاحْ A key, or the *instrument* of opening.

مِيزانْ A scale, or the *instrument* of weighing.

مِكْيالْ A measure of capacity, or the *instrument* of measuring.

مِقْراضْ Scissars, or the *instrument* of cutting.

مِنْشارْ A saw, or the *instrument* of dividing.

مِصْباحْ A lamp, or the *instrument* of giving light.

مِعْيارْ A standard, or the *instrument* of proving money.

مِنْقارْ A bird's beak, or the *instrument* of pecking.

&c. &c. &c.

---

## NOUNS OF TIME AND PLACE, اِسْم, or اَسْمآءِ زَمانْ وَمَكانْ.

These have two Measures, مَفْعَلْ and مَفْعِلْ; both of which are of frequent occurrence in the Persian language; as, مَقْتَلْ "the time and place of slaughter"; مَوْعِدْ "the time and place of promise," &c. &c. Although these Nouns in Arabic often imply both *time* and *place*, yet, when used in Persian, the *place* alone is intended by them; as,

| | | | |
|---|---|---|---|
| مَسْجِد | A mosque, or the *place* of worship. | مَسْكَن | A habitation, or the *place* of dwelling. |
| مَنْزِل | A station, or the *place* of resting. | مَكْتَب | A school, library, or the *place* of keeping books. |
| مَشْرِق | The East } or the *places* where the sun rises and sets. | مَعْبَر | A ford, or the *place* of crossing a river. |
| مَغْرِب | The West } | | |

&c. &c. &c.

There are a number of Nouns in Arabic, which, although destitute of a Feminine *sense* or termination, are applied as of the Feminine Gender, and therefore denominated, in Arabic Grammar, مُؤَنَّثَاتِ سَمَاعِيَّة, or IRREGULAR FEMININES. Many of them are of frequent occurrence in Persian; but there they are merely treated as Substantives, without any regard to their Gender. The following are some of them:—

| SIGNIFICATION. | NOUNS. | | SIGNIFICATION. | NOUNS. | |
|---|---|---|---|---|---|
| The hand, | يَد | 7. | The eye, or fountain, | عَيْن | 1. |
| The arm, | عَضُد | 8. | The neck, | عُنُق | 2. |
| A cubit, or half the arm, | ذِرَاع | 9. | The back of the neck, | قَفَا | 3. |
| The palm of the hand, | كَفّ | 10. | The shoulder, | كَتِف | 4. |
| A finger, | اِصْبَع | 11. | The tongue, | لِسَان | 5. |
| The liver, | كَبِد | 12. | The ear, | أُذُن | 6. |

| | NOUNS. | SIGNIFCATION. |
|---|---|---|
| 13. | كَرْش | The stomach, |
| 14. | اسْت | The buttock, |
| 15. | وَرِك | The hip, |
| 16. | فَخِذ | The thigh, |
| 17. | ساق | The leg, |
| 18. | رِجْل | The foot, |
| 19. | قَدَم | A step, |
| 20. | عَقِب | The heel, |
| 21. | رَحِم | The womb, |
| 22. | كُراع | The feet of the cloven-footed animals, |
| 23. | نَفْس | The soul, or life, |
| 24. | رُوح | The spirit, |
| 25. | سِنّ | Age, |
| 26. | سَراوِيل | Trowsers, |
| 27. | نَعْل | A shoe, |
| 28. | دار | A house, |
| 29. | خَمْر | Wine, |
| 30. | كاس | A cup, or bason, |
| 31. | سِكِّين | A knife, |
| 32. | فاس | A hatchet, |
| 33. | قَوْس | A bow, |
| 34. | دِرْع | Coat of mail, |
| 35. | رُمْح | A spear, or lance, |
| 36. | مَنْجَنِيق | A sling, |
| 37. | حَرْب | War, |
| 38. | سِلْم | Peace, |
| 39. | عَصا | A stick, or staff, |
| 40. | سُلَّم | A ladder, |
| 41. | قِدْر | A pot, or kettle, |
| 42. | مِلْح | Salt, |
| 43. | مِسْك | Musk, |
| 44. | سُرَي | A night journey, |
| 45. | غُول | A demon, or satyr, |
| 46. | ثَعْلَب | A fox, |
| 47. | ضَبُع | A hyæna, |
| 48. | فَهْد | A panther, |
| 49. | عَنْكَبُوت | A spider, |
| 50. | عَقْرَب | A scorpion, |

| SIGNIFICATION. | NOUNS. | |
|---|---|---|
| A hare, | أَرْنَب | 51. |
| A fish, | حُوت | 52. |
| A boat, | فُلْك | 53. |
| A well, | بِير | 54. |
| A bucket, | دَلْو | 55. |
| The sky, | سَمَآء | 56. |
| The earth, | أَرْض | 57. |
| Wind, | رِيح | 58. |
| The sun, | شَمْس | 59. |
| The forenoon, | ضُحَى | 60. |
| A garden, also Paradise, | فِرْدَوْس | 61. |
| Flaming fire, | سَعِير | 62. |
| Fire, | نَار | 63. |
| Hell, | جَحِيم | 64. |
| | سَقَر | 65. |
| Hell, | جَهَنَّم | 66. |
| Hell-fire, | لَظَى | 67. |
| A road, | طَرِيق | 68. |
| | سَبِيل | 69. |
| Prosody, | عَرُوض | 70. |
| An oath, | يَمِين | 71. |
| The north (wind), | شِمَال | 72. |
| Armour, | سِلَاح | 73. |
| A market-place, | سُوق | 74. |
| A palm-tree, | نَخْل | 75. |
| A rib, | ضِلْع | 76. |
| The breast (of a a woman), | ثَدْي | 77. |
| A mill-stone, | رَحَى | 78. |
| A horse, | فَرَس | 79. |

## OF THE ARABIC PLURALS.

One of the important classes of Arabic words, which are of most frequent occurrence in the Persian language, consists of the Plurals. Of the Plural, in the Arabic language there are various descriptions and forms. It has first, by the Grammarians, been resolved into صَحِیح, or سالِم, and مُکَسَّر; terms which literally signify *whole* or *perfect*, and *broken* or *imperfect*: but the former may with equal propriety be termed *regular*, and the latter *irregular*.

Of the first, or *Regular* Plurals, we have no occasion to treat at large, as they scarcely ever occur in Persian; with the exception of a few in the Feminine forms, which are invariably to be recognised by the termination or Feminine sign of Plural, آت; as, خَطَرات *dangers*, the Plural of خَطَر; واقِعات *events*, the Plural of واقِعَة; مُهِمّات *important affairs*, the Plural of مُهِمّ; مَکْتُوبات *letters*, or *epistolary writings*, the Plural of مَکْتُوب; &c. &c.

It is chiefly of the second, or the *Irregular* Plurals, that I here propose to offer a number of Examples frequently occurring in the Persian language. The *Irregular*, or *Broken* Plurals, جَمعِ مُکَسَّر, have again been divided into two distinct species, corresponding, in their technical appellation, to the peculiar uses for which they were originally invented, and to which they are still for the most part, although by no means (especially in Persian) uniformly, applied. The first of these species has been pronounced applicable to limited and small numbers; *i.e.* extending from *three inclusive* to *ten*, and therefore denominated جَمعُ القِلَّة, or *Plural of Paucity;* and the second, as extending in its application to all numbers beyond *ten* without limit, has received the appellation جَمعُ الكَثرَة, or *Plural of Multitude;* a subdivision of which has again been termed مُنتَهِي الجُمُوع, or جَمعُ الجُمُوع, *i.e. the extreme*, or *the Plural of Plurals.* The first of these species, or the Plural of Paucity, comprehends only four measures ; namely, أَفْعُل , أَفْعَال , أَفْعِلَة , and فِعْلَة : but each of these is the common measure for the Plurals of a number of Nouns which themselves are of different measures when in the *Singular Number*.

1. Nouns which form their *Plurals of Paucity* in Measure أَفْعُل

| PLURAL. | SIGNIFICATION. | SINGULAR. | MEASURES. | |
|---|---|---|---|---|
| أَنْفُس | The soul, | نَفْس | فَعْل | 1. |
| أَذْرُع | A cubit, | ذِرَاع | فِعَال | 2. |
| أَيْمُن | An oath, | يَمِين | فَعِيل | 3. |
| أَرْجُل | A foot, | رِجْل | فِعْل | 4. |
| أَعْنُق | A female kid, | عَنَاق | فَعَال | 5. |
| أَكْرُع | A cow's hoof, | كُرَاع | فُعَال | 6. |

2. Nouns which form their *Plurals of Paucity* in Measure أَفْعَال

| PLURAL. | SIGNIFICATION. | SINGULAR. | MEASURES. | |
|---|---|---|---|---|
| أَلْوَاح | A tablet, | لَوْح | فَعْل | 1. |
| أَحْكَام | An order, | حُكْم | فُعْل | 2. |
| أَمْلَاك | Possession, | مِلْك | فِعْل | 3. |
| أَبْطَال | Brave, | بَطَل | فَعَل | 4. |
| أَعْقَاب | The heel, | عَقِب | فَعِل | 5. |
| أَعْضَاد | The arm, | عَضُد | فَعُل | 6. |
| أَعْنَاق | The neck, | عُنُق | فُعُل | 7. |

3. Nouns which form their *Plurals of Paucity* in Measure أَفْعِلَةٌ

| PLURAL. | SIGNIFICATION. | SINGULAR. | MEASURES. | |
|---|---|---|---|---|
| أَطْعِمَةٌ | Food, | طَعامٌ | فَعالٌ | 1. |
| أَحْمِرَةٌ | An ass, | حِمارٌ | فِعالٌ | 2. |
| أَغْرِبَةٌ | A raven, | غُرابٌ | فُعالٌ | 3. |
| أَرْغِفَةٌ | A loaf of bread, | رَغِيفٌ | فَعِيلٌ | 4. |
| أَعْمِدَةٌ | A pillar, | عَمُودٌ | فَعُولٌ | 5 |

4. Nouns which form their *Plurals of Paucity* in Measure فِعْلَةٌ

| PLURAL. | SIGNIFICATION. | SINGULAR. | MEASURES. | |
|---|---|---|---|---|
| غِلْمَةٌ | A boy, or slave, | غُلامٌ | فُعالٌ | 1. |
| غِزْلَةٌ | A young deer, | غَزالٌ | فَعالٌ | 2. |
| خِلَّةٌ | A friend, | خَلِيلٌ | فَعِيلٌ | 3. |
| ثِيرَةٌ | A bull, | ثَوْرٌ | فَعْلٌ | 4. |
| وِلْدَةٌ | A son, | وَلَدٌ | فَعَلٌ | 5. |

The Plural of Multitude, جَمْعُ الكَثْرَةِ, comprises nineteen Measures; according to each of which, several Nouns, differing also, in most instances, in their *Measures of Singular*, form their *common Plurals*. It is to be observed, however, that the *particular Measures* assigned to various Nouns under the respective *heads* of the *several Plurals* do by no means restrict the Plurals of those Nouns to those *particular Measures* only; for it often happens, that a Noun has a Plural of Paucity *as well as a Plural of Multitude*. For instance, غُلامٌ "a boy"; رَغِيفٌ "a loaf"; نَفْسٌ "the soul," given in the above Tables, formed their Plurals of Paucity, as غِلْمَة, أَرْغِفَة, and أَنْفُس, respectively; while each of those *Nouns* has at the same time a Plural of Multitude, غِلْمان, رُغْفان, and نُفُوس, also respectively. It will be sufficient for our purpose, therefore, to remember that *this* is the Measure of the Plural of Paucity, and *that*, that of the Plural of Multitude; while a Noun may form its Plural according to any *one* or *both* of them; or, having any one or both forms of these Plurals, *may* at the same time have likewise a Plural of Plurals, جَمْعُ ٱلْجُمُوع, hereafter explained.

1. Nouns which form their *Plurals of Multitude* in Measure فُعْل

| PLURAL. | SIGNIFICATION. | SINGULAR. | MEASURES. | |
|---|---|---|---|---|
| حُور | A bright-eyed damsel, | حَوْراء | فَعْلاء | 1. |
| حُمْر | Red colour, | أَحْمَر | أَفْعَل | 2. |
| أُسْد | A lion, | أَسَد | فَعَل | 3. |
| نُوق | A she-camel, | ناقَة | فاعَل | 4. |
| وُغْد | A fool, | وَغْد | فَعْل | 5. |

2. Nouns which form their *Plurals of Multitude* in Measure فُعُل

| PLURAL. | SIGNIFICATION. | SINGULAR. | MEASURES. | |
|---|---|---|---|---|
| كُتُب | A book, | كِتاب | فِعال | 1. |
| رُسُل | A prophet, or messenger, | رَسُول | فَعُول | 2. |
| نُذُر | An admonisher, | نَذِير | فَعِيل | 3. |
| فُلُك | A wheel, or The sky, | فَلَك | فَعَل | 4. |
| سُفُن | A ship, | سَفِينَة | فَعِيلَة | 5. |

3. Nouns which form their *Plurals of Multitude* in Measure فُعَل

| PLURAL. | SIGNIFICATION. | SINGULAR. | MEASURES. | |
|---|---|---|---|---|
| سُوَر | A portion of any thing, and also a chapter of the Korân, | سُورَة | فُعْلَة | 1. |
| أُخَر | The last, | أُخْرَي | فُعْلَي | 2. |
| قُرَي | A village, | قَرْيَة | فَعْلَة | 3. |
| لِحَي | The beard, | لِحْيَة | فِعْلَة | 4. |

4. Nouns which form their *Plurals of Multitude* in Measure فِعَل

| PLURAL. | SIGNIFICATION. | SINGULAR. | MEASURES. | |
|---|---|---|---|---|
| صِيَغ | A tense, or person, | صِيغَة | فِعْلَة | 1. |
| نِعَم | A benefit, | نِعْمَة | | |
| مِحَن | Trouble, | مِحْنَة | | |
| حِرَف | Trade, or occupation, | حِرْفَة | | |
| حِيَل | Deceit, | حِيلَة | | |

5. Nouns which form their *Plurals of Multitude* in Measure فَعَلَة

| PLURAL. | SIGNIFICATION. | SINGULAR. | MEASURES. | |
|---|---|---|---|---|
| طَلَبَة | A student, or searcher after any thing, | طَالِب | فَاعِل | 1. |
| سَادَة | A Lord, or a descendant of Mohammad, | سَيِّد | فَعِّل | 2. |
| بَرَرَة | Virtuous, | بَرّ | فَعْل | 3. |
| خَبَثَة | Vicious, | خَبِيث | فَعِيل | 4. |

6. Nouns which form their *Plurals of Multitude* in Measure فُعَلَة

| PLURAL. | SIGNIFICATION. | SINGULAR. | MEASURES. | |
|---|---|---|---|---|
| قُضَاة | A judge, | قَاضِي | فَاعِل | 1. |
| كُمَات | Brave, | كَمِيّ | فَعِيل | 2. |

7. Nouns which form their *Plurals of Multitude* in Measure فِعَلَةٌ

| | PLURAL. | SIGNIFICATION. | SINGULAR. | MEASURES. | |
|---|---|---|---|---|---|
| in Measure فِعَلَةٌ | قِرَدَةٌ | A monkey, | قِرْدٌ | فِعْلٌ | 1. |
| | رِكَبَةٌ | A rider, | راكِبٌ | فاعِلٌ | 2. |
| | قِرَطَةٌ | Ear-ring, | قُرْطٌ | فُعْلٌ | 3. |

8. Nouns which form their *Plurals of Multitude* in Measure فُعَّلٌ

| | PLURAL. | SIGNIFICATION. | SINGULAR. | MEASURES. | |
|---|---|---|---|---|---|
| in Measure فُعَّلٌ | كُمَّلٌ | Perfect, | كامِلٌ | فاعِلٌ | 1. |
| | سُخَّلٌ | Weak, or Infirm, | سَخْلٌ | فَعْلٌ | 2. |
| | هُطَّلٌ | Incessant rain, | هَطِلٌ | فَعِلٌ | 3. |
| | عُزَّلٌ | Unarmed, | اَعْزَلٌ | اَفْعَلٌ | 4. |

9. Nouns which form their *Plurals of Multitude* in Measure فُعَّالٌ

| | PLURAL. | SIGNIFICATION. | SINGULAR. | MEASURES. | |
|---|---|---|---|---|---|
| in Measure فُعَّالٌ | جُهّالٌ | Ignorant, | جاهِلٌ | فاعِلٌ | 1. |
| | تُجّارٌ | A merchant, | تاجِرٌ | | |
| | عُمّالٌ | A Government agent, | عامِلٌ | | |
| | كُفّارٌ | An infidel, | كافِرٌ | | |
| | خُدّامٌ | A servant, | خادِمٌ | | |
| | سُرّاقٌ | A thief, | سارِقٌ | | |
| | زُرّاعٌ | A farmer, | زارِعٌ | | |
| | حُكّامٌ | A governor, | حاكِمٌ | | |
| | نُوّابٌ | A deputy, | نائِبٌ | | |
| | حُذّاقٌ | Skilful, | حاذِقٌ | | |
| | سُكّانٌ | A dweller, | ساكِنٌ | | |

## 10. Nouns which form their *Plurals of Multitude* in *Measure* فِعَالٌ

| PLURAL. | SIGNIFICATION. | SINGULAR. | MEASURES. | |
|---|---|---|---|---|
| عِظَامٌ | Great, | عَظِيمٌ | فَعِيلٌ | 1. |
| عِبَادٌ | A servant, or slave, | عَبْدٌ | فَعْلٌ | 2. |
| ظِبَآءٌ | A fawn, | ظَبْيَةٌ | فَعْلَةٌ | 3. |
| رِقَابٌ | The neck, | رَقَبَةٌ | فَعَلَةٌ | 4 |
| حِبَالٌ | Pregnant, | حُبْلَيٌ | فُعْلَيٌ | 5. |
| جِمَالٌ | A camel, | جَمَلٌ | فَعَلٌ | 6. |
| رِمَاحٌ | A spear, | رُمْحٌ | فُعْلٌ | 7. |
| ذِيَابٌ | A wolf, | ذِئْبٌ | فِعْلٌ | 8. |
| نِقَاطٌ | A point, | نُقْطَةٌ | فُعْلَةٌ | 9. |
| كِرَامٌ | Generous, | كَرِيمٌ | فَعِيلٌ | 10. |
| حِذَارٌ | Cautious, | حَذِرٌ | فَعِلٌ | 11. |
| خِيَارٌ | Benevolent, or virtuous, | خَيِّرٌ | فَيْعِلٌ | 12. |
| عِطَاشٌ | Thirsty, | عَطْشَانٌ | فَعْلَانٌ | 13. |
| خِمَاصٌ | Hungry, | خُمْصَانٌ | فُعْلَانٌ | 14. |
| نِدَامٌ | Ashamed, | نَدْمَانَةٌ | فَعْلَانَةٌ | 15. |
| عِجَافٌ | Lean, | عَجْفَآءٌ | فَعْلَآءٌ | 16. |
| رِجَالٌ | A man, | رَجُلٌ | فَعُلٌ | 17. |
| نِسَآءٌ | A woman, | نِسْوَةٌ | فِعْلَةٌ | 18. |
| سِرَاحٌ | A wolf, | سِرْحَانٌ | فِعْلَانٌ | 19. |

11. Nouns which form their *Plurals of Multitude* in Measure فُعُول

| PLURAL. | SIGNIFICATION. | SINGULAR. | MEASURES. | |
|---|---|---|---|---|
| عُلُوم | Science, | عِلْم | فِعْل | 1. |
| قُلُوب | The heart, | قَلْب | فَعْل | 2. |
| بُرُوج | A turret, or Sign of the Zodiac, | بُرْج | فُعْل | 3. |
| ذُكُور | A male, | ذَكَر | فَعَل | 4. |
| صُخُور | A stone, | صَخْرَة | فَعْلَة | 5. |
| رُقُود | A sleeper, | راقِد | فاعِل | 6. |
| مُلُوك | A king, | مَلِك | فَعِل | 7. |

12. Nouns which form their *Plurals of Multitude* in Measure فُعْلان

| PLURAL. | SIGNIFICATION. | SINGULAR. | MEASURES. | |
|---|---|---|---|---|
| سُودان | Black, or an Ethiopian, | اَسْوَد | اَفْعَل | 1. |
| رُغْفان | A loaf of bread, | رَغِيف | فَعِيل | 2. |
| رُهْبان | A Christian devotee, | راهِب | فاعِل | 3. |

13. Nouns which form their *Plurals of Multitude* in Measure فِعْلان

| PLURAL. | SIGNIFICATION. | SINGULAR. | MEASURES. | |
|---|---|---|---|---|
| غِلْمان | A boy, or slave, | غُلام | فُعال | 1. |
| رِطْبان | Fresh dates, | رُطَب | فُعَل | 2. |
| ضِيفان | A guest, | ضَيْف | فَعْل | 3. |
| نِيران | Light, | نُور | فُعْل | 4. |
| صِبْيان | An infant, | صَبِيّ | فَعِيل | 5. |
| غِزْلان | A fawn, | غَزال | فَعال | 6. |

14. Nouns which form their *Plurals of Multitude* in Measure فَعْلَى

| PLURAL. | SIGNIFICATION. | SINGULAR. | MEASURES. | |
|---|---|---|---|---|
| قَتْلَى | Slain, | قَتِيلْ | فَعِيلْ | 1. |
| مَوْتَى | Dead, | مَيِّتْ | فَعِّلْ | 2. |
| هَلْكَى | Perishing, | هالِكْ | فاعِلْ | 3. |
| حَمْقَى | Foolish, | اَحْمَقْ | اَفْعَلْ | 4. |

15. Nouns which form their *Plurals of Multitude* in Measure فِعْلَى

| PLURAL. | SIGNIFICATION. | SINGULAR. | MEASURES. | |
|---|---|---|---|---|
| حِجْلَى | A partridge, | حَجَلْ | فَعَلْ | 1. |
| ظِرْبَى | A civet-cat, | ظَرِبانْ | فَعِلانْ | 2. |

16. Nouns which form their *Plurals of Multitude* in Measure فُعَلآءْ

| PLURAL. | SIGNIFICATION. | SINGULAR. | MEASURES. | |
|---|---|---|---|---|
| شُرَفآءْ | Noble, | شَرِيفْ | فَعِيلْ | 1. |
| نُجَبآءْ | Well-bred, | نَجِيبْ | | |
| شُرَكآءْ | A partner, | شَرِيكْ | | |
| فُقَرآءْ | Poor, | فَقِيرْ | | |
| غُرَبآءْ | Stranger, | غَرِيبْ | | |
| خُلَفآءْ | A successor, | خَلِيفَةْ | فَعِيلَةْ | 2. |
| سُمَحآءْ | Generous, | سَمْحْ | فَعْلْ | 3. |

17. Nouns which form their *Plurals of Multitude* in Measure أَفْعِلَاءُ

| PLURAL. | SIGNIFICATION. | SINGULAR. | MEASURES. | |
|---|---|---|---|---|
| أَغْنِيَاءُ | Rich, | غَنِيّ | | |
| أَنْبِيَاءُ | A prophet, | نَبِيّ | | |
| أَوْصِيَاءُ | A legatee, | وَصِيّ | | |
| أَوْلِيَاءُ | A friend (of God), | وَلِيّ | | |
| أَذْكِيَاءُ | Acute, | ذَكِيّ | فَعِيْلٌ | 1. |
| أَشْقِيَاءُ | Wicked, | شَقِيّ | | |
| أَتْقِيَاءُ | Pious, | تَقِيّ | | |
| أَصْدِقَاءُ | A faithful friend, | صَدِيْقٌ | | |
| أَحِبَّاءُ | A beloved friend, | حَبِيْبٌ | | |

18. Nouns which form their *Plurals of Multitude* in Measure فَعَالِي

| PLURAL. | SIGNIFICATION. | SINGULAR. | MEASURES. | |
|---|---|---|---|---|
| فَتَاوِي | Decision of law, | فَتْوِي | فَعْلَي | 1. |
| دَفَارِي | A bone behind the car, | ذِفْرِي | فِعْلَي | 2. |
| سَعَادِي | A woman's name, | سُعْدَي | فُعْلَي | 3. |
| عَذَارِي | A virgin, | عَذْرَاءُ | فَعْلَاءُ | 4. |
| سَكَارَي | Drunk, | سَكْرَانٌ | فَعْلَانٌ | 5. |
| يَتَامِي | Orphan, | يَتِيْمٌ | فَعِيْلٌ | 6. |
| أَيَامِي | A widower; also a widow, | أَيِّمٌ | فَعِلٌ | 7. |

19. Nouns which form their *Plurals of Multitude* in Measure فُعَالَي

| PLURAL. | SIGNIFICATION. | SINGULAR. | MEASURES. | |
|---|---|---|---|---|
| سُكَارَي | Drunk, | سَكْرَانٌ | فَعْلَانٌ | 1. |
| فُرَادَي | An unit; also an attribute of the Deity, | فَرْدٌ | فَعْلٌ | 2. |
| قُدَامِي | Ancient; also an attribute of the Deity, | قَدِيْمٌ | فَعِيْلٌ | 3. |

### OF THE PLURAL OF PLURALS, جَمْعُ الْجُمُوعِ ; OR, THE EXTREME BOUNDARY OF PLURALS, مُنْتَهِي الْجُمُوعِ.

Of the origin and signification of this *term*, it will be sufficient for our present purpose to state, that the Arabs often form Plurals from Nouns *already* in the *Plural Number;* as, سَفِينَةٌ "a ship": First Plural, سُفُنْ; Second Plural, سَفَائِنْ. رُكْن "a pillar": First Plural, أَرْكَانْ; Second Plural, أَرَاكِنْ; Third Plural, أَرَاكِيْنْ. &c. &c.

The last of these, then, from which it is not allowable to form another Plural, goes by the above names. But the student is not to imagine that every Plural of this kind, that he meets with, *is absolutely* formed from *another Plural;* for there are many Arabic Nouns, the Plurals of which are confined to the *above form* only, and, in reality, have no other Plurals.

This class of Plurals comprises Seventeen Measures, according to the following table.

| SIGNIFICATION. | SINGULAR. | PLURAL. | MEASURES. | |
|---|---|---|---|---|
| A claim, | دَعْوَيْ | دَعاوِيْ | فَعالِيْ | 1. |
| Mankind, | اِنْسانْ | اَناسِيّ | فَعالِيّ | 2. |
| A book, letter, &c. &c. | رِسالَةٌ | رَسائِلْ | فَعائِلْ | 3. |
| Precious stone, &c. &c. | جَوْهَرْ | جَواهِرْ | فَواعِلْ | 4. |
| Regulation, | قانُونْ | قَوانِيْنْ | فَواعِيْلْ | 5. |
| Greater, | اَكْبَرْ | اَكابِرْ | اَفاعِلْ | 6. |
| Climate, | اِقْلِيْمْ | اَقالِيْمْ | اَفاعِيْلْ | 7. |

| SIGNIFICATION. | SINGULAR. | PLURAL. | MEASURES. | |
|---|---|---|---|---|
| Object, | مَطْلَبْ | مَطالِبْ | مَفاعِلْ | 8. |
| A lamp, | مِصْباحْ | مَصابِيحْ | مَفاعِيلْ | 9. |
| Experience, | تَجْرِبَةْ | تَجارِبْ | تَفاعِلْ | 10. |
| A picture, | تَصْوِيرْ | تَصاوِيرْ | تَفاعِيلْ | 11. |
| Eloquence, | بِلْغَنْ | بَلاغِنْ | فَعالِنْ | 12. |
| A sovereign, | سُلْطانْ | سَلاطِينْ | فَعالِيْنْ | 13. |
| A register, | دَفْتَرْ | دَفاتِرْ | فَعالِلْ | 14. |
| Paper, | قِرْطاسْ | قَراطِيْسْ | فَعالِيْلْ | 15. |
| A Kushmeerian, | كَشْمِيْرِيّ | كَشامِرَةْ | فَعالِلَةْ | 16. |
| An Afghan, | اَفْغانْ | اَفاغِنَةْ | اَفاعِلَةْ | 17. |

[N.B. The Arabic words, with the Forms and Measures in which they appear under the various heads in this Appendix, have been chiefly taken from Baillie's Arabic Tables—the most useful and correct compilation of the kind ever offered to Arabic Students in the English language.

In the selection of them, however, I have felt it necessary to introduce some further explanations; and to make such alterations in the arrangement and disposition of them as seemed to me proper and desirable.

I only wish it had been more in accordance with the nature and the plan of this work to have availed myself more copiously of the use of this most valuable auxiliary.]

PRINTED BY RICHARD WATTS, CROWN COURT, TEMPLE BAR.

| بخوان Read | سطر Line | صفحه Page |
|---|---|---|
| سفره | 10 ۱۰ | 16 ۱۶ |
| ظرف | 11 ۱۱ | .. .. |
| گرم | 10 ۱۰ | 18 ۱۸ |
| طلا | 5 ۵ | 19 ۱۹ |
| نقره | .. .. | .. .. |
| ارزیز | 6 ۶ | .. .. |
| حمّام | 5 ۵ | 21 ۲۱ |
| حدّاد | 8 ۸ | .. .. |
| شمائید | 14 ۱۴ | 44 ۴۴ |
| امّا | 7 ۷ | 115 ۱۱۵ |
| شش | 19 ۱۹ | 10 ۱۰ |
| هفت | 2 ۲ | 11 ۱۱ |
| بیست | 5 ۵ | .. .. |
| شش | .. .. | .. .. |
| ششصد | 7 ۷ | 12 ۱۲ |
| ششم | 2 ۲ | 13 ۱۳ |
| سیزدهم | 3 ۳ | .. .. |
| سیب | 2 ۲ | 15 ۱۵ |
| سنجاق | 8 ۸ | .. .. |
| ریسمان | .. .. | .. .. |
| ابریشم | .. .. | .. .. |

*Published by*

**Facsimile Publisher**
Ashok Vihar, Delhi-110052 (India)
Website: www.facsimilepublishers.com

*Distributed by*

**Gyan Books Pvt. Ltd.**
5, Ansari Road, Daryaganj, New Delhi-110002 (India)
E-mail: books@gyanbooks.com, Website: www.gyanbooks.com

9 788121 266789